# A Guide to...
# Colour Mutations & Genetics in Parrots

*By Dr Terry Martin BVSc*

Published and Edited by ABK Publications ©

**First Published 2002 by**
**ABK Publications**
**PO Box 6288,**
**South Tweed Heads,**
**NSW 2486, Australia.**

**ISBN 0 9577024 6 9 (paperback)**
**ISBN 0 9577024 7 7 (hardback)**

DISTRIBUTED BY
HAMPSHIRE BREEDERS
& BOOKS
12 INWOOD ROAD
LISS, HANTS, GU33 7LZ
TEL/FAX 01730 301340
MOBILE 0421 598637

**Front Cover:**
Top left: Melanistic (Blackface) Greygreen Budgerigar – D Mervilde
Bottom left: Creamino Crimson Rosella – H Kremer
Top right: Blue Eclectus Parrot – J Postema
Bottom: L to R: Cobalt (Turquoise), Turquoise, Lutino and
Mauve (Turquoise) Lineolated Parrots – J Chou
**Back Cover:**
Lutino Red-lored Amazon – J Postema

All Photographs by the author unless otherwise specified.

Design, Type and Art: The TAG Studio and PrintHouse Multimedia Graphics
Printing: Fergies

# DEDICATION

I would like to dedicate this book to my grandfather, the late
Thomas Robert Hunt, who began the family tradition in aviculture.
He would have loved this book and I know he is
sitting under a tree smiling.

# Contents

# PART TWO 113

# FOREWORD

Life is becoming more complicated for the parrot colour breeder. Not only are an increasing number of colour varieties or mutations appearing across a broader range of species but, in many instances, it is also becoming increasingly difficult to understand the relationships between these colour forms. No longer is it sufficient to be able to recognise a small number of easily distinguished colour forms and assign to each one just three simple forms of inheritance pattern: dominant, recessive or sex-linked. Even the novice breeder is now liable to acquire birds, whether of normal appearance or one of the more common colour forms, which have within their genetic make-up hidden factors which may surface in the young they produce. Exciting though it may be to marvel at a mixture of colours unfolding in a nest of fledglings, there may be many a subsequent headache in determining the correct name to identify the colour of each one and to understand the reasons for its occurrence.

Finding the answers to such questions, particularly for the novice breeder, has not been as straightforward as it should be. The worldwide spread of aviculture has led to problems of translation and communication with no single centre of expertise. Even where the same language is spoken, differences of naming and insufficient understanding of genetic principles can, and do, cause confusion. Although some few authors wilfully ignore established naming practices, the errors which arise are more usually the result of a lack of knowledge and insufficient research on the part of the authors concerned. Too many experienced breeders and writers alike perpetuate mistaken beliefs by repeating parrot fashion what they have heard or read.

Fortunately the broad genetic principles involved were explained, and a workmanlike system of naming developed many years ago by scientists and informed amateur breeders who were fascinated by the many colour forms then appearing in the Budgerigar. This body of knowledge was adopted by the Budgerigar Society in the UK, which had sufficient authority to see it established in many parts of the world. As other parrots entered into what became known as aviculture, and mutant colour forms of these started to occur, it soon became apparent that the same principles were involved throughout this Family of birds.

In this book Dr Terry Martin BVSc, who has already established an international reputation in this field through the medium of the internet, builds upon this earlier understanding to introduce and elaborate on the new genetic relationships which have become apparent. As such, this is a book in which both novice and expert alike will make new discoveries.

Many will purchase this book for the photographs alone; for the author and his publisher have gathered together a stunning collection of over 700 studies of most of the colour forms in all the commonly, and not so commonly, bred parrot species. What is more, these are carefully placed so that they appear adjacent to relevant discussions in the text.

The author writes in an easy conversational style which, nevertheless, does not hide a complete and authoritative mastery of the subject at both practical and theoretical levels. This is evident from the opening pages, explaining how colour is formed in parrot feathers, right through to the sealed section (Part 3) where more complex genetic and other matters are discussed in some detail.

I know you will enjoy and benefit from this book. Besides being a thoroughly good read and a rich visual experience, it is an essential reference for the parrot breeder; more than deserving of its place in your avian library for many years to come.

Clive Hesford
Cheltenham, UK

# ABOUT THE AUTHOR

Terry was born in 1965 at Bankstown in Sydney, New South Wales and grew up at Macquarie Fields. His interest in birds started at the age of 10 when Terry was given his first pair of Zebra Finches by his father and thus started a continuous history of aviculture up to the present day. Having started with Zebra Finches and all their different colour mutations, naturally his interest in genetics also began early and this allowed him to form a sound basis of knowledge to work upon in later years.

Terry began his secondary schooling at Hurlestone Agricultural High School. To this day Terry can remember his English teacher Mrs Llewelyn informing his parents that he would never write a novel, but that he had adequate language skills to write a technical manual! At the age of 16 he moved to Brisbane, Queensland and finished his schooling at Sunnybank High School where his Biology teacher Mr O'Driscoll found it difficult to adjust the genetics course for Terry. His solution was to give Terry his university textbook on genetics, a move which opened the door of knowledge even further, resulting in even more difficult questions for the teacher!

In 1984 Terry began studying Veterinary Science at the University of Queensland and he graduated in 1988. His training at university level expanded Terry's genetic knowledge once again and taught him how to use scientific method to expand his knowledge.

Upon graduation, Terry moved back to Sydney to work. His interest in birds naturally led to adding avian medicine to his veterinary skills. He was asked regularly to speak at local bird club meetings and in 1990 began studying parrot mutations and genetics in depth.

In 1995, Terry was a speaker at the first Grass Parrot and Lorikeet Society convention held in Sydney. It was at this time that Nigel Steele-Boyce first suggested that he write a book on parrot mutations and genetics. Also in 1995, Terry decided to move back to Brisbane. He married Sharyn in 1997 and later that year they purchased the Sunnybank Veterinary Clinic. The stability of married life provided the last ingredient required to begin work upon this book in 1998.

Writing the genetics book became an even greater stimulus for knowledge and has led to contact with experts in parrot genetics worldwide. In 1999 Terry initiated the formation of an international genetics discussion group (Genetics-Psittacine@ yahoogroups.com) which operates via e-mail. The existence of this group has helped Terry make his book the most up-to-date and comprehensive book ever produced on colour mutations in parrots.

In 2000, Terry presented three papers on avian genetics and colour mutations at the annual scientific meeting of the Australian College of Veterinary Scientists. Later that year he also spoke at the Birds 2000 conference held in Melbourne by the Post Graduate Foundation in Veterinary Science University of Sydney. In 2001 he spoke at the Aviculture Federation of Australia (AFA) conference in Adelaide on colour mutations in parrots.

Terry has written a number of articles for *Australian Birdkeeper Magazine* as well as for various club magazines. He also has written a significant number of papers currently available through the internet.

Currently Terry keeps a wide range of parrots including *Neophema* species, Red-rumped Parrots, Eastern and Western Rosellas, Indian Ringnecked Parrots, Peachfaced and Masked Lovebirds and, of course, Zebra Finches. As always, his main interest is genetic understanding of the behaviour of colour morphs and he currently has breeding experiments under way to learn more about complex gene interaction in Zebra Finches, Red-rumped Parrots and Peachfaced Lovebirds.

# ACKNOWLEDGEMENTS

This book has taken quite a few years to produce and would have been impossible to complete without the enormous help of a very long list of people. I have spent many hours on the internet conversing with aviculturists worldwide or visiting Australian breeders to photograph their birds and discuss mutations with them.

None of this would have been possible without the support of my wife, Sharyn, who has often had to 'mind the fort' whilst I travelled to conferences, as well as tolerating my 'absence' for hundreds of hours spent on the internet. The cliché about only being as good as your supporting partner is never truer than in this instance.

A few people stand out as requiring special mention. This book would not be successful without their help and foremost amongst them is my friend, Glenn Roman, whom I have known most of my life. The photographs within this book are as essential as the words and Glenn has supplied almost 20% of them. Without this resource, I would have had many substantial gaps in the photographic record and the book would be poorer as a result.

Clive Hesford, whom I have not yet met in person, runs a close second. I first made contact with Clive just over four years ago via the internet and immediately found a like mind with whom to discuss parrot genetics. His knowledge and experience, based on years of Budgerigar breeding in the UK, is equal to my own and he has been invaluable in proofreading the manuscript and ensuring that my writings would be understood by all. He hosts an excellent web site dedicated to genetics in all species of parrots, for which he has gained international recognition.

Inte Onsman may not have contributed directly to the book, however if it were not for Inte dedicating years of his life studying colour morphs in all species of parrots, we would not know as much as we do today. He has always been willing to add his expert advice to the Genetics-Psittacine discussion group and without the knowledge I have gleaned from him over the past four years, my book would be riddled with errors.

A special mention is also in order for Herman Kremer. He not only enthusiastically supplied a large range of his own photographs, but he also organised photographs from a number of other European breeders.

In fact I greatly appreciate the efforts of every one who has supplied me with photographs, as each and everyone is an important piece in 'illustrating the puzzle' of parrot genetics. The following people supplied photographs specifically for use in this book.

| **Australia:** | Mike Anderson | Sam Nastasi | Ken Shepherd |
| --- | --- | --- | --- |
| | Neville Armstrong | Peter Odekerken | Harry Smith |
| | Janelle Deegan | Greg Paul | Eddie Stephens |
| | Sharon House | Russell Pringle | Willie Stobart |
| | Barry Leggett | Peter Rankine | Pantcho Tomas |
| | Toby Martin | Glenn Roman | Steve Wilkinson |
| | David Marshall | John Scull | Ken York |
| | Andrew Mathews | Mark Scull | |

| **Europe:** | Belgian Vereniging Agaporniden Society (BVA) | | |
| --- | --- | --- | --- |
| | Emil Antonin | Martin Gerritsen | Bill Pearson |
| | Jacque Bastiaan | Johan Goessens | Jan Postema |
| | Dirk Van den Abeele | Herman Kremer | M. Zahir T. Rana |
| | Thierry Duliere | Rosemary Low | Jack Suikerbuik |
| | Pat Fielding | Didier Mervilde | |
| | Gerard Geraedts | Brian Nielsen | |

| **North America:** | Kent Benton | Rainer Erhart | Tony Silva |
| | Linda Brandt | Sharon Garsee | Royan Webb |
| | Jim Chou | Darlene Johnson | |
| | Richard Cusick | Bob Nelson | |
| | Scott Doak | Gary and Lynn Redden | |
| **South Africa:** | Ysuf Arendze | Cary Cairncross | Deon Smith |
| **Asia:** | Yutthana Imanothai | | |

I also appreciate and acknowledge the contribution of photographs from the following people:

Diana Andersen, Phil Bender, Michael Blake, Bob Bortolo, Bob Branston, Bob Brown, Danny Brown, Kate Buckley, Alan Chalmers, Michael Christian, Peggy Cross, William Caldwell (late), Gordon Dosser, Frank Doyle, Damian Dunneman, Mark Goodsell, Herb Graf, Chris Hunt, Rick Jordan, R, B & D Kamer, Russell Kingston, Jonathon Lamshed, Nancy Lansom, Nick Livanos, Malcolm Loveland, Glenn Matheson, Jim McCormick, Mike Nash, Todd Osborne, Andre Ozoux, Greg Radcliffe, Gerry Rutte, Athol Shelton, Stan Sindel, Chris Smith, Phil Smith, Richard Smith, Syd and Jack Smith, Roger Sweeney, Cliff Walsh, David Vremec.

I would like to add to that list all the names of breeders who have allowed either myself, Glenn Roman or any of the other photographers access to their birds. However, the list would be nearly as long as this book! Apart from many of the names above, whom I have visited personally, I would like to mention Russell McAlister, Bill Connors and Alan and Thea Lynch who have always welcomed me to visit their aviaries and view the latest in new colours in their birds.

It is also important to acknowledge the 'fathers of parrot genetics' who have over the years piqued my interest in this subject and therefore helped set in motion the ideas which have evolved into this book. I speak of people like George Smith and Jim Hayward, who themselves have been striving for uniform naming in parrot species for 20–30 years, and authors like Stan Sindel whose thorough and precise documentation of colour morphs in many different parrot species has contributed greatly towards completing the 'bigger picture', which is now developing in psittacine genetics.

Finally, but not least, are Nigel and Sheryll Steele-Boyce who have never wavered from the ideal of producing the most complete book ever written on parrot colour mutations. Without their support of aviculture as a whole, with their magazine and all the books they have published, we would all be worse off. Australian aviculture, and indeed the world as a whole, should extend a heartfelt thanks to *ABK Publications* for the tremendous efforts they have made over the years, which has led to the dissemination of so much knowledge to the benefit of all.

Thank you all

*T. Mt—Bh*

Terry Martin

# INVITATION TO READERS

I extend an open invitation to all aviculturists who wish to discuss colour mutations in parrots to contact me either by e-mail to sbankvet@bigpond.com or by conventional mail via the publisher, *ABK Publications*. In particular, I would like to hear about suggestions for possible improvements to this text, as well as information regarding new mutations or those mutations with limited information in this book.

I would greatly appreciate photographs of any and all colours (in any parrot species) not illustrated in this book, with the aim to make future editions even more thorough.

Anyone who has a genuine interest in parrot genetics and mutations is also welcome to join the genetics discussion group at http://www.yahoogroups.com/group/Genetics-Psittacine.

# PUBLISHER'S NOTE

The quality of each image published in this title is generally of a high definition and standard and is a fair and accurate representation of a specific colour mutation. However, it must be stated that there may be slight variances in colour from the original subject due to lack of definition or inadequate light conditions at time of photographing. As described in detail within the text, much of the colour in parrots is created through light distortion, so it is not surprising that insufficient or excessive light would greatly alter the perceived colours we see. We have, in all cases, accurately reproduced the original image supplied.

Terry Martin has conducted intensive research of avian genetics on a worldwide basis via the internet, particularly via communication with like-minded people through Genetics-Psittacine@yahoogroups.com. This form of interaction and communication has not been available until recent times and expands our ability to communicate internationally manyfold. With increased communication, theories and ideas can be brought together from many different aviculturists who would otherwise only have local experience. The outcome is that knowledge is refined at a higher rate and a broader perspective is achieved. Technological advances and the ongoing exploration of genetics in all animal forms are continuing and within a few years even this document will need to be updated.

Enjoy this study and learn from it. We encourage you to contribute your own input into this important and valuable communication.

Nigel and Sheryll Steele-Boyce
ABK Publications

S DOAK

**Lime (Pallid) Blue
Quaker Parrot.**

# INTRODUCTION

This book has two major aims: firstly to present information about genetics and mutations in a readily understandable format and, in Part Three of the book, to discuss the more complex topic of the genetic theory of colour mutations in parrots.

Developing an understanding of genetics is a gradual process that cannot be rushed. I believe part of the problem people have with genetics is 'too much too soon'. The symbolisation is difficult to remember and confusing to say the least. When I first learnt the basics of genetics, it was from books that used only common words. The only scientific terms used were 'sex-linked' and 'recessive'. Whilst the reality of avian genetics requires an understanding of far more complex systems and terms, everyone must crawl before they can walk and walk before they can run. Therefore, the first part of this book avoids the use of technical words and symbols. Sometimes I think that a complete understanding of genetics is akin to flying – beyond all of us!

Whilst the first part of the book is not always technically correct in its use of terminology, I have tried to keep Parts One and Two of the book as simple as possible. For readers with a more advanced knowledge of genetics (or the more adventurous) Part Three explores as many aspects as possible of the whole colour mutational spectrum. Some of the theories presented in this section may seem to challenge convention but none are without sound reason. Do not feel compelled to struggle through Part Three, the technical section, as it is not essential reading.

It is also important to realise that knowledge is a continual struggle for truth. As time goes by, more colour mutations occur and each tells us something more, often giving us a new insight into an old problem. Consequently, what is taken as true now, may need to evolve into new ideas as new information is discovered.

For instance, no-one would have grouped the Pearl Cockatiel with the Opaline Budgerigar when it first appeared. However, with the appearance of a further four or five Opaline mutations, the picture is now a lot clearer and we have no trouble grouping the Pearl Cockatiel with these other mutations.

This is a normal scientific process. Ideas must be theorised, assessed and then developed to fit the facts. Sometimes we get things wrong, but overall the search is for the truth. Critics point out the mistakes, but fail to see where the answer has already evolved.

The important thing is to develop a sound logical base, because it is only from a sound foundation that you can add the upper storeys that will take you into the stratosphere.

## Addendum

*In the beginning, this book was aimed primarily at the Australian reader. However, the need for a comprehensive book covering mutations across all parrot species is universal. If we add to this the tremendous ability we have to communicate internationally through the internet, it becomes imperative that we all understand each other and use names in a consistent fashion. These facts have compelled my book to become international in context.*

*The global nature of aviculture has forced me to expand my knowledge further and to accept different ideas from all over the world. To achieve universal acceptance of naming systems will require us all to accept changes in common usage of different names, but overall the reader will see that the majority of names are consistent with what they already understand.*

*One area that may attract comment is my use of 'unique' common names for certain combination colours. Without doubt, it is technically correct to call these colours by the combination of their component mutations. However, I recognise that the average breeder will always desire simple attractive names that can be applied to colours being sold to the general public. In my opinion, there is nothing wrong with common names, as long as they are applied consistently. So whilst Part Two may appear to promote these names, my real aim is to promote consistent application when these names are used.*

# GLOSSARY OF TERMS – PARTS 1 AND 2

**Allele –** see *Multiple alleles.*

**Background colour** – the component of plumage colour, due to melanin pigments lying deep within the medulla of the feather, which makes possible the production of greens and blues.

**Body colour** – the colour of plumage regions where background melanin is present in the wildtype appearance; excluding areas coloured by foreground melanin and regions of special colouration or markings (eg face masks, differential stripes or bands, etc).

**Carotenoid pigments** – a class of pigments derived from the diet. In parrots these are generally referred to as **Psittacin pigments** as they are different from similar pigments found in finches and other species of birds.

**Chromosome** – a unit of DNA comprising part of the genetic make-up of the individual. They are long strings of genes occurring as a set number of pairs, with one chromosome of each pair inherited from one parent and the second from the other parent.

**Co-dominant gene** – a gene that is neither dominant nor recessive to its wildtype counterpart. Instead they express themselves equally when both are present.

**Colour morph** – any colour appearance other than the Normal colour. The words mean 'alternate colour'.

**Constructive interference** – the correct term for the light distortion effect creating the appearance of green and blue colours in feathers.

**Cortex** – the outer regions of the feather structure that may carry either melanin or psittacin pigments.

**Cream ground** – a ground colour part way between yellow and white.

**Crossover** – the mechanism by which linked genes recombine.

**Dihybrid cross –** the classical step from Mendelian genetics whereby two 'double split' parents are mated together, thereby allowing two different mutations to be combined in the one offspring for the first time.

**DNA (deoxyribonucleic acid)** – the chemical compound from which genetic material is made.

**Dominant gene** – a gene that overpowers the wildtype gene to which it is paired, producing the same appearance whether one or two genes are present.

**Double factor/single factor** – refers to the number of genes present for a particular trait. Only normally used for dominant and co-dominant mutations.

**Foreground colour** – the regions of the plumage where melanin pigment is found in the cortex of the feather and generally produces dark colours like black and dark brown.

**Gene** – the basic unit of genetic control. Each gene has a specific function and is found on a specific section of a specific chromosome.

**Gene family** – correctly known as a multiple allelic series for a given locus, genes belonging to a family interact in special ways.

**Gene linkage – linked genes** – genes that lie on the same chromosome and within a short distance of one another. They require crossover to allow them to be collected on the one chromosome and therefore be passed together to the one offspring. Crossover is also required to separate them again.

**Genotype** – the genetic make-up of the bird.

**Grey family pigments** – an easy way to remember what melanin pigments are – the pigments that produce black, grey and brown colours. They also contribute to the production of blue and green colouration.

**Ground colour** – the base of psittacin pigments found in the plumage. Can be yellow ground, cream ground or white ground. Ground colour influences the choice of name for certain colour combinations.

**Halfsider** – a genetic aberration whereby one half of the bird is one colour whilst the other half is a different colour, eg half green and half blue or half yellow and half white.

**Locus –** the location on the chromosome occupied by a gene.

**Master gene –** a gene that controls other genes.

**Medulla** – the central portion of the feather structure. Is important for producing constructive interference through special structural aspects. This works in concert with the presence of melanin pigments to create the appearance of green and blue colours. The colour produced by the medulla forms the basis of the bird's body colour.

**Melanin** – the scientific name of the black pigment found in different regions of the feather giving it certain colours. For ease, I refer to them as Grey family pigments.

**Modifying gene** – a gene whose action upon the plumage colour is small or whose action only occurs secondarily to another gene.

**Multigenic inheritance** – when multiple genes control a single trait, (eg height in humans). The resultant appearance is the result of a number of different genes all working in concert.

**Multiple alleles** – alternative genes (see *Gene family* above) for a single position on a chromosome. (See also technical section – Part Three.)

**Mutant gene** – a gene that has been altered from the wildtype form.

**Mutation** – the act of creating a mutant gene. Is colloquially used as referring to the mutant gene.

**Normal/Wildtype** – the natural 'wild' colour of the bird is known as Normal. Genetically, the Normal or wildtype is a hypothetical bird taken to be carrying only wildtype genes unless hidden recessives are indicated, eg Normal/Blue.

**Phenotype** – the physical appearance of the bird, created by its genotype.

**Pigment** – a chemical substance that can be deposited in feathers or other tissue to give it colour. Feathers of parrots can carry two different classes of pigment commonly known as melanin and psittacin.

**Pigment distribution mutation** – a colour mutation that alters distribution of pigment through the plumage, but does not alter the process of forming the pigment.

**Primary colour mutation** – a mutant gene whose action produces a significant change to plumage colouration. A colour change which is produced by a single mutant gene.

**Psittacin** – the name given to the carotenoid type pigments found in parrot feathers. They produce yellow, red, orange and pink colours. For ease, I refer to them as Yellow family pigments.

**Recessive gene** – a gene that is only allowed to express itself when two copies are present in the genetic make-up. A single copy is suppressed by the opposing wildtype gene.

**Sex-linked inheritance** – a form of recessive inheritance linked to the X chromosomes. As hens only have one X chromosome, they only require one copy of the gene for it to express itself, whilst the cock requires two copies as with standard recessive mutations.

**Sexual dimorphism** – the occurrence of different plumage colours and/or patterns for cocks and hens in the same species.

**Split** – indicates that a bird is carrying a hidden gene for a recessive or sex-linked trait.

**Structural colour** – the portion of the plumage colour produced through special feather structure via the effect known as constructive interference. Primarily green and blue colours.

**Structural (affecting) mutation** – a mutation that alters feather structure, thereby affecting its ability to produce structural colour.

**Tyndall effect** – a light distortion effect commonly credited with the production of structural colour in birds, now known to be caused by constructive interference.

**White ground** – a ground colour totally lacking all psittacin pigment.

**Yellow family pigments** – an easy way to remember what psittacin pigments are: yellow, red, orange and pink colours.

**Yellow ground** – a ground colour retaining full psittacin pigment levels. These can include reds, oranges and pinks.

# PART ONE

*Blue (or Turquoise?)
King Parrot cock.*

# UNDERSTANDING MUTATIONS

## The Creation of Colour in Parrots

When we think of parrots, we imagine many bright colours, all the colours of the rainbow! It might come as a surprise, but all those different colours are the result of just three basic elements of colour that can be altered and combined in different ways to provide this variety. These elements are **yellow family pigments** (or **psittacins**), **grey family pigments** (or **melanins**) and **structural colour**.

Let us start by considering the colour green, the predominant colour in parrots. To produce this colour one needs all three elements working together. Green, as we see it in parrots, is not a real colour. It is not created by green pigments, but is actually the result of a combination of other colours. Just like mixing paint, green is a combination of yellow and blue.

You begin with Grey family pigments.

Yellow in parrots is **real** and is produced by pigments commonly called **psittacins.** There are other related colours also produced by this class of pigment – reds, oranges and pinks. All these colours are produced by pigments, which I will refer to as **yellow family pigments** throughout the first part of the book. The relationship between yellow, red, orange and pink is important to understand before exploring colour mutations further. Yellow family pigments create what is known as the **ground colour** of the bird. If they are present, the ground colour is yellow, if they are absent the ground colour is white. This classification system will be used in later sections.

The other component needed to create green colouration is blue, which in parrots is also not a pigment either. Instead it is itself created by the combination of the final two elements of colour in parrots – **grey family pigments** and

Add light distortion to create Blue.

**structural colour**. These two elements are both essential if you want the colour blue and therefore green to occur in the bird.

Grey family pigments are correctly known as **melanins** and are, in reality, black in their natural state. Under most circumstances, however, they will appear as shades of grey to the human eye. Therefore I have chosen to call them *grey family pigments* for simplicity in this book. Grey family pigments can also be altered slightly to produce all the shades of brown that are found in parrots.

Grey family pigments can be found in two areas of the feather. These two areas produce slightly different components which contribute to the bird's overall colour. For simplicity I will call these components **background colour** and **foreground colour** although, elsewhere, you may also come across the more technically correct terms

**background melanin** and **foreground melanin**. Foreground colour is produced by large amounts of black pigments lying close to the surface of the feather. This results in dark colours such as black, dark grey and dark brown. These areas have no structural colour element.

Background colour, however, represents those areas where the grey family pigments are lying deeper within the feather and the third element known as **structural colour** is superimposed as an overlay. Together, the structural colour and the central grey family pigments create the blue colour we see. The grey family pigments are still the same colour as those present in any foreground areas of the bird. The blue we see (and therefore all green colours as well) is merely a trick of the eye. The various combinations of background colour, structural colour and yellow family pigments result in what is known as **body colour**.

It is the structural colour element that creates the magic. Any feather that produces blue or green colour has a special structure that causes light to be distorted as it passes through the feather. This distortion creates the illusion for our eyes that we see as blue or green. It is similar to the **Tyndall effect** that makes the sky appear blue. However, researchers have recently classified this effect in birds as **constructive interference**. The change does not alter our knowledge of what is happening, just the name by which we should call it. The various shades of blue and green are produced by slight alterations to this structural element.

With three basic elements for colour, yellow family pigments, grey family pigments and structural colour, the parrot has been able to create virtually any colour in the rainbow and hence all the appeal as both a pet and aviary bird.

For a more detailed explanation of colour production in parrots, refer to Clive Hesford's web site *The Genetics of Colour in Budgerigars and other Parrots* or the book *Genetics for Budgerigar Breeders* by Taylor and Warner.

*Then add Yellow family pigments.*

*And all together you have Green.*

*The three basic elements of colour combine to produce all the colours of the rainbow – Normal Eastern Rosella.*

Page 21

## The Value of Mutations

Over the past decade, mutation bashing has become fashionable. This is not based on logic or commonsense, but merely on whims combined, in this case, with a little fear. This fear is caused by their own misunderstandings and concern about negative comments being directed towards aviculturists by misguided groups in society.

Breeding mutations is an accepted practice. Monetary greed, however, has accompanied the breeding of some new mutations and this frequently leads to poor breeding decisions being made by aviculturists. However greed is a transgression to which many people are susceptible.

The colour mutation itself is not at fault and poses no realistic threat to the existence of any species. A few points can place this into perspective:

- Mutations occur in all species at a constant but low rate. They occur just as frequently in the wild as in captivity. A bird carrying a colour mutant gene has only one altered gene out of thousands of 'normal' genes. That mutant gene can be selected against to remove it from the population at any time.
- Any animal bred in captivity (wild or domesticated) is immediately altered genetically by man, whenever we select one individual to breed from over another. We cannot play Mother Nature, selecting an individual for survival traits within its natural environment. The 'normal' animals bred by aviculturists or zoos have no greater survival ability than any colour mutant. However, that should not matter, as restocking of wild populations will rarely happen except in special circumstances and is rarely the purpose of keeping animals in captivity.
- All animals kept and bred by humans have equal value. They offer us a chance to learn more about other organisms beside ourselves. They give us pleasure and relaxation to watch and observe. They also teach people, particularly children, how to be responsible and care for others.
- Without domestication of animals, humans would not have been able to evolve to our current level of civilisation. It is only now that we have gained so much from our captive animals, that we are in a position to consider their welfare. This creates a situation of great responsibility whenever we choose to keep animals, but should never lead to an ending of our relationship with animals, nor place a ban on our domestication of new species. Breeding animals is too important a piece of what makes us human.

Besides all these arguments, I view mutations as being potentially more valuable than Normal birds because they are able to teach us something about the way the body functions. They pinpoint what function a particular gene has in the Normal bird, knowledge that in humans has taught us much about diseases and even life itself. By studying mutations and their effects, we can earn a little peek into one tiny aspect of what makes an animal what it is.

I acknowledge that to many people, a colour mutation is just a pretty bird that someone may want and is willing to pay for. However, every time I see a new mutation, I learn something new. Mutations represent new insights into the nature of that particular species of bird. They also add to our knowledge of the universe. I hope that reading this book will give you a new understanding and greater appreciation of mutations.

## The Value of Normals

Whilst the existence of colour mutations is not a threat to the survival of normal-coloured birds, Normal birds are vitally important for the existence of mutations. They will always be necessary when establishing a new mutation. They serve as a reservoir of genetic diversity and they are the standard against which any mutation is evaluated. A mutation can reveal many things about the Normal bird, and conversely the Normal bird can often tell us much about a mutation.

*Study the Normal Blue-winged Parrot (L) to understand the Blue Blue-winged Parrot (R).*

Although I am enthusiastic about every mutation I see, I value the study of normal-coloured birds just as much. We need to look closely at these birds and learn to appreciate what is before us. Only then can we fully appreciate colour mutations and start to understand what they truly represent.

Regardless of the species of parrot you breed, take time to look closely at the Normal bird. Observe the shades of colour, the areas which contain differing pigments, and the areas which have structural colour. Then consider the colour mutation and you can understand why it looks the way it does.

For instance, if you look at the body colour of the Blue-winged Parrot, you should notice that it is basically a grey-green bird, with structural colour only on the face and wing areas. Once you understand this, look at the Blue mutation of the Blue-winged Parrot and you will note that the body colour is grey, with blue primarily on the face and wings. This is not an uncommon pattern for Australian parrots.

When establishing a new mutation, a good stud of Normal birds will come into its own. They are essential for establishing the genetics of a new mutation, and can also introduce vital traits such as vigour and fertility to ensure a successful outcome for a new mutation. Many new mutations are lost through excessive inbreeding and poor use of outcrossing to Normal birds.

Aviculturists provide many reasons for the breeding of Normal birds. No matter how many reasons there may be, I recognise the necessity of breeding Normal birds for their value to the success of my main hobby – the breeding and understanding of mutations.

*Normal Scarlet-chested Parrot cock.*

*No matter what species you breed, study its Normal form closely.*
*Above: Normal Masked Lovebird.  Above right: Normal Red-rumped Parrot cock.*

## Naming Mutations

This is an extremely contentious area for some very basic reasons. The first problem is that some breeders of new mutations feel that they must have the right to name the mutation to show ownership and provide recognition for their achievement. Breeders should always be recognised and recorded for their efforts, but early names are generally later proven wrong. It is extremely difficult to name a new mutation without years of research!

The second problem is simply a lack of suitable names. We have fewer names than we have mutations, so the temptation is there to use the wrong name rather than think of a new one. In addition, we have a number of names that have never been defined in aviculture.

The third and most difficult problem stems from the desire of all aviculturists to have descriptive names that tell them what colour the bird is. Unfortunately this is an impossible aim. But why?

The appearance of any bird is the sum of the action of all the 'Normal' genes that it carries for colour production, not the result of any one colour mutant gene. In other words, for every species the Normal bird is different, therefore the appearance of any given mutation will be different for each species.

Not only will the one mutation look different in each species, but different mutations in different species can also look very similar. No single colour appearance is produced by the one mutation across the board. It is the gene action that is the same each time and this is what must be identified and classified.

Many people (probably most) want to subscribe to the 'name the colour' system, where you choose a name to describe the colour you see, without considering the genetics. However, half the names we use are not even colours! What colour is Fallow, Opaline, Dilute or even Cinnamon? These are names that identify a mutation, a genetic process. It is simply not possible to describe a mutation's colour in one or two words. However, if the mutation is correctly named and you are aware of the appearance of the Normal bird for the species, then you can visualise what it should look like, but only if a system is used to name the mutation.

The only systematic way to name mutations logically is to use genetics and gene action, irrespective of the physical appearance of the bird.

**It is not currently possible to fully identify the following colours to their correct mutation.**

B PEARSON

ANON

1. 'Black-eyed Yellow' Eastern Rosella – is it a Dilute or a Black-eyed Clear?
2. 'Aqua' Rainbow Lorikeet – a new dominant mutation yet to be correctly classified.
3. Young 'Aqua' and Normal Rainbow Lorikeets.
4. Greygreen 'Aqua' Rainbow Lorikeet.
5. 'Avocado' Fischer's Lovebird – this Australian mutation has yet to be studied and classified.

ANON

B BORTOLO

ANON

*Above: 'Pied' Sun Conure (foreground) – not a true Pied. It has features in common with the 'Golden' Eastern Rosella.*
*Right: 'Olive' (L) and Blue (Whiteface) 'Olive' (R) Cockatiels – true Olive is not possible in Cockatiels, therefore this colour has yet to be correctly identified.*

## Mutation versus Colour

At this point I think it is necessary to define an important difference. Despite the way aviculturists generally use the word 'mutation', there is a distinction between 'mutation' and 'colour'. The bird itself is not a mutation; it merely carries a **colour mutant gene** that alters its colour. So when we refer to a bird's mutation, we are really referring directly to the altered genes the bird carries. When we refer to its colour, we are discussing how it physically appears. A bird's colour

is a result of all the genes it carries, both those altered by mutations and those unaffected. [In a technical sense, when we refer to a bird's mutation we are referring to its genetic make-up (**genotype**), whilst when talking about its colour we are referring to its physical appearance (**phenotype**).]

It therefore becomes incorrect to refer to a bird whose colour is a combination of mutations as either 'a such and such mutation' or as 'a secondary mutation'. It is a combination colour, some of which have special names (such as Albino, Cobalt, Lacewing etc) and these should never be called 'mutations', or alternatively we refer to all the mutations the bird carries (and call it a Blue Lutino or a Dark Factor Blue or a Cinnamon Lutino).

There are also instances where the official name given to the mutation differs from that given to the colour it produces. For instance the Dark Factor mutation is the correct term for the gene that produces Dark Green and Olive. Also the mutation that produces the Greygreen colour is more correctly called the Grey mutation (the grey colour is only produced as a combination colour). To avoid

*'Yellow' Crimson Rosella – is it a Black-eyed Clear?*

*Below: Cleartail Indian Ringnecked Parrot cock – this mutation is unique and does not fit any recognised category.*
*Right: Turquoise Grey Cleartail Indian Ringnecked Parrot hen.*

confusion for breeders, I have only used the absolutely correct naming in the technical section (Part Three) of the book, however it is essential that all breeders start learning the distinction between a mutation and a colour.

## Common Colour Mutations in Parrots

Each bird has a set number of normal genes which, when combined, produce plumage colour as we see it. Colour mutations occur, almost without exception, through damage to one of the bird's normal genes for colour production. These statements have significance for two reasons. Firstly, these genes are inherited through evolution and therefore related species of birds (in this case the whole parrot family) carry the same genes as each other. Therefore each species has the ability to develop the same colour mutations. Secondly, the number of possible colour mutations is finite. It is set for each species by the number of genes it has which control colour production.

Some of these genes can be destroyed by the simplest mistake in their genetic code and become non-functional. Examples are the Cinnamon gene and the structural genes like Greygreen and Dark Factor. Other genes can be partially altered, as well as

R PRINGLE

T DULIERE

*Left: 'Yellow-headed' Eastern Rosella – found worldwide and often incorrectly called 'Pied', it has been selectively enhanced by European breeders to produce attractive combinations.*
*Below: 'Double Factor Yellow-headed' Lutino Eastern Rosella.*

inactivated, to give a range of outcomes, for example the Blue gene, the Lutino gene and some Dilute genes.

Whilst there exists an enormous range of colour mutations in many different species of parrots, there are common denominators running through the existence of those mutations. The fact that each colour mutation belongs to a particular gene increases the necessity for naming each one correctly. Names for colour mutations were assigned in a logical manner by our earliest aviculturists. However with the increase of new mutations in recent years, as well as translation problems from European languages into English and a lack of suitable names, we now have many new colours being named in a haphazard fashion. This situation is intolerable; we cannot call every brown-looking mutation Cinnamon without reason. It is up to aviculturists to start applying names with logic. To do this, we need the mutations defined in a simple way, readily understood by all.

In the sections which follow, I will attempt to explain the correct use of different names. Some names have never been defined or have had changing definitions over time. Some mutations are in desperate need of a name but none have been consistently applied.

What has to be understood before I go further, is that it is impossible to give descriptive names to all colour mutations. Many different mutations produce similar colours; therefore the only suitable system involves naming the mutation by the gene responsible. There are many aviculturists who oppose this method, because they cannot accept a Blue mutation in the Cockatiel or a Lutino mutation in the Galah. Whilst I understand their argument, it is difficult to accommodate their ideas in a logical system that identifies a mutation's true genetic form.

Although I have said that most colour mutations recur across all species of parrots, some occur in genes that are restricted to one species only. These are mutations in genes that have probably evolved at the same time as the species and do not occur in other parrots. However, some of those mutations presently thought of as 'species-specific' may eventually be seen merely as the first of their kind. Only time will tell!

# UNDERSTANDING BASIC GENETICS

G ROMAN

*Above: Normal or Green Indian Ringnecked Parrot.*
*Below: Normal Cockatiel.*

The aim of this chapter is to explain some genetic principles in a very basic form, which can be readily understood by everyone. For this reason, technical terminology and descriptions have been simplified and analogies used to aid comprehension. As I mentioned in the introduction, you must crawl before you can walk. This section allows you to crawl, get on your feet and take your first steps.

## Normal versus Green

The terms **Normal bird** and **Normal** refer to the appearance of the wild form of the species under discussion. Throughout the book I have used this term except under special circumstances. It is standard to refer to the **wildtype** bird as Normal so as to avoid confusion over the differing colours of wildtype birds. However, in the sections dealing with **structural mutations** and their combinations, I have replaced the use of the word 'Normal' with 'Green', because only green-coloured Normal birds can exhibit mutations which alter **structural colours** (eg Olive, Greygreen, Violet). If you start with a grey bird (eg Cockatiel) or a brown bird (eg Bourke's Parrot) you cannot ever have these mutations. Therefore calling the Normal bird 'Green' is inappropriate. (Bourke's Parrots do have small areas of structural colour to produce the blue colours on the brow, wings and rump – structural colours would occur and be visible there, but would be easily overlooked by many people. This is an area for an observant breeder to establish a new colour.)

The most important point to understand about genetics is that a **Normal bird is not a mutation.** Often you will hear someone describe the Normal bird as a dominant mutation. It is not dominant and it is not recessive. It is simply the appearance you have if no colour mutations are able to express themselves. It is actually the sum of thousands of working wildtype genes all doing their job and culminating in what we see as the Normal bird.

M LOVELAND

## Written Genetic Make-up and its Meaning

When describing the genetic make-up of a bird, we could list all the wildtype genes the bird has along with its colour mutant genes. However, this would be superfluous and redundant. Therefore it is traditional to record only those genes that are altered from Normal.

The traditional way to write the genetic make-up is along the lines of the following example:

Cinnamon Blue / Fallow / Dilute

G ROMAN

*Normal Bourke's Parrot.*

*Normal or Green Peachfaced Lovebird.*

This bird is expressing both the Cinnamon gene and the Blue gene and is split for Fallow and split for Dilute.

There is also further information, which we are conveying in this statement of genetic make-up. For recessive mutations, if the bird is expressing that mutation then we have two genes for that mutation. If it is said to be split, then we have one gene only. If the mutation is sex-linked, then expression of the mutation implies two genes if it is a cock and one gene if it is a hen.

If dominant mutations are involved, it is traditional to use the Single Factor (SF) and Double Factor (DF) terminology to indicate how many genes we have for these mutations. For co-dominant mutations, we generally have two names – one for the Single Factor form and one for the Double Factor form. Some organisations have attempted to change the naming of co-dominant mutations to Single Factor and Double Factor to better explain to breeders what is happening.

## Dominant and Recessive Inheritance

How do we use this information? Each individual has its chromosomes arranged in pairs that separate and are inherited independently by their offspring. If the bird has two genes for the mutation, then it does not matter which chromosome from the pair is inherited by the young, they must always get one of these identical genes. However, if the bird only has one gene for a mutation, any youngster has a 50% chance of either receiving it or missing out.

For any mating between two birds, we consider each mutation involved from each parent separately and determine

*A typical recessive mutation – the Fallow Hooded Parrot.*

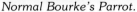

G ROMAN

*A typical dominant mutation – the Greygreen Rainbow Lorikeet.*

what genes the youngster is likely to inherit and in how many possible combinations. We then simply add up the genes to determine which mutation the bird will express. For a **dominant** mutation to appear, the bird only needs to inherit *one gene* from either parent. For a **recessive** mutation to appear, the bird must inherit a gene for the mutation from each parent thereby giving it *two genes* for the colour. If a bird only inherits one gene for a recessive mutation, it will remain hidden by the bird's genetic make-up and the bird is referred to as 'split' for the recessive colour.

In this basic system, we ignore the presence of wildtype genes. If the bird does not have two genes for a mutation, then it has at least one wildtype gene to oppose the mutation. Therefore if we simply concentrate on the colour mutation genes, and if we do not have enough for any mutation to appear, then we must have a bird of Normal appearance.

Congratulations, you are now beginning to crawl and are well on your way to walking. However, if you are finding the system I am describing difficult to follow, do not despair. You may find it helpful to refer to a different system of terminology used in another book such as *A Guide to Cockatiels*. This book also makes use of excellent diagrams which can help you visualise the process of genetic inheritance.

## Sex-linked Inheritance

You now need to learn how **sex-linked** mutations work. The trick with these mutations is that cocks have two *X chromosomes*, but hens have only one. In the hen the other chromosome of the pair is a *Y chromosome* which is too small to carry any genes. As a result, it does not carry any of the wildtype genes that oppose mutations carried on the X chromosome. This means that a hen only needs one gene for a sex-linked mutation to be expressed, but a cock needs two.

It also means that a hen cannot pass a sex-linked mutation on to her daughters, because they receive her Y chromosome instead. If a chick receives its mother's X chromosome, it has to be a cock because it can only inherit another X chromosome from its father.

In other words, hens only pass sex-linked

*A typical sex-linked mutation – the Cinnamon Turquoise Parrot.*

mutations to their sons, whilst cocks pass them to both sons and daughters. The daughters will be visual for the mutation, but the sons will only be visual if they inherit the mutation from both the father and the mother.

If you are still with me, you should be crawling at a fair speed now and ready to take your first steps.

## Gene Families

There are two special situations that can alter the results we achieve. Firstly, if we have more than one mutation from the one **gene family** and, secondly, if we have any **linked genes** involved. Both of these special conditions alter the standard outcomes that we might expect in the basic systems described.

Gene families occur when more than one mutation occurs at the same site or location. Mutations within a family can be viewed as alternatives for one another. Mutations occur only through alteration of an existing gene for colour production. If a pre-existing gene is altered in two different ways, then this will result in two different mutations that belong to the same gene family. If it happens three times, we might have three family members. In the Budgerigar, we have four members of the Blue gene family – two Blue genes and two Parblue genes.

Gene families are special because members of a family can work together in special ways. Since they represent different forms of the same gene, they act as partial copies of one another. It is as though the bird has two genes for the one mutation, instead of two different mutations.

The appearance of the bird that inherits two different genes from the one family varies depending on the gene family involved and some special interactions that occur. The important thing to understand at this stage is that you do not see a Normal appearance when a bird has two different genes belonging to the one gene family, as you would if the mutations were not related.

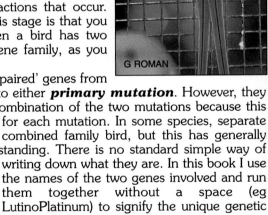

G ROMAN

Generally speaking, these birds with 'paired' genes from one family have a differing appearance to either **primary mutation**. However, they cannot be written down as a standard combination of the two mutations because this would signify that they carry two genes for each mutation. In some species, separate unique names have been given to the combined family bird, but this has generally happened purely through lack of understanding. There is no standard simple way of writing down what they are. In this book I use the names of the two genes involved and run them together without a space (eg LutinoPlatinum) to signify the unique genetic interaction between the two genes.

The most common gene families are the Blue gene family, the Lutino gene family and the Dilute gene family (in Budgerigars).

*All Blue and Parblue mutations form a genetic family.*
*Above: The Turquoise Indian Ringnecked Parrot.*
*Left: The Blue Indian Ringnecked Parrot.*

# Linked Genes and Crossover

Up until now we have been treating all mutations as being inherited separately. However, this is not always the case. Genes live on chromosomes and each has a special address (called a ***locus***) which cannot be altered. Chromosomes are inherited separately, but genes are inherited carried on the chromosome where they live. Therefore if two different mutations have addresses that are on the same chromosome, they are said to be linked and will be inherited together if *coupled* (when both are on the same chromosome) or individually if in *repulsion* (when one is on each chromosome of a pair).

This phenomenon is responsible for the difficulty in combining certain mutations such as Blue and Olive as well as the various sex-linked mutations. In fact, if it were not for another special condition known as ***crossover***, you could never combine two linked mutations.

Crossover is a form of genetic rearrangement that occurs during the process of forming ova or sperm. It is a kind of genetic 'deckchair swapping' between ships on separate voyages. The 'deckchair' on one chromosome (one voyage) can be swapped with a 'deckchair' on the other chromosome (the other voyage), but only with the 'deckchair' that lives at the same address on the other chromosome.

Through this process of swapping genes between chromosomes of a pair, genes that were destined to be inherited apart can then be inherited together. They are then said to be inherited together through crossing over. However, do not forget that crossing over can separate two mutations that were linked together in a reverse of the process. It works in either direction just as effectively.

So how difficult is crossover? This depends on how close the addresses of the two mutations are to each other. The process is random, but relatively common along the tremendously long lengths of chromosomes. If two mutations live right next door to each other, it is less likely that chance will separate them, but if they are further apart the chances increase. The likelihood that swapping will occur is measured as a percentage (eg 3% means three crossovers occur in every 100 young).

There is also another aspect to the written terminology of gene linkage that must be mentioned and has to do with the way the genetic make-up of each bird is written down. Consider these two birds:

Normal/Cinnamon/Opaline cock and Normal/Cinnamon-Opaline cock

The genetic name of each cock identifies its genetic make-up. Both cocks are Normal birds double split for Cinnamon and Opaline. The first bird has the Cinnamon gene on one X chromosome and the Opaline gene on the other X chromosome. The second bird has both the Cinnamon and the Opaline genes linked on the one X chromosome and the other X chromosome carries only wildtype genes. The hyphen signifies that the two genes are linked on the one chromosome. (Refer to page 176 for breeding results that highlight these differences.)

If the two linked mutations are both recessive or both sex-linked the above method works well. However, in the case of the linkage between a dominant mutation and a recessive mutation, a differing designation needs to be used. In these cases, we use the terms ***Type 1*** and ***Type 2.*** It can be quite confusing trying to remember which is which and under which circumstances a linkage is designated as either Type 1 or Type 2. (For further information refer to page 274.)

## Linked Genes and Crossover – Another Way of Looking at It

I shall attempt to explain what these terms mean by using an analogy. Let us start by considering only the sex chromosomes (X and Y). (The same process applies to all the other chromosomes as well, except that both sexes have two chromosomes of the same length which carry the same genes for each pair of chromosomes in the genetic make-up.) Visualise the chromosomes as strings of beads, all normal-coloured beads. Imagine that the X chromosome is a string with ten beads on it and the Y chromosome

**Sex-linked mutations are linked to one another, as well as the X chromosome.**
*Right: Lutino Red-rumped Parrot.*
*Centre right: Cinnamon Red-rumped Parrot.*
*Bottom right: Opaline Red-rumped Parrot cock.*

G ROMAN

is a short string without any beads. Each of these normal beads has an important function in the bird and they all act together to produce the end product we see – the Normal bird.

The cock has two X chromosomes and therefore two strings of ten beads each, whilst the hen has only one string of ten beads (X) and a short string with no beads (Y). If we substitute one of the hen's beads with a yellow bead (representing ino), she will now appear as a Lutino. This yellow bead cannot go just anywhere, it can only lie in its special position, say the third bead from the end of the string of beads.

If this hen breeds with a Normal cock, a son receives a string of beads from each parent. From the father he receives one string with ten normal beads and from the mother one string of beads with the yellow bead at the third position. This young cock then has two strings of beads, with one yellow bead like his mother, however, he is normal in appearance because at the third position on the string from the father, there is a normal bead to oppose the yellow bead from the mother. If he were to be mated back to a Lutino hen, Lutino cocks could be produced with two yellow beads (one at the third position on each string of beads). This is standard *sex-linked inheritance*.

Let us make things a little more complicated. Consider the Cinnamon mutation. A Cinnamon hen has a brown bead at the fourth position on her long string of beads, but a normal bead at every other position including the third position. We then mate her to the Lutino cock to produce Lutino daughters and double split sons.

These double split cocks have one string from their father and one from their mother. The father's string has a yellow bead at position three and the mother's string has a brown bead at

G ROMAN

position four. He does not show either colour because he still has one normal bead at both the third and fourth positions.

We then breed from this bird. To simplify things let us only consider his daughters. Half of his daughters receive the string with the yellow bead and become Lutino and half receive the string with the brown bead and become Cinnamon. This would be all you get except for the rare occurrence of crossing over between the strings.

Crossover (for X chromosomes) only occurs in the testes whilst sperm are being produced by the father. (For non sex chromosomes it occurs in the respective testes or ovaries for each sex of bird.) In crossover, the two strings swap a bead. However, they can only swap beads that belong to the same position on each string. In the above double split cock, crossover could result in the two coloured beads (yellow and brown) both being on the one string or it could result in no coloured beads (ie only normal beads) on the string. Therefore a small percentage of young daughters will receive two coloured beads and become a Lacewing (Cinnamon Lutino), whilst a similar (but still small) number will be pure Normals (only normal beads). The percentage you get depends on how close together the two beads are. In this case they are side by side, so crossover occurs only 3% of the time.

Now let us mate the Lacewing hen to a Normal cock. Their sons will receive two coloured beads from their mother (a yellow and a brown) but none from their father. They will also be double splits, but quite different from the other double split mentioned above. This time when we breed from this double split, half the daughters get a string with no coloured beads (only normal beads) and half get the string with two coloured beads and become Lacewings. If crossover occurs (remember that there is only a 3% chance) you can also get a few Lutino hens and a few Cinnamon hens.

What is a Lacewing cock? He must have four coloured beads (two yellow and two brown) occupying the third and fourth positions respectively of both strings. If we breed with him and crossover occurs, a yellow bead swaps with a yellow bead, or a brown bead swaps with a brown bead and the result does not change. You still get 100% Lacewing hens.

In the above examples, it is the positions on a respective string where particular beads must lie, which are linked together by the string. When it is said that Lutino and Cinnamon are linked, we are referring to their locations, not simply the **mutant alleles** themselves. The beads are only linked if they are on the one string. If they are on separate strings, they are still linked, but in this situation they are linked to normal beads sitting in those positions.

Linkage can also apply to non sex chromosomes, but in this case the crossover may occur in the hen as well, as she has two full strings just like her mate. This linkage occurs between Blue and Dark Factor. These two mutations lie on the one chromosome with a crossover rate of 14%.

# ESTABLISHING NEW MUTATIONS

When discussing genetics with breeders I am often asked 'I have this unusual coloured bird, what is it?' and 'what should I mate it to?' These are two of the most common questions asked of me when discussing genetics. Remember that you cannot name the mutation correctly until it has been bred for a number of years. Unfortunately the mistakes made in pairing these mutations often delay, or even prevent your finding out what kind of mutation it is.

This occurs because the first advice given to most owners of an apparent new colour is either 'mate it to its parent' or 'mate it to its sibling'. This often sounds the death knell for the new

*A 'Cinnamon' Military Macaw – this is an albinistic mutation, but unlikely to be a true Cinnamon.*

mutation because inbreeding suppresses fertility. It is doubly worse because inadvertent (or sometimes deliberate) inbreeding is often the reason why the mutation 'appeared' in the first place. Such advice is often given freely and in large quantities by breeders who may be quite experienced. However, free advice is generally only worth what you paid for it.

If you believe you have a new and different mutation, what should you do? Before deciding what to mate it to, you need to consider the 'new' bird itself. Most new mutations appear in their final form with their first appearance and most desirable mutations are significantly different from the original wild form. However, if the new mutation occurs in a bird already expressing another colour mutation it can sometimes be difficult to detect. There are also some mutations that appear in the opposite manner, being more noticeable in combination with a second mutation (eg Blue) than on the wild colour form.

Most of the possible 'new' colours I am shown fall into the category of variations of either the Normal bird or, sometimes, established mutations. This is not to denigrate or reject these new birds, but simply to try and place them in context. If the change is small, it

**It is often impossible to correctly identify new mutations before they are fully established and studied in great detail.**

*Above: 'Olive' Hooded Parrot.*
*Right: Yellow Regent Parrot.*
*Far right: 'Olive Pied' Alexandrine Parrot.*

is probably a variation. Therefore it may never be any different and this must be considered before starting a long involved project to establish it. However, the possibility is always there that the 'new' mutation can be selectively enhanced to create an appearance deemed desirable by the public if it has **multigenic inheritance** (eg Red-fronted in Turquoise and Scarlet-chested Parrots). The road is still going to be long and difficult, with improvement being reduced by the necessary outcrosses needed to maintain fertility.

If the change from Normal is large, then the likelihood is that it represents a **primary mutation** of a single gene. This means that it will be inherited simply and can be established much more easily (if the correct approach is taken).

P ODEKERKEN

*This new colour in the African Grey Parrot has been called a 'Red Pied'. However, the appearance is not consistent with what we would expect from a Pied mutation and the exact nature is yet to be determined.*

## Establishing Primary Mutations

### Step 1

At this stage we all try to guess what form of inheritance the new colour is, but it is only a guess and is irrelevant for the first mating. **For the first mating, always use an unrelated Normal bird of the highest quality (including fertility) that is available**. (Try not to use Normal birds split for other colours as their appearance in subsequent generations may confuse the inheritance and disguise the appearance of the new colour.) Breed as many young as possible from this mating in the first season. Consider breeding techniques such as fostering of eggs and young to increase output and to lessen the workload for the 'new' bird.

During the first year, there is one other very important mating that should not be forgotten – the mating between the parents of the new colour bird.

K BUCKLEY

*'Partial-ino' Red-tailed Black Cockatoo – wild colour morphs may never be properly identified.*

These two should be kept together in the hope that they will produce more offspring of the new colour in subsequent years. These birds have the best chance of producing more of the new colour in the first few years.

M GERRITSEN

*Unnamed Cloncurry Parrot – clearly a form of albinism.*

Siblings of the new colour bird can also be considered for matings, however, I reiterate that inbreeding with these birds should be avoided. If room is a luxury, any siblings may be held for later matings, because outcrossing them to Normal birds will produce large numbers of young with unknown value to the process. If the new colour is a possible sex-linked mutation, then mating a sibling brother to a Normal hen would be useful and could help prove the inheritance form.

ABK

Left: 'Cinnamon' Twenty-eight Parrot – colours like this one are sometimes a Lime mutation rather than a true Cinnamon and cannot be proved until test mated to a Lutino mutation. The Lime Red-rumped Parrot had to wait 60 years before being correctly identified.
Below: 'Golden' Eastern Rosella – a unique mutation that does not fit any recognised group.

T DULIERE

Otherwise, siblings of the original new colour are possibly best held in reserve until as late as Step 3 below.

The results of your first season will tell us a lot (but not everything) about the genetics and will set the course for the next season, however not in the way you might expect. Everyone wants to take the first offspring of the opposite sex to the original 'new colour' bird and mate it back to its parent. This only falls for the inbreeding trap once again and this path should never be followed.

What we do is assess and interpret the results of our first generation outcross. If the original 'new colour' bird is a hen, then any 'new colour' young from this first mating would indicate that we have a dominant (or co-dominant) mutation. It is more difficult to rule this out with the lack of 'new colour' young unless you have bred at least 20 youngsters in the first generation. Even then you cannot be certain if the 'new colour' is simple recessive or sex-linked.

If the original 'new colour' bird is a cock, then 'new colour' sons would indicate a dominant (or co-dominant) mutation, whilst daughters could indicate either dominant or sex-linked inheritance. To say it is recessive from this mating would require approximately 20 Normal hens being bred from the cock to be reasonably certain that the 'new colour' is not sex-linked. Do not worry too much about determining recessive inheritance, it will be proven by further generations.

Theoretically a sex-linked mutation will not first appear as a cock. That is, if you know the mother and she is not a 'new colour', then the son is not sex-linked. However if he came from an unknown source, consider that he may already be a second generation and the original breeder did not identify what it was. This situation must also be considered when other mutations are involved with the original production of the 'new colour'. Many mutations can hide or mask other mutations. This is one of the reasons why it is always advisable to use Normal birds for outcrossing until such time as the mutation is established.

J POSTEMA

'Clearhead' Alexandrine Parrot – could be a Fallow mutation like a similar colour in the Indian Ringnecked Parrot.

## Step 2

If the results of the first mating indicate a dominant (or co-dominant) mutation, you have a relatively easy path to follow.

Mate any new coloured young produced to unrelated Normal birds, using as many differing unrelated bloodlines as possible. Next to consider are the future matings for the parents. If good numbers of young were produced from the first pairing then mate this pair again to continue producing as many young as possible. If not, then consider a new mate that might be more compatible or productive. Dominant mutations can be continually outcrossed each generation, but after two or three outcrosses, the breeder can consider trying to produce Double Factor birds as well as combinations with other mutations.

'Dilute' Lineolated Parrot – a new mutation being established in the USA.

If the results of the first mating indicate that the 'new colour' could be of recessive or sex-linked inheritance, then the path to follow differs slightly. In these cases it is best to pair the original 'new colour' bird to a new bird for the second mating. Once again the bird used should be a Normal of good bloodlines which is unrelated to the first Normal bird used. This mating will hopefully produce reasonable numbers of further split birds that are only one quarter related to the young from the first mating.

If young from the first mating are sufficiently mature, they can be mated together for one season whilst you are awaiting less related matings to become available. If production is poor from these matings, do not be too concerned as this is the effect of inbreeding. Brothers and sisters have half of their genes in common, and if deleterious traits exist in their make-up, there is a good chance they will appear. This generally manifests itself as reduced fertility.

It is interesting to note that young share exactly the same proportion of genes with either parent and this is why father–daughter and mother–son matings can have the same trouble. Many breeders think that these latter matings are less deleterious than brother–sister matings. Some of this thinking may originate from the book by Taylor and Warner (1986) *Genetics for Budgerigar Breeders*, which mistakenly claims that there is a difference. This is a sad error in an otherwise important book.

## Step 3

Hopefully by the third season, you should have two partly related lines of splits who share one parent in common, but not both. As many pairings as possible should be made between these birds to increase the odds of producing 'new colour' young. Remember that if two splits are paired together, one in four young can be expected to be coloured.

This generation should prove whether the mutation is recessive and your results should go a long way to proving sex-linked inheritance if that is the mode being followed. Breeders who chose the ill-advised path of inbreeding, will not have been able to prove any inheritance at all at this stage. By always mating a 'new colour' bird to a related bird, you can never be sure whether you have splits or not. Many dominant mutations have been considered recessive because of this path, thereby creating a confusing myth of two forms of inheritance for the one mutation.

By the end of the third step, you should then consider the results to this stage. If fertility is good and production high, then cautious matings between 'new colour' and

'Cinnamon' or 'Dilute' Maroon-bellied Conure.

split birds can be tried, as well as attempting the first matings for combination with other mutations.

However, if fertility is still poor and numbers produced are still low, then it is advised that the original bird be mated to a third Normal bird and that any 'new colour' chicks from the third step be outcrossed to Normals for the next generation.

Always remember that you cannot lose a recessive mutation if you have lots of splits and that there is no point in inbreeding if you have a dominant mutation. The original bird has two of the mutant genes (one only if it is a dominant mutation or a sex-linked hen) and every youngster will have one gene for the mutation. Therefore ten young bred from one original bird is equivalent to five of the new mutation with twice the likelihood that they will breed (twice as many birds equals twice as many chances).

## Establishing Selective Traits

To achieve this aim requires a different approach to that for a primary single gene mutation. By their very nature, selective traits rely upon selection of multiple genes from each parent. With time these multiple genes must be collected into one individual to increase or alter the trait to the desired outcome. This will always require some degree of inbreeding to achieve its aim. The successful breeder needs to find the balance between inbreeding to enhance a desired trait and outcrossing to maintain vigour and fertility. It is a fine path to tread and many efforts end in failure.

If you have what appears as a possible selective trait, I would still recommend outcrossing to Normal for the first generation. Because of the multigenic action of selective traits, you will almost always find that they act as dominant to Normal, with the resultant young simply expressing a lesser effect than the parent. I would still recommend outcrossing the original bird to a second Normal bird and then combining the young from the two lines following the method for recessive traits. (See previous section page 37.) This way you have reduced the degree of inbreeding before you start. At this point you could also consider mating the original parent back to an offspring to explore whether the trait can be enhanced. Many attempts run aground at this stage; or the breeder loses interest because of lack of results.

If your first outcross suggests that the trait is recessive, follow the same path as for a primary mutation, as this is probably what it is. However, you must consider whether it is likely to have any potential for selection and development. Often the answer is no, if the original change from Normal is small.

## Summary

It should be obvious from reading the above discussion on establishing mutations, that it is not an easy process. You should also realise that it is a numbers game. The more pairs you have, the more successful you will be. Many people try to establish a mutation when they only have room for one or two pairs. This will never work. If you do not have the room, build some more aviaries. Alternatively give the birds to someone who has the room and hopefully the experience to succeed. For every new mutation that is established at least as many fail and become lost to aviculture.

# PRIMARY COLOUR MUTATIONS

Primary colour mutations are created by a **single** mutation, as opposed to combinations where more than one primary colour mutation is involved, or variations of colour created by the action of modifying genes. The following sections deal with all the common primary colour mutations.

## Blue

Possibly the simplest mutation is the one that inactivates the production of the yellow family pigments. We call this mutation Blue because in any common green-coloured parrot, the presence of this mutation results in a blue appearance for the bird. Remember that the colours blue and yellow create green. If the yellow is removed you are left with blue. It is that simple. In a grey-coloured species such as the Cockatiel or the Galah, the Blue gene still performs the same function, ie to remove the yellow, red, orange and pink colours. Therefore, the Blue mutation in these species is grey and white. In these limited cases it may be acceptable to use species-specific names such as Whiteface in the Cockatiel. However, it is important that breeders understand that they are dealing with the Blue gene.

Blue mutations can vary in shade, depending on the colours in the wildtype for the species. In some species (eg Indian Ringnecked Parrot) the colour may be even and intense because the green of the Normal bird is strong and even. In other species (eg Twenty-eight Parrot) the blue comes in many shades, once again because the Normal wildtype bird has many shades of green. With so many shades of colour, it can sometimes become difficult to determine if a blue-coloured bird represents the Blue mutation or the closely related Parblue mutation. The only way to be certain is to combine the mutation with the Lutino gene. In this way grey family pigments (and therefore blues, blacks and browns) are removed, thereby revealing any residual underlying yellow family pigments that would make the mutation a Parblue rather than a Blue mutation.

Normal-coloured parrots are known as **Yellow Ground** because of the presence of these yellow family pigments. Birds exhibiting the Blue gene are known as **White Ground** due to the absence of the yellow family pigments. This distinction is important for understanding the naming of some colours such as Cinnamon, Fawn, Lutino and Albino. Parblue birds (those with reduced yellow family pigments but not total absence) are known as **Cream Ground**, hence the combination known as Creamino.

Blue mutations are not only very attractive and common in parrot species, they are also one of the most useful mutations for combining with other mutations. Unfortunately, many of these combinations have suffered

ABK

*Blue Budgerigar – breeders traditionally call it 'Sky Blue', however this is superfluous.*

TOBY MARTIN

*Blue Scarlet-chested Parrot.*

*Blue Blue-winged Parrot.*

*Blue Red-rumped Parrot.*

*Blue Mallee Ringnecked Parrot.*

*Blue Port Lincoln Parrot.*

from misnaming. The following is a list of names for Blue combination colours:

Albino  – Blue Lutino
Ivory   – Cinnamon Blue
White   – Yellow Blue
Silver  – Dilute Grey, Dilute Blue or Faded Blue
Fawn    – Cinnamon Greygreen Blue
Cream   – Dilute Cinnamon Greygreen Blue
Grey    – Greygreen Blue
Cobalt  – Dark Green Blue
Mauve   – Olive Blue

The true Blue mutation is established or has occurred in a large number of species and will no doubt occur in all, given time. The following species have produced examples of the Blue mutation:

Budgerigar (two forms)
Scarlet-chested Parrot
Blue-winged Parrot
Red-rumped Parrot
Mallee Ringnecked Parrot
Port Lincoln Parrot
Twenty-eight Parrot
Eastern Rosella
Pale-headed Rosella
Crimson Rosella
Western Rosella
Princess Parrot
King Parrot
Eclectus Parrot
Cockatiel
Galah
Rainbow Lorikeet (extinct)
Scaly-breasted Lorikeet
Masked Lovebird
Nyasa Lovebird
Fischer's Lovebird
Black-cheeked Lovebird
Indian Ringnecked Parrot
Alexandrine Parrot
Plum-headed Parrot
Moustache Parrot
African Grey Parrot
Pacific Parrotlet
Blue-winged Parrotlet
Plain Parakeet
Scarlet Macaw
Blue and Gold Macaw
Quaker Parrot
Yellow-naped Conure
Golden-crowned Conure
Dusky-headed Conure
Blue-fronted Amazon
Yellow-naped Amazon

*Blue Twenty-eight Parrot.*

*Blue Princess Parrot.*

1

G ROMAN

2

P RANKINE

6

J POSTEMA

3

G ROMAN

1. *Blue Crimson Rosella.*
2. *Blue Pale-headed Rosella.*
3. *Blue (Whiteface) Cockatiel.*
4. *Blue (White-fronted) Galah.*
5. *Blue Western Rosella.*
6. *Blue Eclectus Parrot.*

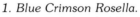

5

E ANTONIN

4

T OSBORNE

W CALDWELL

S & J SMITH

P ODEKERKEN

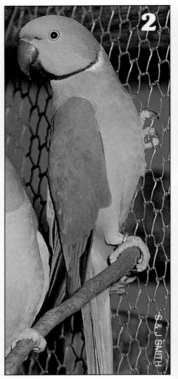

R ERHART

1. *Blue Rainbow Lorikeet.*
2. *Blue Indian Ringnecked Parrot.*
3. *Blue Scaly-breasted Lorikeet.*
4. *Blue Pacific Parrotlet.*
5. *Blue Eastern Rosella.*
6. *Blue Scarlet Macaw.*
7. *Blue Alexandrine Parrot.*
8. *Blue Masked Lovebird.*

J POSTEMA

R SWEENEY

P RANKINE

R LOW

J POSTEMA

J POSTEMA

R LOW

1. Blue Golden-crowned Conure.
2. Blue Moustache Parrot.
3. Blue Quaker Parrot.
4. Normal Blue and Gold Macaw (L) and Blue mutation (R).
5. Blue Fischer's Lovebird.
6. Blue King Parrot.
7. Blue Blue-fronted Amazon.

B BRANSTON

R ERHART

C CAIRNCROSS

It is interesting to note that in the Budgerigar there are two Blue mutations, which are both related but interact in an unexpected fashion. Budgerigar breeders know the second mutation by the name Yellowface Mutant 1. When the two different Blue genes are combined, a parblue-coloured bird results. This has been an extremely difficult concept for everyone to understand. (For more information refer to page 241.)

The Blue mutation is always a recessive mutation following the standard rules, which give the following outcomes from matings:

| | |
|---|---|
| **Blue x Normal** | = 100% Normal/Blue |
| **Normal/Blue x Blue** | = 50% Normal/Blue<br>+ 50% Blue |
| **Normal/Blue x Normal/Blue** | = 25% Normal<br>+ 50% Normal/Blue<br>+ 25% Blue |
| **Blue x Blue** | = 100% Blue |

## Parblue

The same gene that, when fully inactive creates the Blue mutation, can be partially activated to create intermediate colour mutations (part way between green and blue) known as Parblue. Together, these colour mutations form a genetic family with the Blue mutation. Therefore, whilst all Parblues are recessive mutations, they are dominant to the Blue mutation as it is part of their family. Unfortunately, the true nature of this genetic relationship can only be described accurately in genetic terms. (If the reader feels up to the challenge, for further information refer to page 241.) The correct terminology for this genetic interaction is that the Blue and Parblue mutations are ***multiple alleles*** for the same locus.

R CUSICK

*Above: Turquoise Green-cheeked Conure.*
*Below: Parblue (L) and ParblueBlue (R) (Goldenface) Budgerigars.*

The existence of this genetic family has long been the bane of Budgerigar breeders who, through their show circuit, have learnt that all birds are either green or blue in colour. The truth is that they can be Parblue (in the Budgerigar these mutations are known as Goldenface and Yellowface Mutant 2) as well, giving four base colours! This complication has led to the false belief that Parblue is somehow dominant or co-dominant and that green birds simply mask the colour. It has also created the mistaken belief that these mutations add yellow family pigments to the bird, when in effect they simply remove less than the true Blue mutation. It is true that they do produce some yellow family pigments, but compared to the Normal bird they are defective.

D VREMEC

Some Parblue mutations can remove all yellow from part of the bird, but leave some present in other areas (eg the 'Whiteface Blue' Peachfaced Lovebird and probably the

*Turquoise Peachfaced Lovebird – commonly referred to as 'Whiteface Blue', a misleading name for a Parblue mutation.*

*Applegreen Peachfaced Lovebird – incorrectly called 'Seagreen' in the USA.*

*Aqua Peachfaced Lovebird – incorrectly called 'Pastel' or 'Dutch Blue'.*

*Right: Turquoise Alexandrine Parrot.*

G ROMAN

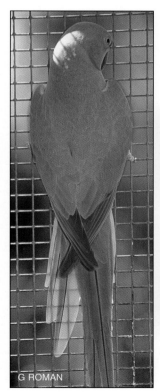

G ROMAN

*Turquoise Indian Ringnecked Parrot – this colour should never be called 'Pastel'.*

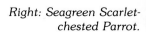

G ROMAN

*Above: Aqua Scarlet-chested Parrot – generally known by breeders as Parblue.*

*Right: Seagreen Scarlet-chested Parrot.*

TOBY MARTIN

C SMITH

B NIELSEN

Australian 'Blue' Western Rosella). Jim Hayward (1992) has proposed the alternative name of Lavender for Parblues that act this way. He also favours the use of the name Marine instead of Parblue. Marine superficially appears as an apt and unique name, however the avicultural world has been reluctant to accept these names. Part of the problem is that when translated into various European languages, Marine becomes Navy Blue, obviously a poor choice.

Various names are also being used for Parblues in different species, including Turquoise, Marine, Pastel Blue, Pastelface, Seagreen and even Seablue. All these names are synonymous and it would be best to simply call all of them by the same name. It is preferable to apply the name Parblue to the overall class of colours, whilst possibly retaining its use for those mutations that are almost blue in colour (this use could cause confusion). Seagreen is the best choice for those ranging from 50% loss of yellow family pigments through to those closer to the normal green colour. Turquoise is favoured as a better alternative for Parblue mutations closer in colour to a true Blue mutation. Finally, for mutations that are currently being called Marine, Aqua is a suitable alternative that is easily adapted into other languages as well. *Note: the use of the name 'Pastel' for Parblue mutations (as is common in Australia and the UK) should be discontinued, as Pastel correctly refers to a grey family pigment diluting gene. (See pages 67.)*

*Top: The Australian 'Blue' Western Rosella appears to be a Parblue type mutation rather than a true Blue.*
*Above: The Turquoise Lineolated Parrot is commonly misnamed 'Blue'.*

The action of the Parblue gene is to give the bird what has been called a Cream Ground colour. Hence, when combined with the Lutino mutation, we get the Creamino. In effect the change of ground colour is part way between the natural yellow colour and the pure white colour of White Ground – a lighter shade of yellow.

All Parblue mutations are recessive to Normal. However, as mentioned earlier, they belong to the Blue gene family and interact with Blue genes in various ways. The standard interaction is for co-dominance between Blue and Parblue (the intermediate result being midway between Blue and Parblue). When a bird receives one gene for Parblue and one gene for Blue, the resultant young are part way between parblue and blue in colour. Sometimes the combination produces more yellow than either mutation, almost a sum of the two (giving a more green-coloured bird than the Parblue). I call the genetic pairing of Parblue and Blue genes a ParblueBlue without a space in the name to signify that it is not a standard combination. (See page 32.)

*Left: The Australian Parblue Crimson Rosella appears to be a Turquoise mutation.*

*Right: The European Parblue Crimson Rosella known as 'Orange' appears to be a Seagreen mutation.*

G ROMAN

H KREMER

The following are some standard mating results:

| | |
|---|---|
| **Parblue x Normal** | = 100% Normal/Parblue |
| **Normal/Parblue x Parblue** | = 50% Normal/Parblue<br>+ 50% Parblue |
| **Normal/Parblue x Normal/Parblue** | = 25% Normal,<br>+ 50% Normal/Parblue<br>+ 25% Parblue |
| **Parblue x Blue** | = 100% ParblueBlue |
| **Parblue x ParblueBlue** | = 50% Parblue<br>+ 50% ParblueBlue |
| **ParblueBlue x Blue** | = 50% ParblueBlue<br>+ 50% Blue |
| **Normal/Parblue x Blue** | = 50% Normal/Blue<br>+ 50% ParblueBlue |
| **Normal/Blue x Parblue** | = 50% Normal/Parblue<br>+ 50% ParblueBlue |
| **Normal/Parblue x Normal/Blue** | = 25% Normal<br>+ 25% Normal/Blue<br>+ 25% Normal/Parblue<br>+ 25% ParblueBlue |
| **Normal/Blue x ParblueBlue** | = 25% Normal/Parblue<br>+ 25% Normal/Blue<br>+ 25% ParblueBlue<br>+ 25% Blue |

The Parblue mutation combines well with most other mutations, creating subtle effects with shades of green, blue, yellow and white.

Above: Aqua(marine) Quaker Parrot.
Right: The Parblue Cockatiel is generally known as
'Pastelface', an incorrect name. An acceptable
alternative could be 'Paleface'.

The Parblue mutation is established or has occurred in the following species:
Budgerigar (two forms)
Turquoise Parrot (extinct?)
Scarlet-chested Parrot (two forms)
Red-rumped Parrot
Eastern Rosella
Crimson Rosella (two forms)
Western Rosella (probably)
Cockatiel
Peachfaced Lovebird (two forms)
Indian Ringnecked Parrot
Alexandrine Parrot
Plum-headed Parrot
Moustache Parrot
Lineolated Parrot
Quaker Parrot

At present the real situation with regard to the two mutations known as 'Parblue' and 'Seagreen' in the Scarlet-chested Parrot is still unclear. It is still possible that in this species (alone at this point) we have a Seagreen mutation that is not part of the Blue gene family. The problem is that the various Blue and Parblue genes have been so interbred that the genetics of any particular bird is totally confused. We also know from Budgerigars that unusual results are sometimes produced even when all genes belong to the one family. For now it is best to consider that these mutations behave according to the standard rules, with the hope that future research might shed further light on the subject.

In the Peachfaced Lovebird the two Parblue forms also interact in an unusual way, with the combined bird being closer to Normal in colour. This form is often called Applegreen (and known incorrectly in the USA as Seagreen). It has one gene for each of the two Parblue colours: Aqua ('Pastel Blue') and Turquoise ('Whiteface Blue').

# Lutino – Sex-linked

The sex-linked Lutino mutation is the simplest 'grey family pigment affecting' mutation to explain. It is also one of the most common mutations across species and after the Blue mutation, the easiest to recognise. The standard Lutino gene is a sex-linked recessive mutation and represents the same gene as the Albino gene in mammals. No **single** gene known can prevent production of both grey family pigments and yellow family pigments and this is why no single Albino gene exists in parrots that have yellow family pigments in their Normal form. You need the Blue gene to remove the yellow family pigments and the Lutino gene to remove the grey family pigments. Together they create an Albino.

*Lutino Budgerigar.*

The best way to imagine how the Lutino gene works is to visualise a leaking tap that governs production of black, grey and brown pigments. That is the effect of the Lutino mutation. It does not alter the yellow family pigments, the structural aspects of colour production, or the distribution of pigments. However, it does seem that the tap leaks and can never be totally turned off. Some species have Lutino mutations with suspect green tinges. It has also been shown in some species that combination with the Cinnamon mutation highlights this leak.

*Lutino Scarlet-chested Parrot.*

Another feature of the Lutino gene is that it can be partially effective in the same way that the Blue gene can. The result is a bird part way between the Normal green bird and the Lutino bird in colour. This mutation has been called Sex-linked Dilute by Jim Hayward (1992), and Parino by George Smith (AVES 95), but neither name has been adopted by the avicultural world. Instead, an ever increasing range of names have been used with little consistency. Some of these include Clearbody, Isabel, Lacewing, Yellow, Cinnamon and Platinum. Many of these names apply to completely different mutations and have been used erroneously. As the name Lime has been used for the recessive 'Partial-Lutino' in lovebirds and has not been used for other purposes to date, I favour its use for these members of the Lutino gene family. (Refer also to the section on Lime and Platinum mutations on page 56.)

There is some debate over the use of the name Lutino in species that have little yellow pigment but a lot of pink or red. The argument is that the name Lutino is not descriptive in these cases, and that these mutations should be called 'Rose-ino' or 'Rubino' or something similar. This debate is no different from the argument against calling a Cockatiel or Galah, Blue. If the correct name is not used for the mutation, confusion will arise as to the real attributes of the mutation. We already have Lutino Opaline combinations in the Eastern Rosella and the Bourke's Parrot being called by the same names. We must have consistency if nothing else, even at the sacrifice of description. In reality no name fully describes any bird or any mutation.

*Lutino Bourke's Parrot.*

G ROMAN

J LAMSHED

*Above: Lutino Red-rumped Parrot.*
*Right: Lutino Adelaide Rosella.*
*Below: Lutino Eastern Rosella.*

J POSTEMA

G MATHESON

J POSTEMA

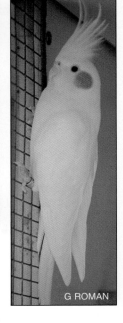

G ROMAN

*Above: Lutino Galah.*
*Left: Lutino Rainbow*
*Lorikeet.*
*Right: Lutino Cockatiel.*

For the sex-linked Lutino mutation, the following matings apply:

| | |
|---|---|
| **Lutino cock x Normal hen** | = Normal/Lutino cocks and Lutino hens |
| **Normal cock x Lutino hen** | = Normal/Lutino cocks and Normal hens |
| **Normal/Lutino cock x Normal hen** | = Normal and Normal/Lutino cocks + Normal and Lutino hens |
| **Normal/Lutino cock x Lutino hen** | = Normal/Lutino and Lutino cocks + Normal and Lutino hens |
| **Lutino cock x Lutino hen** | = Lutino cocks and hens |

The true Lutino mutation is established or has occurred in a large number of species and will no doubt occur in all, given time. The following species have produced examples of the Lutino mutation:

Budgerigar
Bourke's Parrot
Scarlet-chested Parrot
Red-rumped Parrot
Eastern Rosella
Crimson Rosella
Adelaide Rosella
Cockatiel
Galah
Yellow-fronted Kakariki
Red-fronted Kakariki
Scaly-breasted Lorikeet
Peachfaced Lovebird
Red-faced Lovebird (extinct?)
Indian Ringnecked Parrot
Alexandrine Parrot
Moustache Parrot
African Grey Parrot
Blue-winged Parrotlet
Lineolated Parrot
Blue-fronted Amazon

*Above: Lutino Peachfaced Lovebird.*
*Below: Lutino Red-collared Lorikeet.*

S SINDEL

A Lutino Yellow-tailed Black Cockatoo was photographed in the wild during the mid 1980s. A Lutino of unknown inheritance exists in the Superb Parrot. It may be recessive like the Lutino mutation in the closely related Princess Parrot. There are (or have been) Lutino mutations of uncertain inheritance in the Western Rosella, Yellow Rosella, Twenty-eight Parrot, Blue and Gold Macaw, Red-lored

1. Lutino Scaly-breasted Lorikeet.
2. Lutino Indian Ringnecked Parrot.
3. Lutino Alexandrine Parrot.
4. Lutino Lineolated Parrot.
5. Lutino Blue-winged Parrotlet.
6. Lutino Red-fronted Kakariki.

Amazon, Festive Amazon, Nanday Conure, Sun Conure and White-headed Pionus Parrot.

## Addendum

*Recently the sex-linked Lutino gene has been introduced into the Rainbow Lorikeet and the Red-collared Lorikeet through hybridisation with the Scaly-breasted Lorikeet.*

**The following Lutino mutations are of unknown inheritance.**

J POSTEMA

J POSTEMA

S GARSEE

G RADCLIFFE

1. Lutino Red-lored Amazon.
2. Lutino Blue-fronted Amazon.
3. Lutino Superb Parrot.
4. Lutino Western Rosella.
5. Lutino Festive Amazon.
6. Lutino Twenty-eight Parrot.
7. Lutino Dusky-headed Conure.

ANON

T SILVA

E ANTONIN

# Lime and Platinum – Sex-linked

As mentioned in the section on the Lutino mutation, it is possible for intermediate mutations to occur as part of the Lutino gene family. They are quite common and in one species (the Red-rumped Parrot) at least two forms exist. These colour mutations are able to produce some grey family pigments, but not as much as a Normal bird. As a result, the birds are often mistakenly identified as Cinnamon mutations, another sex-linked mutation. However, Cinnamon birds are clearly brown without grey traces and are not reduced in the amount of pigment deposited, whereas Lime and Platinum mutations often contain grey tones and are always reduced in the amount of pigment deposited.

I have chosen to use the name Lime for birds of this mutation because it is used here in Australia for the recessive form of this mutation in lovebird species and has not been misused for

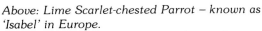

other purposes. For the same reason I have retained the name Platinum which was given by the Cockatiel fraternity to the version in their species. In the Red-rumped Parrot, there are two different versions of this mutation, a darker one (which I call Lime) and a lighter one (which I call Platinum to distinguish it).

---

*Above: Lime Scarlet-chested Parrot – known as 'Isabel' in Europe.*
*Left: Lime Red-rumped Parrot – known by numerous incorrect names.*
*Below left: Comparison of Red-rumped Parrot hens – Lime (L), Platinum (above) and Cinnamon (R).*
*Below: Platinum Red-rumped Parrot.*

In the same way that Parblue interacts with the Blue gene (members of the same family), Lime and Platinum interact with the Lutino gene whose family they belong to. As a result, some interesting breeding results occur with examples below. When a bird receives one gene for Lime and one gene for Lutino, the resultant young are part way between lime and lutino in colour. I call these birds LutinoLime or LutinoPlatinum without a space in the name to signify that they are not standard combinations. (Refer to page 32 for further information on these birds.)

| | |
|---|---|
| **Lime cock x Normal hen** | = Normal/Lime cocks and Lime hens |
| **Normal cock x Lime hen** | = Normal/Lime cocks and Normal hens |
| **Normal/Lime cock x Normal hen** | = Normal and Normal/Lime cocks + Normal and Lime hens |
| **Normal/Lime cock x Lime hen** | = Normal/Lime and Lime cocks + Normal and Lime hens |
| **Normal/Lime cock x Lutino hen** | = Normal/Lutino and LutinoLime cocks + Normal and Lime hens |
| **Lime cock x Lime hen** | = Lime cocks and hens |
| **Lime cock x Lutino hen** | = LutinoLime cocks and Lime hens |
| **Lutino cock x Lime hen** | = LutinoLime cocks and Lutino hens |
| **LutinoLime cock x Normal hen** | = Normal/Lutino and Normal/Lime cocks + Lutino and Lime hens |
| **LutinoLime cock x Lime hen** | = LutinoLime and Lime cocks + Lutino and Lime hens |
| **LutinoLime cock x Lutino hen** | = LutinoLime and Lutino cocks + Lutino and Lime hens |

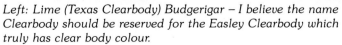

*Left: Lime (Texas Clearbody) Budgerigar – I believe the name Clearbody should be reserved for the Easley Clearbody which truly has clear body colour.*
*Centre: Lime (Pallid) Peachfaced Lovebird – known incorrectly as Australian 'Cinnamon'.*
*Right: Platinum Cockatiel.*

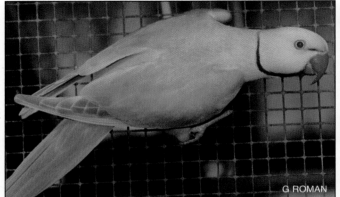

G ROMAN    R JORDAN

*Above: Lime Indian Ringnecked Parrot – should never be referred to as 'Lacewing'.*
*Above right: Green-cheeked Conure – is this mutation a Lime or a Cinnamon?*

S DOAK

*Lime (Pallid) Quaker Parrot – known incorrectly as 'Cinnamon'.*

The true Lime and Platinum mutations are established or have occurred in the following species and will no doubt occur in all species, given time:

Budgerigar
Scarlet-chested Parrot
Red-rumped Parrot (two forms)
Cockatiel
Swift Parrot (uncertain)
Peachfaced Lovebird
Indian Ringnecked Parrot
Quaker Parrot
Green-cheeked Conure (probably)

In Budgerigars the mutation has been called Clearbody. In Scarlet-chested Parrots it has been called Isabel. In Peachfaced Lovebirds it has been called Isabel (in Europe), Australian Ino (in the USA) and Australian Cinnamon (worldwide). In the Red-rumped Parrot the darker mutation has been called Yellow in Europe and UK Cinnamon in Australia, whilst the Indian Ringnecked Parrot mutation has been called Lacewing (a name which indicates the Cinnamon Lutino combination). The Swift Parrot is called Yellow (Kremer, 1992), the Quaker Parrot is known as the Dark-eyed Cinnamon and the Green-cheeked Conure is called Fallow. As you can see, some form of standardisation is in dire need.

### Addendum
*European clubs have recently chosen the name Pallid for this mutation.*

## Lutino – Recessive
There are Lutino genes in some species that are not sex-linked, but are simple recessive. They are in the minority however. Therefore I will concentrate on the sex-linked type in this book.

For the mating results for various combinations of the Recessive Lutino, use those provided for the Dilute mutation and substitute Lutino for Dilute as follows:

| Normal x Lutino | = 100% Normal/Lutino |
|---|---|
| Normal/Lutino x Normal | = 50% Normal<br>+ 50% Normal/Lutino |
| Normal/Lutino x Normal/Lutino | = 25% Normal<br>+ 50% Normal/Lutino<br>+ 25% Lutino |
| Normal/Lutino x Lutino | = 50% Normal/Lutino<br>+ 50% Lutino |
| Lutino x Lutino | = 100% Lutino |

Perhaps with time more Recessive Lutino mutations will occur in other species. There is a belief that the Lutino mutation may prove to form genetic families with recessive Dilutes or possibly Fallow in those species in which they occur.

The Dutch expert Inte Onsman believes that in the Budgerigar, the German Fallow mutation is part of the Recessive Lutino gene family. If this is correct, then other Fallow mutations may also form families with Recessive Lutino genes.

The action of the Recessive Lutino gene is no different from the sex-linked Lutino gene; it turns off (or nearly off) black, grey and brown pigments. In some species the Recessive Lutino mutation is not as effective in reducing these pigments as we would normally expect. Some people are therefore arguing against the name Lutino in these species (eg Princess Parrot). What is

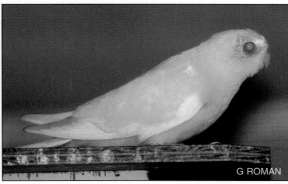

clear is that they represent a member of the Recessive Lutino gene family. If a more effective gene is recognised in the future, then these current birds should be called Lime, but perhaps they are simply as effective as the gene can be in certain species. Only time will tell.

*Above: Recessive Lutino Adelaide Rosella.*
*Left: Recessive Lutino Pacific Parrotlet (foreground).*
*Below left: Recessive Lutino Nyasa Lovebird.*
*Below: Recessive Lutino Elegant Parrot.*

*Above left: Recessive Lutino Slaty-headed Parrot.*

*Above right: Recessive Lutino Princess Parrot.*

*Left: Recessive Lutino Quaker Parrot.*

*Right: Recessive Lutino Fischer's Lovebird.*

The true Recessive Lutino mutation is established or has occurred in the following species:

Budgerigar (historically)
Elegant Parrot
Eastern Rosella (historically)
Crimson Rosella
Adelaide Rosella
Western Rosella
Princess Parrot
Masked Lovebird
Nyasa Lovebird
Fischer's Lovebird
Plum-headed Parrot
Pacific Parrotlet
Quaker Parrot

George Smith (AVES '95) has also reported a Recessive Lutino Indian Ringnecked Parrot.

## Lime – Recessive

Just like the sex-linked Lutino and Lime gene family, there is a Recessive Lutino and Lime gene family. At present the Recessive Lime mutation is only found in three of the White Eye-ring Lovebird group of *Agapornis*. However, as mentioned in the previous section, the German Fallow Budgerigar may be a

*Recessive Lime Princess Parrot.*

member of this mutation group and therefore other Fallow mutations, in other species, may also belong in this group. However, we cannot be certain until Recessive Lutino mutations occur to confirm the inheritance interaction. There is some evidence to suggest that the Fallow Elegant Parrot may fall into this category.

I also suspect that certain variations seen in the 'Recessive Lutino' Princess Parrot are due to one or more Recessive Lime genes. It is possible that our genetic population in this species comprises more than one gene belonging to the Recessive Lutino gene family.

## Cinnamon

The Cinnamon mutation is a sex-linked mutation with a specific effect; it prevents the conversion of brown pigment into black pigment. Therefore, a Cinnamon bird cannot produce black or grey in any colour shade, yet there is no reduction in the amount of pigment found in

*Recessive Lime Fischer's Lovebird – known worldwide as 'Pastel'.*

feathers. Other mutations (eg Fallow) also interrupt production of black pigments, but they do so at earlier stages. Their mode of inheritance is also different.

1. *Cinnamon Scarlet-chested Parrot.*
2. *Cinnamon Crimson-winged Parrot.*
3. *Cinnamon Elegant Parrot.*
4. *Cinnamon Red-rumped Parrot.*
5. *Cinnamon King Parrot.*

G ROMAN

H KREMER

Cinnamon Crimson Rosella.

A CHALMERS

Cinnamon Eastern Rosella.

Cinnamon Adelaide Rosella.

Because of the existence of two types of Lutino genes and of the superficial similarity of other mutations to the Cinnamon, many aviculturists have started calling various recessive mutations 'Cinnamon'. They are not. There is also the previously mentioned confusion between Lime and Cinnamon mutations. This confusion could be excused in that it is another sex-linked mutation. **If it is not sex-linked, it cannot be Cinnamon.** The true Cinnamon gene occurs across many different species of birds from various Families and Orders including parrots and even in reptiles.

Of the birds being incorrectly called 'Cinnamon' most are not even fully brown, but retain large amounts of grey colouration in their plumage, whilst others are clearly Fallow mutations. There is a recessive gene that creates only brown pigment and it is correctly called the Brown mutation. The only known example is the Brownwing mutation in the Budgerigar, which was thought to be lost but may be making a comeback.

How can we be certain that a mutation is a Cinnamon? Firstly, it must be inherited in a sex-linked manner. Secondly, it must not have any grey or black pigment in it. To determine this, either the feathers must be studied microscopically or the mutation must be combined with other mutations; one that removes yellow family pigments, (ie the Blue gene) and, if possible, eliminate structural colour distortion with a Greygreen gene. This will allow clear visualisation of any grey, black or brown pigments in the bird. Many breeders become excited about the presence of a red-brown eye (generally described as plum eyes) in a hatchling. The eye colour darkens as the bird ages. It is true that all Cinnamon chicks have this trait, but other mutations have shades of red-brown eyes as well, so it is not a distinguishing feature for the mutation when taken alone.

It is also vitally important to test mate any bird of apparent 'Cinnamon' colouration to a bird visual for the sex-linked Lutino mutation to rule out the Lime possibility.

Aviculturists who breed species other than parrots will also have heard of the Fawn mutation. This is the same mutation as the Cinnamon mutation. The difference in use for these names is in the ground colour of the bird. Cinnamon is the correct name in a Yellow Ground bird and Fawn is the correct name in a White Ground bird. A species without any yellow family pigments (eg Zebra Finch) has a Fawn mutation whilst others (eg Canary or Star Finch) have Cinnamon mutations. The same rules should apply to parrots; therefore a White Ground Cinnamon could be called a Fawn. As the name Ivory has also been used for White Ground Cinnamon (Cinnamon Blue), I am reserving use of the name Fawn for the Cinnamon Grey combination. (See pages 118 and 122.)

G ROMAN

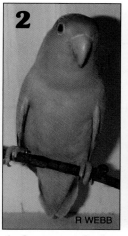

R WEBB

1. *Cinnamon Cockatiel.*
2. *Cinnamon Peachfaced Lovebird.*
3. *Cinnamon Galah.*
4. *Cinnamon Turquoise Parrot cock.*
5. *Cinnamon(wing) Budgerigar.*
6. *Cinnamon Quaker Parrot.*
7. *Cinnamon Red-fronted Kakariki.*
8. *Cinnamon Indian Ringnecked Parrot.*

S & J SMITH

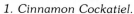

B PEARSON

G ROMAN

B NELSON

P TOMAS

The following are some basic matings for the Cinnamon mutation:

| | |
|---|---|
| **Cinnamon cock x Normal hen** | = Normal/Cinnamon cocks<br>+ Cinnamon hens |
| **Normal cock x Cinnamon hen** | = Normal/Cinnamon cocks<br>+ Normal hens |
| **Normal/Cinnamon cock<br>x Normal hen** | = Normal and Normal/Cinnamon cocks<br>+ Normal and Cinnamon hens |
| **Normal/Cinnamon cock<br>x Cinnamon hen** | = Normal/Cinnamon and Cinnamon cocks<br>+ Normal and Cinnamon hens |
| **Cinnamon cock x Cinnamon hen** | = Cinnamon cocks and hens |

The true Cinnamon mutation is established or has occurred in a large number of species and will no doubt occur in all, given time. The following species have produced examples of the Cinnamon mutation:

Budgerigar
Bourke's Parrot
Turquoise Parrot
Scarlet-chested Parrot
Elegant Parrot
Red-rumped Parrot
Blue-bonnet Parrot
Eastern Rosella
Crimson Rosella
Adelaide Rosella
Yellow Rosella
Western Rosella
Crimson-winged Parrot
King Parrot
Cockatiel
Galah
Red-fronted Kakariki
Rainbow Lorikeet
Peachfaced Lovebird
Indian Ringnecked Parrot
Plum-headed Parrot
Blue-winged Parrotlet
Quaker Parrot
Blue-fronted Amazon

H KREMER

*Above: Cinnamon Western Rosella.*
*Below: Cinnamon Bourke's Parrot.*

There are possible Cinnamon mutations in the Rock Parrot, Port Lincoln Parrot, Moustache Parrot, Alexandrine Parrot and White Eye-ring Lovebird group, which only breeding results will clarify.

There are a number of Amazon and conure species where new mutations are being developed, some of which are being called Cinnamon. Whether any are true Cinnamon mutations will require time to be determined. The so-called 'Cinnamon' Hooded Parrot mutation is in fact a Fallow mutation

TOBY MARTIN

because it is recessive in inheritance. I have seen a photograph of a pale fawn Red-tailed Black Cockatoo that may be a Cinnamon mutation. It exhibited the typical fading caused by the sun that is seen commonly in Cinnamon (but not others). However, other photographs of the bird show it as a grey-coloured bird, which suggests it is a Dilute type mutation.

The Cinnamon mutation combines best with mutations that alter yellow family pigments (eg Blue or Parblue), structural colour mutations (eg Olive or Greygreen) or those that alter pigment distribution (eg Opaline, Pied and Melanistic). Some interesting combinations can also be created through combination with other grey family pigment-altering mutations, but as the pigment from this group is reduced, the effects become less visible. Unusual results are obtained in some species when Cinnamon is combined with Lutino, creating the Lacewing combination.

P ODEKERKEN

*Cinnamon Rainbow Lorikeet.*

***The following group of mutations are commonly known as Cinnamon, but the correct identification has yet to be proven.***

C CAIRNCROSS

*Above: 'Cinnamon' Blue-fronted Amazon.*
*Above right: A different 'Cinnamon' Blue-fronted Amazon.*
*Right: Another different 'Cinnamon' Blue-fronted Amazon from South Africa which may be the true Cinnamon mutation.*

J POSTEMA

S SINDEL

R CUSICK

TOBY MARTIN

T SILVA

1. 'Cinnamon' or 'Isabel'
   Superb Parrot.
2. 'Cinnamon' Blue-
   bonnet Parrot.
3. 'Cinnamon' Rock
   Parrot – this mutation
   has red eyes and is
   probably a Fallow.
4. 'Cinnamon' Twenty-
   eight Parrot – this
   mutation is sex-linked,
   but the degree of
   pigment reduction
   suggests that it may
   be a Lime mutation.
5. 'Cinnamon' Golden-
   crowned Conure.
6. 'Cinnamon' White-
   fronted Amazon.

E STEPHENS

## Dilute (Yellow)

There exists a loose grouping of mutations that are called Yellow or sometimes Dilute. The term Yellow is generally used for the lighter, more yellow forms, whilst Dilute is used for the darker, more green forms. Technically these are all Dilute mutations. In Europe, it is standard to call the darker mutations, Pastel and the lighter mutations, Green Suffused. I call this grouping 'loose' because the

K YORK

Above: Comparative photograph of the Dilute Budgerigar (L) and the version commonly exhibited which is actually a Cinnamon Dilute (R).
Left: Greywing – the second Dilute mutation of the Budgerigar.
Below left: Clearwing – the third Dilute mutation of the Budgerigar.

S HOUSE

J SCULL

exact genetic relationship is uncertain between species. Some species have multiple forms that all belong to one genetic family, whilst other species clearly have forms that are unrelated genetically. The difficulty is in defining a difference that will hold between species and it may be that it is only resolved by microscopic examination.

All birds in this group have greatly reduced amounts of grey family pigments (this includes black and brown). They all retain dark eyes, even from hatching and they are all inherited in a recessive fashion. Some Dilute mutations are very dark, almost normal in colour. (See the section on *Faded or Isabel* on page 72.) If a red eye is retained into adulthood, then the name Fallow may or may not be more appropriate.

The name Dilute has received some criticism for being ill-defined and not descriptive, but it is exactly what these mutations do to any grey family pigments. It has been argued (Smith G, 1995) that a Parblue could be called a Dilute because it dilutes yellow family pigments and that is true. However, we must understand what is meant by the name Dilute – that grey family pigments not yellow family pigments are diluted.

Dilute mutations do not alter the yellow family pigment group, the structural colour or the pigment distribution. Because they reduce grey family pigments so much, they only combine well with yellow family pigment-altering mutations (eg Blue and Parblue) and structural mutations (eg Greygreen and Olive). The darker forms sometimes combine well with Cinnamon, but the Yellow forms leave little pigment for the Cinnamon gene to act upon.

In species that are primarily grey in colour, the Dilute mutations have generally been called Silver. It is only in these species that the true effect of these mutations can

*Dilute Mulga Parrot – one of two types being established in Australia.*

*Dilute Mulga Parrot – the second type of Dilute being established in this species.*

*Yellow King Parrot – an Australian mutation that may be a Black-eyed Clear.*

*Dilute King Parrot – the European mutation that is a typical Dilute.*

*Dilute Eastern Rosella – the European Pastel.*

*Dilute Eastern Rosella – the Australian mutation is very similar to the European bird – is it the same mutation?*

normally be seen, unless they are combined with other mutations to give the same effect as a grey species (ie combination with the Blue gene and the Greygreen gene). Silver is therefore correctly used for the Dilute Blue or Dilute Grey combinations. Many aviculturists have incorrectly chosen to use the name 'Silver' for the Cinnamon Blue or Cinnamon Grey combinations and this must cease. (See page 126.)

Some basic matings for the Dilute are as follows:

| | |
|---|---|
| **Normal x Dilute** | = 100% Normal/Dilute |
| **Normal/Dilute x Normal** | = 50% Normal<br>+ 50% Normal/Dilute |
| **Normal/Dilute x Normal/Dilute** | = 25% Normal<br>+ 50% Normal/Dilute<br>+ 25% Dilute |
| **Normal/Dilute x Dilute** | = 50% Normal/Dilute<br>+ 50% Dilute |
| **Dilute x Dilute** | = 100% Dilute |

The true Dilute mutation is established or has occurred in a large number of species and will no doubt occur in all, given time. The following species have produced examples of the Dilute mutation:

TOBY MARTIN

*Dilute Turquoise Parrot – commonly known as 'Yellow'.*

Budgerigar (three forms)
Bourke's Parrot
Turquoise Parrot
Elegant Parrot (possibly)
Rock Parrot (possibly)
Red-rumped Parrot (possibly)
Mulga Parrot (possibly two forms)
Blue-bonnet Parrot
Port Lincoln Parrot
Regent Parrot
King Parrot (possibly two forms)
Eastern Rosella (possibly two forms)
Pale-headed Rosella
Crimson Rosella
Yellow Rosella (extinct?)
Western Rosella
Superb Parrot
Cockatiel (two forms)
Galah
Rainbow Lorikeet
Scaly-breasted Lorikeet
Purple-crowned Lorikeet
Peachfaced Lovebird (two forms)
Indian Ringnecked Parrot
Pacific Parrotlet (two forms, perhaps three)
Quaker Parrot (possibly)

In the Budgerigar, the three mutations known as Greywing, Clearwing and Dilute (or Black-eyed Yellow in some countries such as Australia) form a genetic family. In other species, such as the Peachfaced Lovebird and the Cockatiel, different Dilute mutations are unrelated genetically, producing Normal double splits when they are crossed. No doubt with time, more examples of Dilute mutations will occur and investigations will show that many form genetic families. Much research is needed before the true nature of these mutations becomes clear.

*Left: 'Silver Spangle' Cockatiel – an Australian mutation that may be a second Dilute mutation. Below: Dilute Cockatiel – the true Silver Cockatiel is an Australian mutation generally known as 'Pastel Silver'.*

D ANDERSEN

G ROMAN

R ERHART

*Left: (American) Yellow Pacific Parrotlet – one type of Dilute known for this species. Right: (European) Pastel Pacific Parrotlet – the second Dilute mutation.*

B NIELSEN

B NIELSEN

*Left and right: 'Isabel' Pacific Parrotlet – is this a third Dilute mutation?*

B NIELSEN

In Australian lorikeets, various Dilute mutations are being commonly called 'Cinnamon'. This is incorrect for all the reasons already discussed and should be corrected before greater confusion develops. Some may be Fallow mutations, but most appear to be simple Dilute mutations incorrectly named.

American Yellow Peachfaced Lovebird – known as Edged Dilute in Europe. Confusion exists in some countries between this colour and the rare Japanese Yellow.

Japanese Yellow Peachfaced Lovebird – a rare mutation reported to have fertility problems.

'Yellow' Madagascan Lovebird – unfortunately now extinct.

Superb Parrot – is this a Dilute mutation?

Dilute Scaly-breasted Lorikeet – generally incorrectly known as 'Cinnamon'.

Dilute Rainbow Lorikeet – generally incorrectly known as 'Cinnamon'.

Dilute Purple-crowned Lorikeet – generally incorrectly known as 'Cinnamon'.

*'Yellow' Yellow Rosella.*

*Dilute Crimson Rosella.*

*Above: 'Black-eyed White' Galah – may be a Black-eyed Clear rather than a Dilute. There is another mutation known as Silver which may be the true Dilute.*
*Right: Suffused Indian Ringnecked Parrot – the true Dilute mutation has been known by a variety of names.*

## Faded or Isabel

Isabel is a name that has long been misused and I am reluctant to use it. Perhaps there is a better name for this group of mutations, but that is a difficult issue. The name Isabel was first used in the 1960s in Europe as a synonym for the Cinnamon mutation. When European texts were translated into English, the name entered English usage without the translation and without any understanding of what it was. As a result it has been applied to numerous different mutations that breeders thought 'looked' like a Cinnamon. Some of these are dark Dilutes and some are Lime mutations. Even today, in texts translated from European languages there appears to be no consistency in its use.

I have recently been made aware of standards written by Dutch and Belgian breeders in the early 1970s that define Isabel as a mutation where all or most grey family pigments are lost, but retain another type of melanin which is red-brown in colour. This pigment is not present in most species of parrots and if we use this system, the name Isabel should be banned from use!

In Australia the name has primarily been given to colours that would otherwise have been incorrectly called 'Recessive Cinnamon'. If all aviculturists agreed to drop the name Isabel and adopt Faded instead, then I would support the idea.

The Faded (Isabel) mutation, as defined for Australian birds, is recessive in inheritance. It slightly reduces the amount of black pigment in the bird, often giving it a browner appearance, but it does not actually change the pigment produced into brown. It only makes any natural brown pigments in the bird more noticeable. These birds all still carry shades of grey when viewed in good light. (Remember a true Cinnamon or Brown bird can never have any black pigment or shades of grey in it.)

*Above: Faded Bourke's Parrot – has been called Dilute in Australia. Below: Faded Turquoise Parrot – known as 'Isabel' in Europe.*

I believe that the following species have examples of the Faded (Isabel) mutation:

Budgerigar
Bourke's Parrot
Turquoise Parrot
Red-rumped Parrot
Eastern Rosella
Crimson Rosella
Princess Parrot
Cockatiel
Galah
Swift Parrot
Fischer's Lovebird (possibly)
Indian Ringnecked Parrot (possibly)
Nanday Conure (possibly)

In the Budgerigar the mutation is called Faded, which, in my opinion, is the best suggestion for an alternative name. In the Cockatiel (in Australia) it is called West Coast Silver which obviously cannot be used in other species. In other species the name Recessive Cinnamon has been used incorrectly.

As the mutation is recessive in mode of inheritance, breeding expectations are the same as for any other recessive trait (eg Blue or Dilute).

Faded Red-rumped Parrot – an Australian mutation incorrectly known as 'Recessive Cinnamon', which may now be extinct.

Some basic matings for the Faded (Isabel) mutation are as follows:

| | |
|---|---|
| **Normal x Faded** | = 100% Normal/Faded |
| **Normal/Faded x Normal** | = 50% Normal<br>+ 50% Normal/Faded |
| **Normal/Faded x Normal/Faded** | = 25% Normal<br>+ 50% Normal/Faded<br>+ 25% Faded |
| **Normal/Faded x Faded** | = 50% Normal/Faded<br>+ 50% Faded |
| **Faded x Faded** | = 100% Faded |

*Faded Galah – known also as 'Isabel'.*

Faded (Isabel) combines well with many other mutations, creating subtle changes for the breeder to investigate. Unfortunately they often become overlooked when other more distinct mutations become established within a species.

### Addendum
*The 'Pastel' Swift Parrot almost certainly is a Faded mutation. The photographs of the mutation in 'The Swift Parakeet' by Cyril Laubscher shows the typical features of slight melanin reduction (far less than the 50% reduction required to fit the Pastel definition), changes to eye colour and loss of pigment in the feet which are consistent with a Faded mutation.*

S NASTASI

D BROWN

1. *Faded Cockatiel – known in Australia as 'West Coast Silver'.*
2. *A new mutation of the Blue-winged Parrot which may be a Faded.*
3. *Faded Nanday Conure – known incorrectly as 'Cinnamon'.*
4. *Faded Princess Parrot – known incorrectly as 'Cinnamon'.*
5. *Faded Budgerigar (R).*

# Dominant Dilute

The Dominant Dilute gene is not a common mutation in parrots. To date only two examples are known to aviculture. They are the Dominant Silver Cockatiel and the incorrectly named 'Fallow' Indian Ringnecked Parrot. I have also seen reports of a similar mutation in the Eastern Rosella but cannot confirm it.

*Dominant Dilute Cockatiel.*

The photographs of the Cockatiel form show 'patchiness' to the wing and body colour, along with a general dilution to the grey pigments of the bird. It is a co-dominant mutation, with the Double Factor Silver bird being a lighter shade of silver.

The 'Fallow' Indian Ringnecked Parrot also has this 'patchiness' but shows a less distinct dilution of colour, except on the extremities of the wings. In many specimens, the only clear indication of the presence of this mutation is in the flight feathers. It is a standard dominant mutation and therefore is unlikely to represent the same mutation as the Cockatiel form. One thing is certain about the Indian Ringnecked form; it is not a Fallow, which has red eyes and strong dilution of all grey pigment to light browns. In the USA it is known as Isabel and recently has been called a 'Dominant Cinnamon', which it is also clearly not.

Possibly the most significant feature of these two mutations is that they are dominant (or co-dominant), an uncommon form of inheritance except for mutations that affect structural components of colour. To date they are the only examples of grey pigment altering mutations that are dominant. This does not ensure they are one and the same mutation, but is enough to group them together until further is known. Each may simply be a one off species-specific mutation.

*Above: Blue (Whiteface) Dominant Dilute (DF) Cockatiel hen.*
*Right: Blue (Whiteface) Dominant Dilute (SF) Cockatiel pair.*

G ROMAN    N ARMSTRONG

*Left: Dominant Dilute (Edged) Indian Ringnecked Parrot – known incorrectly as 'Fallow'.*
*Far left: Dominant Dilute Blue Indian Ringnecked Parrot.*

Some basic breeding expectations are as follows:

| | |
|---|---|
| **Dominant Dilute (SF) x Normal** | = 50% Dominant Dilute (SF) <br> + 50% Normal |
| **Dominant Dilute (SF)** <br>    **x Dominant Dilute (SF)** | = 25% Normal <br> + 50% Dominant Dilute (SF) <br> + 25% Dominant Dilute (DF) |

### Addendum

*There is a new mutation being established in Lineolated Parrots in Europe and the USA that appears to belong to this category. It is very similar in appearance to the Dominant Dilute Indian Ringnecked Parrot.*

## Fallow

The Fallow is a mutation with a strong definition, yet the name is still misused for other mutations. To complicate the issue, some species may have more than one unrelated gene that can produce a Fallow colouration (eg Budgerigar and Peachfaced Lovebird) and some Fallow genes may have a genetic relationship with the Recessive Lutino and may, in fact, be Recessive Lime mutations.

To be a Fallow mutation, a gene must produce red eyes in the adult bird, be recessive in inheritance and change all black pigment (or grey colours) to light brown shades without altering any other pigments or distribution. Because black and grey are reduced to light brown, the bird loses any deep colours of green or blue, becoming more yellow or white in appearance and lighter in colour overall.

**Change of eye colour alone does not constitute a Fallow mutation**, merely an eye colour mutation. Although some mutations like Fallow do alter eye colour, it should not be used alone to determine the identity of a mutation, as eye colour can be inherited separately from plumage colour.

### Addendum

*As a direct result of increased communication between breeders interested in genetics on the internet, I have come to accept that there are some colours that must be considered Fallow, but which do not fit the standard definition I have always used. Some of the oldest Fallow mutations, such as the English Fallow*

Budgerigar, have their grey family pigments altered to a grey-brown colour rather than pure brown. As a result it is necessary to break fallow colours up into at least four different groups which probably represent different mutations. They are as follows:

- **Ashen or Smokey Fallow** have grey family pigments reduced to light grey.
- **Dun Fallow** have grey family pigments reduced to grey-brown.
- **Bronze Fallow** have grey family pigments reduced to brown.
- **Pale Fallow** have grey family pigments reduced to light brown.

There are also other features that help distinguish each of these Fallow groups and if you are game, I refer you to the Fallow section in Part Three. (See page 239.)

*Bronze Fallow Bourke's Parrot – commonly known as 'Cream'.*

When more than one Fallow mutation exists in a species, mating them together will produce only Normal birds in the first generation.

As Fallow reduces the grey family pigments so strongly, it does not combine well with other grey family pigment-altering mutations. Instead it is best to combine it with mutations from the other groups (eg yellow family pigment, distribution or structural mutations).

The following matings apply when breeding Fallow mutations. (Be aware, however, that strange results may indicate the presence of multiple Fallow genes in your flock.)

| | |
|---|---|
| **Fallow x Normal** | = 100% Normal/Fallow |
| **Normal/Fallow x Normal** | = 50% Normal<br>+ 50% Normal/Fallow |
| **Normal/Fallow x Normal/Fallow** | = 25% Normal<br>+ 50% Normal/Fallow<br>+ 25% Fallow |
| **Normal/Fallow x Fallow** | = 50% Normal/Fallow<br>+ 50% Fallow |
| **Fallow x Fallow** | = 100% Fallow |

Above: Bronze Fallow Hooded Parrot – known incorrectly as 'Cinnamon'.
Right: An Australian Fallow Budgerigar – believed to be identical to the Bronze Fallow from Germany.

*Left: Bronze Fallow Rainbow Lorikeet – one of two Fallow types being established in Australia.*

*Far left: A second Fallow Rainbow Lorikeet mutation – the breeder has chosen to dub it 'Purple Fallow' until we are able to correctly identify the mutation.*

*Right: Bronze Fallow (Type 1) Peachfaced Lovebird.*

*Far right: Pale Fallow (Type 2) Peachfaced Lovebird.*

*Right: Dun Fallow (Type 1) Red-rumped Parrot.*

*Far right: Bronze Fallow (Type 2) Red-rumped Parrot – commonly known as 'Golden Fallow'.*

*Above left: Type 1 Fallow Turquoise Parrot – an Australian mutation known also as 'Isabel'.*
*Above right: Type 2 Fallow Turquoise Parrot – another Australian mutation, a distinctly different second Fallow type also being called 'Isabel'.*

At least one Fallow mutation is present in the following species:

Budgerigar (three forms)
Bourke's Parrot (two forms)
Turquoise Parrot (two forms)
Scarlet-chested Parrot (two forms)
Red-rumped Parrot (two forms)
Hooded Parrot
Western Rosella
Cockatiel (two forms)
Rainbow Lorikeet (two forms)
Masked Lovebird
Peachfaced Lovebird (two forms)
Indian Ringnecked Parrot (two forms)
Plum-headed Parrot
Moustache Parrot
Pacific Parrotlet

In Australia the so-called 'Cream' or 'Yellow' Bourke's Parrot is in fact a Fallow mutation. It fits all the criteria set out above for Fallow mutations. There is also a second Fallow Bourke's Parrot mutation in Europe. The Europeans also have a 'Yellow' or 'Pastel', which by definition is not a Fallow but most likely is a Dilute mutation. The bird the Europeans call Isabel appears to be very similar to the Australian named 'Cream' Bourke's Parrot. In Budgerigars there are three unrelated genes that produce Fallow birds, with one suspected as being related to the Recessive Lutino gene. Remember too that the so-called 'Fallow' Indian Ringnecked Parrot is not a Fallow at all.

1. *Dun Fallow Elegant Parrot.*
2. *Ashen Fallow Scarlet-chested Parrot – known also as 'Isabel'.*
3. *Fallow Quaker Parrot.*
4. *Dun Fallow Pacific Parrotlet.*
5. *Australian Fallow Cockatiel – this mutation needs to be compared to the Bronze Fallow from other countries.*
6. *Ashen Fallow Cockatiel – known incorrectly as 'Recessive Silver' in Europe and the USA.*

B PEARSON

B BRANSTON

S DOAK

R ERHART

T DULIERE

The poor use of the name Fallow is all the more criminal because there are two true Fallow mutations in the Indian Ringnecked Parrot. One is known as Buttercup or Yellowhead. The other is known by the unfortunate misnomer of 'Recessive Cinnamon'.

There is a mutation in the Turquoise Parrot and the Scarlet-chested Parrot that is being called Fallow, which I am still not prepared to accept in this category. The Turquoise Parrot mutation exists in Europe and the Scarlet-chested Parrot mutation exists in Australia. Visually they have red eyes, but they both appear to change the structural colouration of the bird and I have wondered whether they may be something akin to Violet Green birds. Much greater study is required with these colours to fully understand them, including test matings through Blue mutations to clarify things. There are true Fallow mutations in both of these species to further illustrate the importance of naming mutations correctly.

In the USA there is a mutation of the Green-cheeked Conure that is being called Fallow. As it is sex-linked in inheritance, it is either a Cinnamon or more likely a Lime mutation. This is yet another example of breeders naming mutations without enough knowledge of what these mutations actually do.

---

1. Clearhead Fallow Indian Ringnecked Parrot generally referred to as 'Buttercup' by breeders.
2. Bronze Fallow Western Rosella – known incorrectly as 'Cinnamon' in Australia.
3. The European 'Fallow' Turquoise Parrot is not correctly named – it has features in common with the unclassified Scarlet-chested Parrot mutation.
4. An unclassified mutation of the Scarlet-chested Parrot known incorrectly as 'Fallow'.

## Olive

The Olive or Dark Factor gene is the first of the **structural colour affecting** genes. The effect of the gene is to increase the depth of colour seen. It does not increase pigment to do this, but changes the way light is bent as it passes through cells within the feather. This creates the darker appearance that we see.

Because the effect is created by 'tricks of light', only species with the ability to distort light (through natural green and blue production) are able to produce this mutation. Therefore Olive mutations are not possible in grey species such as the Cockatiel or the Galah. The only hope for blue or green colours in those species is for a dormant gene present in the Normal bird to be reactivated. This can sometimes happen but is rare compared to the simple inactivation of a gene that causes most other mutations.

P TOMAS

The three structural mutations of Olive, Greygreen and Violet are often confused with one another by aviculturists. Under optimum conditions the three effects are easily distinguished, but those conditions include combining it with the Blue gene and sometimes with one another. Therefore, in species without a Blue mutation, these three mutations can be confused.

One of the most important features of the Olive gene is that it is co-dominant. If an olive-looking mutation is fully dominant, then it is probably a Greygreen mutation. This is the problem with the misnaming of the Greygreen mutation in lorikeets. As large numbers of breeders persist in calling them Olive, now that true Olive mutations are appearing we have a difficult period of re-education.

Another aspect of the Olive gene also needs consideration. It is linked to the Blue gene for inheritance purposes. In the Budgerigar this is a fairly tight linkage. To date, very little investigation has been done into linkage in other species, partly because Olive genes are uncommon and when they do occur, a Blue gene is not always present as well (eg Turquoise Parrot). If the apparent Olive mutation is not linked to the Blue gene in a species, but still occurs as a co-dominant mutation, then perhaps it is a Violet mutation. (Alternatively, there may be no direct relationship to mutations in other species.)

As in all co-dominant mutations, the bird that

E ANTONIN

*Top: Dark Green Budgerigar.*
*Centre: Olive Budgerigar.*
*Bottom: Dark Factor Western Rosella.*

R, B & D KAMER

R, B & D KAMER

T DULIERE

Y IMANOTHAI

1. *Olive Masked Lovebird.*
2. *Dark Green Masked Lovebird.*
3. *Olive Abysinnian Lovebird.*
4. *Olive Black-cheeked Lovebird.*
5. *Olive Peachfaced Lovebird.*
6. *Dark Green Peachfaced Lovebird – commonly known as 'Jade'.*
7. *Comparing rump colours is the best way to distinguish Dark Factors in Peachfaced Lovebirds. L to R: no factor, one factor, two factors.*

A MATHEWS

A MATHEWS

Page 82

has one Olive gene and one Normal gene falls part way between normal and olive in colour. This part way colour is called Dark Green. The name Jade is also commonly used for Dark Green birds, but it is best to standardise this, using the name given precedence by the Budgerigar fraternity – Dark Green. In the USA, lovebird breeders call the part way coloured bird 'Medium Green' and the Olive bird 'Dark Green', but using these names tends to add to the confusion.

J POSTEMA

E ANTONIN

*Above: Dark Green Mallee Ringnecked Parrot.*
*Left: Dark Green Indian Ringnecked Parrot.*

Some basic matings involving the Olive mutation are as follows:

| | |
|---|---|
| **Dark Green x Normal** | = 50% Normal<br>+ 50% Dark Green |
| **Dark Green x Dark Green** | = 25% Normal<br>+ 50% Dark Green<br>+ 25% Olive |
| **Olive x Normal** | = 100% Dark Green |
| **Olive x Dark Green** | = 50% Dark Green<br>+ 50% Olive |
| **Olive x Olive** | = 100% Olive |

The true Olive mutation is established or has occurred in the following species:

Budgerigar
Turquoise Parrot
Masked Lovebird
Peachfaced Lovebird
Abysinnian Lovebird
Indian Ringnecked Parrot
Alexandrine Parrot (possibly)
Green-rumped Parrotlet
Lineolated Parrot

*Right: Dark Green (L) and Green (R) Lineolated Parrots.*
*Bottom left: Dark Green Turquoise Parrot – commonly known as 'Jade'.*
*Bottom right: Olive Turquoise Parrot.*

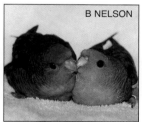

B NELSON

G ROMAN

G ROMAN

The true nature of the Dark Green Indian Ringnecked Parrot is still being debated, with many aviculturists suggesting that it might be a Violet mutation rather than an Olive mutation.

### Addendum
*Recent breeding in the USA has produced a Double Factor bird, establishing that their mutation is in fact a Violet mutation. Concurrently, research in Europe has shown that the similar looking mutation on that continent is in fact the true Olive. Hence we now have both mutations in the Indian Ringnecked Parrot, although the names used by breeders will remain confused for a while yet.*

A possible true Olive mutation is being established in the Rainbow Lorikeet. In Europe there are probable Olive mutations in the Western Rosella and the Mallee Ringnecked Parrot under development.

In Australia there are also mutations called 'Olive' in the Scarlet-chested Parrot and the Port Lincoln Parrot, which are still being investigated. They do not appear to produce an even change to structural colour over the whole plumage. Species-specific factors may be responsible for creating this apparent paradox.

### Addendum
*I have recently learnt of similar mutations in Swift Parrots and Black-cheeked Lovebirds in Europe that probably represent the same mutation. The 'Olive' Rainbow Lorikeet in Australia also appears to be this mutation. They are distinctly different to other structural colour mutations and the European Lovebird Fancy has adopted the name 'Misty'. The name 'Khaki' also comes to mind, which is what the original breeder of the Scarlet-chested Parrot mutation called the birds. (See page 250.)*

In the Pacific Parrotlet, the so-called European 'Dark Factor' or 'Greygreen' is clearly not an Olive mutation. It is now generally recognised as a Recessive Greygreen, although photographs suggest that not all structural

*'USA Dark' Pacific Parrotlet – so far a unique mutation with no recognised classification.*

*Khaki Scarlet-chested Parrot – incorrectly known as 'Olive'.*

*Khaki Rainbow Lorikeet – one of two colours currently known as 'Jade' in Australia.*

*'Jade' Rainbow Lorikeet – a second 'Jade' colour that could be a true Dark Green.*

colouration is lost, raising a small question mark on its identity. A second recessive mutation from the USA also produces a 'Dark Factor' effect, but once again does not fit the genetic inheritance of true Olive mutations.

The Olive gene combines well with the Blue gene, to produce Cobalt and Mauve (sometimes incorrectly called Slate) colours. Its combination with the Cinnamon gene has been called Mustard by the lovebird fraternity in Australia. However, the so-called 'Cinnamon' gene they use is not a Cinnamon but a Lime. Nevertheless, breeders of other species are now using the name Mustard for the Cinnamon Olive or Cinnamon Greygreen combinations.

Olive mutations also combine well with distribution mutations such as Pied and Opaline.

## Greygreen

The Greygreen mutation is responsible for preventing all structural colours in the bird. This is the natural state for some species such as the Cockatiel and the Galah (and birds like canaries).

***The following lorikeet mutations have all been incorrectly known as 'Olive'.***

*Above: Greygreen Red-collared Lorikeet.*
*Above left: Greygreen Musk Lorikeet.*
*Below: Greygreen Rainbow Lorikeet.*
*Below left: Greygreen Scaly-breasted Lorikeet.*

As neither Cockatiels nor Galahs have much yellow pigment through their bodies, neither appears as a typical grey-green colour like the wildtype canary. Instead what we see is closer in appearance to the Greygreen Blue combination known as Grey. Remember, however, that these species do contain some pigments from the yellow family pigments so are not fully grey until these are removed using a Blue gene.

Visually, the Greygreen is close in appearance to the Olive mutation, with many breeders confusing the two colours. Some authors have spoken out against the name Greygreen, preferring to call both mutations Olive. However this ignores the differences between the mutations in how they affect the feather. The Greygreen gene does produce a grey effect; it just cannot be seen until the yellow pigment is removed. The Olive gene can produce a very similar effect (eg Turquoise Parrot) but you cannot ignore the different mode of inheritance.

All Greygreen genes are dominant in inheritance; therefore both Single Factor (SF) and Double Factor (DF) birds exist that are indistinguishable from one another.

Some basic matings are as follows:

| | |
|---|---|
| **Greygreen (SF) x Normal** | = 50% Normal<br>+ 50% Greygreen (SF) |
| **Greygreen (SF) x Greygreen (SF)** | = 25% Normal<br>+ 50% Greygreen (SF)<br>+ 25% Greygreen (DF) |
| **Greygreen (DF) x Normal** | = 100% Greygreen (SF) |
| **Greygreen (DF) x Greygreen (SF)** | = 50% Greygreen (SF)<br>+ 50% Greygreen (DF) |
| **Greygreen (DF) x Greygreen (DF)** | = 100% Greygreen (DF) |

The true Greygreen mutation is established or has occurred in the following species:

Budgerigar
Turquoise Parrot
Scarlet-chested Parrot
Red-rumped Parrot
Rainbow Lorikeet
Red-collared Lorikeet

Scaly-breasted Lorikeet
Musk Lorikeet
Indian Ringnecked Parrot
Alexandrine Parrot
Plum-headed Parrot

I have seen an individual colour mutant of the Blue-crowned Conure which I originally considered a possible Greygreen mutation, however subsequently the bird

*Greygreen Budgerigar.*     *Greygreen Turquoise Parrot.*

moulted to a lighter colour, almost Normal in appearance. I suspect that it represents a form of non-genetic melanism. The breeder is still performing breeding experiments to determine what is actually happening.

There are also new mutations in the Red-rumped Parrot, the Superb Parrot and the Crimson-winged Parrot that may be Greygreen mutations.

The Greygreen gene combines best with the Blue gene to produce a visual Grey. It has also been combined with the Cinnamon gene to produce Mustard. When combined with the Dilute and the Blue gene it creates Silver. Combining Greygreen with Blue and Cinnamon creates Fawn. If you also add a Dilute gene to Fawn you create Cream. The Greygreen mutation also combines well with distribution mutations such as Pied and Opaline.

I will briefly mention the Recessive Grey mutation at this time. (For more information, refer to page 260.) A Grey mutation, recessive in inheritance, is known in the Budgerigar. Although it is very similar to the true Dominant Grey mutation, it actually affects the colour production in a different way. This results in a loss of structural colour and the bird becomes a grey-green colour. Whether this mutation will ever appear in other species is yet to be seen.

As mentioned in the last section, there are two so-called 'Dark Factors' in the Pacific Parrotlet. One is recognised as a Recessive Greygreen whilst the other does not fit easily into any recognised category. The American mutation is recessive in inheritance and may be a species-specific gene. Once again only time will tell.

C CAIRNCROSS

G ROMAN

1. *A mutation of the Blue and Gold Macaw known to breeders as 'Black and Gold'. It appears to be a Greygreen mutation.*
2. *Greygreen Red-rumped Parrot.*
3. *A new mutation of the Superb Parrot which appears to be a Greygreen.*
4. *Greygreen Indian Ringnecked Parrot.*

G ROMAN

P RANKINE

*Above: A new mutation of the Crimson-winged Parrot which is possibly a Greygreen. Left: Greygreen Scarlet-chested Parrot.*

### Addendum

There are reports of a recessive Greygreen mutation of the Turquoise Parrot in Europe. However it is unclear whether this mutation really exists or not. It is listed in a recent book on Neophema spp, however there are many birds incorrectly identified by this book and it cannot be used as a reliable reference. There also seems to be a lack of available information in print on the so-called 'Olivegreen' developed in Denmark in 1983. I am not certain whether it is the same mutation as the Olive developed in Australia around the same time or a distinctly different mutation. I cannot even confirm its form of inheritance at this point in time. If it were recessive, then it could be a Recessive Greygreen. It is distinct from the true dominant Greygreen illustrated in this book, which originated in Holland.

## Violet

The Violet mutation is the third of the structural colour affecting mutations. It gets its name from its action in the Budgerigar where it alters the Cobalt combination into a beautiful violet colour. In its basic state however, it appears simply as a dark green colour. This makes it difficult to distinguish from the Olive gene in some circumstances and is the basis of the Olive/Violet debate in the Indian Ringnecked Parrot. One significant difference however, is that the Olive gene is linked to the Blue gene whereas the Violet gene is not.

Many people consider that Violet is a dominant mutation. In reality it behaves in a co-dominant manner with one shade produced in Single Factor and another deeper shade in Double Factor birds. The difference is seen to a greater degree when combined with the Blue gene. Here a single Violet gene creates a 'cobalt' colour (not to be confused with the true Cobalt) whereas two Violet genes will produce the violet appearance. What is still not known for certain is how much this effect will vary between species, which have different base colours.

*Double (above) and Single Factor (below) Violet Green Masked Lovebirds.*

The true Violet mutation is established or has occurred in the following species:

Budgerigar
Masked Lovebird
Fischer's Lovebird
Peachfaced Lovebird
Indian Ringnecked Parrot

I have also seen Scarlet-chested Parrots that were

possibly Violet Green but are being called 'Fallow' simply because they have a red eye. The effect on the plumage is to darken the green and change the light blue on the face and wings in a manner suggestive of a violet type effect. A similar mutation occurs in the Turquoise Parrot; this has also been called

*Above: Violet Green Budgerigar.*
*Right: Single Factor Violet Green Indian Ringnecked Parrot.*

'Fallow' because it has a red eye. These are further examples of a name being assigned for the wrong reasons or without studying the bird as a whole. (See page 80.)

The Violet gene combines best with the Blue gene and a single Olive gene, the Violet Cobalt being the traditional Visual Violet colour. It also combines well with distribution genes such as Pied and Opaline.

Some basic matings for Violet are as follows:

| | |
|---|---|
| **Violet Green (SF) x Normal** | = 50% Normal<br>+ 50% Violet Green (SF) |
| **Violet Green (DF) x Normal** | = 100% Violet Green (SF) |
| **Violet Green (SF)**<br> **x Violet Green (SF)** | = 25% Normal<br>+ 50% Violet Green (SF)<br>+ 25% Violet Green (DF) |
| **Violet Green (SF)**<br> **x Violet Green (DF)** | = 50% Violet Green (SF)<br>+ 50% Violet Green (DF) |
| **Violet Green (DF)**<br> **x Violet Green (DF)** | = 100% Violet Green (DF) |

Matings for the really spectacular violet colours are covered in the *Combinations of Mutations* section under *Violet Blue* and *Visual Violet*. (See pages 164 and 166.)

## Opaline

The Opaline mutation is the first of the ***pigment distribution*** mutations to be discussed. It is an interesting mutation that produces slightly different effects in each species where it occurs. Therefore, its effects are closely controlled by the genes that make each species what it is.

The true nature of the gene has only recently come to light, as the first examples of this mutation were so disparate that no-one saw the connection. As more examples became known, definite patterns could then be seen.

This mutation has several identifying features. Firstly, it must be sex-linked in inheritance. Secondly, it must alter pigment distribution but not actually create new pigments that the species does not already have. Thirdly, all adults carry enhanced wing

ABK

stripes (like a hen) which become visible above the wing. Underneath the underwing coverts there is also a retained wing stripe. Finally, in species with grey down pigment, this is lost and the down becomes white. However, yellow pigment is not lost from the down.

Along with these identifying features, the Opaline gene reduces the spread of grey family pigments in the bird, whilst enhancing the spread of yellow family pigments. The modified yellow family pigments such as red, orange or pink are emphasised in species where they occur. There is no alteration to structural colour production.

Using these identifying features, it can be seen that the following mutations in differing species all represent the one mutation:

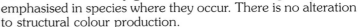

ABK

Budgerigar (Opaline)
Bourke's Parrot (Rose)
Turquoise Parrot (Opaline, formerly called Pied)
Red-rumped Parrot (Opaline)
Eastern Rosella (Red)
Cockatiel (Pearl)

I have also seen photographs of Scarlet-chested Parrots and an African Grey Parrot that could be Opaline mutations. There is also a Peachfaced Lovebird mutation known as 'Rose-headed' that is being classified as an Opaline mutation. Various other mutations have been incorrectly called Opaline due to the failure of breeders and even authors to understand the nature of the mutation. If the 'Rose-headed' Peachfaced Lovebird is an Opaline mutation, then it is the first outside of Australian parrot species. Unfortunately it lacks underwing stripes and therefore cannot be classified as an Opaline with certainty.

There are also mutations in the Plum-headed Parrot, the Green-cheeked and the Black-capped Conures that could fit this mutation category, but like the Peachfaced Lovebird mutation they lack the wing stripe. There are even reports of a true Opaline in Indian Ringnecked Parrots, but do not confuse this with those incorrectly called Opaline in *Ringnecked Parakeets and their Mutations* by T. and G.J.J. Bastiaan.

G ROMAN

L BRANDT

P TOMAS

1 & 2. Opaline (Red) Eastern Rosella
    showing the classical underwing stripes of
    Opaline mutations in Australian
    species of parrots.
3. Opaline (Rose) Bourke's Parrot.
4. Opaline Peachfaced Lovebird – note the
    green rump colour,
    a feature of this mutation in this species.
5. Opaline Budgerigar.

'Yellowsided' Black-capped Conure may also be another Opaline mutation.

Above: Opaline Turquoise Parrot. Right: The 'Yellowsided' Green-cheeked Conure (R) may be another Opaline mutation.

Some basic matings for Opaline are as follows:

| | |
|---|---|
| **Opaline cock x Normal hen** | = Normal/Opaline cocks + Opaline hens |
| **Normal cock x Opaline hen** | = Normal/Opaline cocks + Normal hens |
| **Normal/Opaline cock x Normal hen** | = Normal and Normal/Opaline cocks + Normal and Opaline hens |
| **Normal/Opaline cock x Opaline hen** | = Normal/Opaline and Opaline cocks + Normal and Opaline hens |
| **Opaline cock x Opaline hen** | = Opaline cocks and hens |

The Opaline mutation combines well with almost any other mutation, often producing unexpected results (eg Lutino Opaline). Each combination in each species is a new area to explore and it is well worthwhile trying them all. It ranks with the Blue mutation as possibly the most valuable mutation, particularly for attractive outcomes.

Opaline Red-rumped Parrot cock.

Opaline Red-rumped Parrot hen.

Opaline (Pearl) Cockatiel.

## Pied

Pied mutations are another group of pigment distribution genes. There is more than one gene that will produce a pied pattern. At least four different types can be identified by a combination of visual effect and genetic inheritance:

- Dominant Pied
- Recessive Pied
- Recessive Black-eyed Clear
- Recessive Anti-dimorphism (ADM) Pied

The action of all Pied mutations (irrespective of genetic type) is to interrupt deposition of grey family pigments within feathers in a generally irregular pattern. From basic definitions **they should not alter yellow family pigments or structural colour directly**. However one type of Pied, the ADM Pied, which is recessive in inheritance, interferes with the process by which some species become sexually dimorphic and as a result appear to reduce certain yellow family pigments or structural colours. This type of Pied mutation is the basis for much of the common confusion about the action of Pied mutations. However, there is evidence that some other types of Pied mutations do interfere with red pigment production as well as with the grey family pigments. Why this happens has yet to be determined. (This topic is discussed in more detail in Part Three, see page 255.) It is important to realise that most other types of Pied mutations only alter the grey family pigments.

There are birds that have yellow feathering amongst areas of normally red feathering. They have been commonly labelled as Pied, although their true nature is uncertain. Most appear to be only 'sports' or variations of the Normal bird. In fact there is no known mutation that breaks the pattern of yellow family pigment deposition. If it was possible to have a so-called 'Psittacin Pied', it should have appeared by now, given all the mutations that we already have in different species. Therefore, I doubt that we will ever see birds with patches of blue colour amid the normal green, or if combined with a Lutino mutation, white patches amid the yellow colouration. Dreamers can continue to dream, and I wish them success, but I believe it is a forlorn hope.

*Above: A yellow mark in a region of red colouration does not represent a Pied mutation in this Crimson Rosella.*

Many readers might now be asking about birds they have seen that are half green and half blue. These birds are known as *halfsiders* and are split down the centre into the two colours. The appearance is quite different from the action of Pied mutations. Genetically these birds are always Normal/Blue birds. It is currently believed that they occur

*Left: A Halfsider Eclectus Parrot.*
*Far left: A Halfsider Fischer's Lovebird.*

*A Halfsider Masked Lovebird.*

due to a genetic error as an embryo. This error deletes the Normal gene from one half of the bird, thereby allowing the Blue gene to express itself in that side of the bird. This sort of error, whilst genetic in origin, cannot be passed on to youngsters and, whilst certain family lines are predisposed to producing halfsiders, it is impossible to establish them as an inherited mutation.

There is another aspect regarding Pied mutations that is commonly misrepresented and deserves mention. That is the effect of Pied on other body parts. The original definition for Pied mutations (made early last century) stated that they should not alter the colour of any body parts except feathers. This would exclude many of the current Pied mutations that have pied feet, and these obviously should not be excluded. However it is interesting to note this definition and remember that a Pied mutation may affect nothing else except feathers, a fact forgotten by many modern breeders.

The pied effect of grey family pigment loss can also be caused by conditions other than colour mutations. In particular, certain diseases can cause the bird to appear as an apparent Pied. Liver disease, Polyomavirus and Psittacine Beak and Feather Disease are all common causes. A word of warning to breeders looking for new mutations. They may in fact be introducing a new disease into their flock instead of a Pied mutation. Any bird with patchy grey family pigment loss, particularly on the back, should be treated with caution unless tested for illness and given a clean bill of health.

With Pied mutations, it is common to refer to the areas of grey family pigment loss as the 'pied areas' and the normally pigmented areas as the 'non-pied areas'. Most Pied mutations are highly variable and can be selected for increased 'pied areas'. Some can become fully pied (sometimes misleadingly called 'Reverse Pieds') and are then known as Black-eyed Clears. The typical yellow canary is in fact a Black-eyed Clear (full Pied) and the heavily variegated forms are, in fact, lightly Pied birds. You might also note that a 'Red Factor' Canary is a full Pied, yet is still able to produce red pigment!

All Pied mutations combine well with yellow family pigment mutations, structural mutations (ie Olive, Greygreen and Violet), the Opaline mutation and the darker grey family pigment mutations. Whilst their effects can be visible on even the lightest grey family pigment mutation, the contrast is lost between pied and non-pied areas and therefore their desirability is decreased.

### Dominant Pied

Identifying this mutation is fairly simple; it is a typical Pied that is inherited in a dominant manner. At this time it is impossible to be sure that all Pied mutations of dominant inheritance represent the same mutation. Only microscopic studies of feathers and other body parts can clarify this. In the Budgerigar it is known that two distinct Dominant Pied mutations exist. (They are known as the Dutch Pied and the Australian Pied to distinguish them.) On a functional level they each affect the process of pigment deposition

*Australian Dominant Pied Budgerigar.*

*Dutch Dominant Pied Budgerigar.*

R CUSICK    ABK    B NIELSEN

G ROMAN

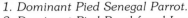

G ROMAN

1. *Dominant Pied Senegal Parrot.*
2. *Dominant Pied Peachfaced Lovebird.*
3. *Dominant Pied Elegant Parrot.*
4. *Dominant Pied Yellow Rosella.*
5. *Dominant Pied Mallee Ringnecked Parrot.*

slightly differently, but the visual effect would not be easily discernible to anyone unfamiliar with Budgerigars.

Like all Pied mutations, patterns vary, but different forms seem to have certain target areas. The Australian Pied Budgerigar typically produces a pied band across the abdomen. (It is also known as the Banded Pied for this reason.) In some instances, the spread of pied markings seems to be increased by the presence of two (Double Factor) genes for Pied.

The true Dominant Pied mutation is established or has occurred in the following species:

Budgerigars (two forms)
Scarlet-chested Parrot
Elegant Parrot
Eastern Rosella
Red-fronted Kakariki
Peachfaced Lovebird

Undoubtedly many other Dominant Pied mutations exist but have not yet been established or identified. The Dominant Pied Elegant Parrot is a European mutation and should not be confused with the Australian Recessive Pied Elegant Parrot.

The following mating results are typical for any dominant mutation:

| | |
|---|---|
| **Dominant Pied (DF) x Normal** | = 100% Dominant Pied (SF) |
| **Dominant Pied (SF) x Normal** | = 50% Normal<br>+ 50% Dominant Pied (SF) |
| **Dominant Pied (SF) x Dominant Pied (SF)** | = 25% Normal<br>+ 50% Dominant Pied (SF)<br>+ 25% Dominant Pied (DF) |
| **Dominant Pied (SF) x Dominant Pied (DF)** | = 50% Dominant Pied (SF)<br>+ 50% Dominant Pied (DF) |

## Black-eyed Clear

There exists a small number of Pied mutations whose primary expression is for a full Pied colour. This is known as the Black-eyed Clear mutation. The two species with clear examples are the Hooded Parrot and the Red-rumped Parrot. Much confusion exists over the genetic nature of these Pied mutations in both of these species. They are often thought of as dominant rather than their true recessive nature. This is because a

Black-eyed (Australian) Yellow Peachfaced Lovebird – viewed as a 'Pied' in Europe and the USA.

G ROMAN

Birds split for Black-eyed Yellow often show break-through 'Pied' markings.

Black-eyed Yellow Red-rumped Parrot – a recessive mutation incorrectly known as 'Australian Dominant Pied'.

percentage of split birds show evidence of pied feathering. However, only some do and these stray pied feathers are simply an indication of variable expression and reduced penetrance of the Normal over the Pied gene. (These are genetic terms, which will be discussed further in Part Three. See page 257.) Suffice it to say that these mutations are not dominant, otherwise splits would never be possible and they definitely do exist.

When these mutations express themselves, an almost full pied effect is seen. They often have stray normal-coloured feathers or patches. The full colour of the patches makes them distinguishable from the Dilute (Yellow) mutation that has diluted pigment in areas of retention. If you view these birds as recessive Black-eyed Clears, with some of the split birds displaying stray pied feathers, their genetics will make sense.

G ROMAN

Black-eyed Yellow Hooded Parrot – commonly known as 'Dominant Pied'.

In both Rainbow Lorikeets and Red-collared Lorikeets there are apparent Yellow birds that have proven very difficult to reproduce. Breeders had believed the colour was not a true mutation, so the colour could not be passed on to any young. However, persistence from breeders has been rewarded with reports of the Rainbow Lorikeet form being reproduced after extensive outcrossing. It now appears that the colour is a typical recessive Black-eyed Clear, with a percentage of splits showing evidence of the gene being carried. The difficulty in establishing the mutation has been just the typical problems experienced with all recessive mutations.

Despite the difficulty in establishing these birds as a mutation, they do allow us to 'peek inside' the bird and look at the true distribution of yellow family pigments. What we find is that the Rainbow Lorikeet has red pigment in its head, whilst the Red-collared does not.

P SMITH

Black-eyed Yellow Rainbow Lorikeet.

J McCORMICK

P ODEKERKEN

*Above: Possible Black-eyed Clear mutation of Chattering Lory.*
*Above left: 'Dark-eyed' Yellow Budgerigar – is a combination*
*of Dominant and Recessive Pied mutations.*

T DULIERE

*'Dark-eyed' Yellow*
*Red-fronted Kakariki –*
*known as 'Gold-checked',*
*is actually a*
*combination colour.*

This is an example of the invaluable insights one can gain into a species from studying mutations.

Another form of Black-eyed Clear exists in the Budgerigar. This mutation is commonly called Dark-eyed Clear by Budgerigar breeders. In fact there are other Black-eyed Clears in this species. (See *Spangle* section on page 101.) The form I am referring to here is actually a combination of two primary mutations, the Dominant Dutch Pied and the Recessive Danish Pied. When these two different Pied mutations are combined on the one bird, their effects are complimentary and the result is a Black-eyed Clear bird. As this is the only species where this is known to occur, I mention it here rather than in ·the section on *Combinations of Mutations*.

## Addendum

I have become aware of an identical interaction between Dominant and Recessive Pied in the Red-fronted Kakariki. In this species the combination has become known as Gold-checked and Golden Yellow. As this pied interaction has been demonstrated in two species, there is good reason to suspect that it will occur in other species as well. It also allows the grouping of Dominant Pied with Recessive Pied interaction as one form of Dominant Pied (equivalent to a Dutch Pied Budgerigar) and those that do not interact into a second group (equivalent to an Australian Pied Budgerigar).

## Recessive Pied

The great majority of Pied mutations have proven to be recessive in inheritance. However, not all Recessive Pied mutations are the same (eg the Black-eyed Clear and the ADM Pied). (See the next section.) It is impossible to know for certain whether the remaining recessive Pieds in this group form only one group or are merely a grouping for convenience. We can be certain that some of the recessive Pied mutations in species that are sexually monomorphic, will be ADM Pieds, but cannot be accurately assigned without extensive scientific analysis.

Like the Dominant Pied mutations, Recessive Pied mutations

ABK

*Recessive Pied*
*Budgerigar.*

can be selectively altered for varying amounts of pied markings. Different breeders of different species prefer different patterns or amounts of pied, but the most common desired feature is bilateral symmetry (each side a mirror image of the other) in pied markings. Achieving this effect is not always the easiest thing to do, due to the variable nature of Pied mutations.

This variable nature tends to flow through to the genetic level as well. Like the Black-eyed Clear mutation, it is not uncommon for some split Pied birds to show occasional pied markings. This should not be taken as an indication that the mutation is dominant.

The following species either have or have had Recessive Pied mutations or Pied mutations of uncertain inheritance that cannot be placed in another of the Pied classes mentioned:

*Pied Red-bellied Parrot of unknown inheritance.*

Budgerigar
Bourke's Parrot (two forms)
Turquoise Parrot
Scarlet-chested Parrot
Eastern Rosella
Pale-headed Rosella
Crimson Rosella
Yellow Rosella
Princess Parrot
Red-tailed Black Cockatoo
Yellow-tailed Black Cockatoo
Red-fronted Kakariki
Rainbow Lorikeet
Varied Lorikeet
Masked Lovebird
Fischer's Lovebird
Indian Ringnecked Parrot
  (multiple forms)
Plum-headed Parrot
Moustache Parrot

*Pied Indian Ringnecked Parrot of unknown inheritance.*

*Above: Pied Blue and Gold Macaw of unknown inheritance.*
*Below: Another Pied Indian Ringnecked Parrot of unknown inheritance.*

The following are typical breeding results for matings involving the Recessive Pied:

| | |
|---|---|
| **Recessive Pied x Normal** | = 100% Normal/Rec. Pied |
| **Normal/Rec. Pied x Normal** | = 50% Normal<br>+ 50% Normal/Rec. Pied |
| **Normal/Rec. Pied**<br>    **x Normal/Rec. Pied** | = 25% Normal<br>+ 50% Normal/Rec. Pied<br>+ 25% Rec. Pied |
| **Recessive Pied x Normal/Rec. Pied** | = 50% Normal/Rec. Pied<br>+ 50% Recessive Pied |
| **Recessive Pied x Recessive Pied** | = 100% Recessive Pied |

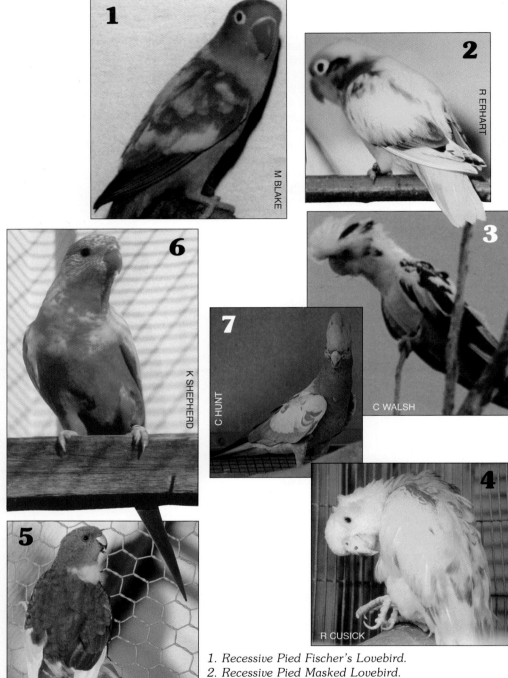

1. Recessive Pied Fischer's Lovebird.
2. Recessive Pied Masked Lovebird.
3. Pied Red-tailed Black Cockatoo of unknown inheritance.
4. Pied Double Yellow-headed Amazon of unknown inheritance.
5. Recessive Pied Red-fronted Kakariki.
6. Recessive Pied Rainbow Lorikeet.
7. Recessive Pied Galah.

1. *Pied Crimson Rosella – a strain being established in Australia.*
2. *Pied Scarlet-chested Parrot of unknown inheritance.*
3. *Pied Mulga Parrot of unknown inheritance.*
4. *Recessive Pied Turquoise Parrot.*
5. *Recessive Pied Bourke's Parrot.*
6. *Recessive Pied Pale-headed Rosella.*

*The 'Hillerman' Pied Indian Ringnecked Parrot exhibits anti-dimorphism traits via the loss of the neck ring in cocks. It also has an unstable pied pattern, with fledglings showing more pied markings than older birds.*

## Anti-dimorphism (ADM) Pied

This is a new category for those recessive Pied mutations that interfere with the normal **sexual dimorphism** of the species in which they occur. Their existence has long been a source of confusion because they seem to alter the distribution of yellow family pigments and in one instance (the UK Pied Red-rumped Parrot) they seem to alter structural aspects of colour. No Pied mutation directly alters these elements, and the clue to the true nature is in looking at the mutations in the correct manner.

To understand what these mutations are doing, the breeder needs to closely examine the appearance of the UK Pied Red-rumped Parrot and compare it closely to the Normal Red-rumped Parrot. What is found is not just the loss of the cock's red rump, but also a change in structural colour towards a grey-green shade. However, this change is not absolute because if we look at a Normal hen, we find patches of structural colour in her plumage. These features result in the Blue UK Pied Red-rumped Parrot mutation being almost totally grey and white in colour, although breeders had been expecting a Blue Pied bird. All the changes created by this mutation are either the pied effect or else relate to loss of normal sexual dimorphism.

The next species to consider is the Pied mutation in the Cockatiel. They have always been notoriously difficult to sex, based on plumage colour. Cocks frequently do not have a bright yellow face and crest like a typical cock of their species. There is also an increased spread of yellow pigment through the body and wings and increased grey family pigments in the face area. This is certainly an unusual combination of traits for any mutation let alone a Pied mutation. All these changes are once again normal features for hens not cocks.

For a long time the simplest examples have been taken for granted, without being considered for what they are. The Recessive Pied Elegant Parrot mutation in Australia is noted for the absence of the orange vent spot in cocks. This means that the only significant dimorphic trait in this species is lost. There is also a Pied Indian Ringnecked Parrot mutation that fails to develop the neck ring of the cock upon sexual maturity. Cocks in some Recessive Pied mutations of the Turquoise Parrot do not have the red shoulder flash.

*ADM Pied Elegant Parrot – an Australian mutation.*

*ADM Pied Cockatiel – the common Pied Cockatiel is an ADM Pied.*

These mutations lose yellow family pigments indirectly; therefore the common belief that Pied mutations can remove red colouration is true but for the wrong reasons. It cannot be stated too strongly – **Pieds do not remove red colouration as a direct action.**

There is one other common feature of this type of Pied mutation. They often have partially coloured, partially pied feathers. This is most notable in the flight feathers if they are not totally pied marked. I mention this feature because early definitions of pied feathering state that this type of mutation has individual feathers which are totally coloured or totally pied, but never have feathers which are partially coloured or partially pied. Mutations which have this trait have been called Grizzle by this old definition. Grizzle is used as a name for certain special Pied type mutations with this feature in other species of birds, but not yet in parrots to my knowledge.

*ADM Pied Red-rumped Parrot – known also as 'UK Pied'.*

The genetic inheritance for this group is the same as the other main group of Recessive Pied mutations. Therefore use the matings for Recessive Pied and its combinations. (See page 97.)

### Headspot Pied

I have become aware of a trait that exists in both Budgerigars and Indian Ringnecked Parrots that may represent a form of sex-linked Pied. It involves a pied spot appearing on the back of the head in otherwise normal-coloured birds. It appears to have a sex-linked inheritance pattern but this has not been properly investigated, as the mutation does not have strong individual appeal as a colour mutation.

In Budgerigars it is often found combined with the other Pied mutations and is not always recognised as a separate entity. In the Indian Ringnecked Parrot, it is often linked with the Lutino mutation. Cocks showing the spot are generally identified as split Lutino birds.

It is obvious that this mutation will never gain a wide appeal, but it is interesting to note for genetic reasons and will be worth noting if found in other species. It cannot be increased in pied area like other Pied mutations.

### Spangle

This is a co-dominant mutation found only in the Budgerigar at this point. I am discussing it in this section on Pieds, because I believe that it should be viewed as a special Pied mutation.

The bird that most people will recognise is the Single Factor bird. In this state, the mutation removes foreground grey family pigments from approximately half of the feather in a strict pattern. It has no effect on background grey family pigments. This means that body colour is unaltered in the Single Factor, but the characteristic wing markings in Budgerigars are reduced to thin stripes. In the Double Factor, the mutation behaves more like the Black-eyed Clear, totally removing all traces of grey family pigments from the

*Single Factor Spangle Budgerigar.*

TOBY MARTIN

M CHRISTIAN

Y IMANOTHAI

*Single Factor Dominant Edged Fischer's Lovebird – is it a Spangle?*

*An Opaline 'Spangle' Bourke's Parrot.*

*Double Factor Spangle Budgerigar.*

Y IMANOTHAI

*Above: The appearance of the Double Factor Dominant Edged Fischer's Lovebird is consistent with a Spangle mutation.*
*Below: The so-called 'Spangle' Bourke's Parrot is reported to be recessive and if this is correct, it cannot be a Spangle mutation.*

TOBY MARTIN

foreground areas, but often leaving areas of background pigment in patches. The appearance of the Double Factor bird is the best clue to the true nature of the mutation and is why I call it a special Pied mutation. The Black-eyed Clear bird should not be confused with the similar looking Dark-eyed Clear created by the combination of Dutch and Danish Pied mutations in the Budgerigar. (See the section on *Black-eyed Clear* on page 97.) This is a case of a similar appearance being possible from birds with a different genetic make-up.

Although no other definite examples of this mutation exist at this time, breeders of other species have used this name a number of times for unrelated mutations. A unique mutation in the Bourke's Parrot has some similarities to the Single Factor form, but its inheritance is reported as recessive, which makes it a different type of mutation altogether. In the Fischer's Lovebird there is also a very similar looking mutation known as Spangle in the USA and Edged in Europe. It is co-dominant like the true Spangle with the Double Factor also producing a Black-eyed Clear appearance. This would suggest that it may be a true Spangle, but debate still exists over its true nature. It may fit into the Dominant Dilute category.

In other species, specimens with mottled wing patterns have also been called Spangles, but once again are clearly different mutations altogether. If the mutation was to reoccur in another species, it is most likely to occur in the Rosella *Platycercus* genus, which carries the black markings across the back similar to the Budgerigar.

Following are some breeding results from various matings involving the Spangle mutation:

(BE Clear = Black-eyed Clear)

| | |
|---|---|
| **Spangle (SF) x Normal** | = 50% Normal<br>+ 50% Spangle (SF) |
| **Spangle (DF) [BE Clear] x Normal** | = 100% Spangle (SF) |
| **Spangle (SF) x Spangle (SF)** | = 25% Normal<br>+ 50% Spangle (SF)<br>+ 25% Spangle (DF) [BE Clear] |
| **Spangle (DF) [BE Clear]<br>    x Spangle (SF)** | = 50% Spangle (SF)<br>+ 50% Spangle (DF) [BE Clear] |
| **Spangle (DF) [BE Clear]<br>    x Spangle (DF) [BE Clear]** | = 100% Spangle (DF) [BE Clear] |

## Melanistic

Melanistic mutations form another ad hoc group of mutations with similar action, but doubtful genetic relatedness. They are grouped together because their basic action is to increase distribution of grey family pigments. As each does it in a different way they probably represent different mutations in different species. These mutations are all recessive in inheritance.

*Melanistic Rainbow Lorikeet – commonly known as 'Blue-fronted'.*

Two Melanistic mutations occur in lorikeets and could possibly be related. The Melanistic Rainbow Lorikeet adds grey family pigments deep within the feathers in areas previously lacking this pigment. In other words body colour is increased, causing green colours to appear where previously only yellow was visible and blue colours to appear where previously red was visible. These blue areas are actually more of a purple-blue, the same colour as the head and abdomen (belly) because red pigment is not lost, only hidden. This mutation is known to lorikeet breeders as 'Blue-fronted'.

*Melanistic Stella's Lory.*

The Melanistic Stella's Lory appears black in photographs. I have not seen these birds in the flesh, but have been advised that they are in fact a dark blue. If this is true, then the increased pigment would also be background grey family pigments in all areas where it was previously absent, which is similar to the changes in the Melanistic Rainbow Lorikeet. The Normal Stella's Lory is predominantly red in colour.

I suspect that both of these mutations represent dysfunction of a gene that normally restricts distribution of grey family pigments into a strict pattern. When it is damaged

G ROMAN

*Melanistic Eastern Rosella.*

D MERVILDE

*Melanistic (Blackface) Budgerigar – this bird is not the base colour, but actually the Melanistic Greygreen combination.*

(in the case of the mutant gene) the grey family pigments are allowed to spread without control.

A similar pattern occurs in the Melanistic Eastern Rosella, but in this case the grey family pigment increase seems to spread from the black wing markings, over most of the bird. The spread of this pigment appears a little variable in extent, with a greater area of black being more desirable to most breeders. I do not believe that there is any loss of yellow family pigments (including red) in this bird, but the breeders trying to combine it with the Lutino will soon discover the truth. Grey family pigments are increased in foreground areas, distinguishing it from the lorikeet forms. The different distribution of pigment results in extensive areas of black colouration instead of blue colouration as seen in the lorikeet species. This mutation is commonly called the Black Eastern Rosella.

The most recent Melanistic mutation is the Blackface Budgerigar. Whilst I would have expected a Melanistic mutation in Budgerigars to be similar to the Melanistic Eastern Rosella, when it did occur it was quite different. This mutation seems to increase grey family pigments in most areas of the bird, including areas where these pigments are already present. Therefore, this results in darker shades of green or blue. There is also a spread of grey family pigments over the face area, but no loss of barring from the wings, as in the Melanistic Eastern Rosella. It will lead to a large number of new possibilities in combination with other mutations. At present, however, it has some of the problems typical for all new recessive mutations. (See page 36.)

A new colour in the Cloncurry Parrot has been reported as a possible Melanistic mutation. Photographs of the bird published in *Australian Broad-tailed Parrots* (Sindel and Gill, 1999) suggest that this is unlikely. The colour is reported as recessive, ruling out Olive, the most likely possibility on appearance. The bird does give the appearance of being very similar to the closely related Port Lincoln Parrot. Therefore, I suspect that it may represent a species-specific gene that 'converted' the ancestors of this parrot into the Cloncurry Parrot. In effect, this mutation reverses this process, making the Cloncurry Parrot look like its ancestors once again!

The following are standard mating outcomes for Melanistic mutations:

| | |
|---|---|
| **Melanistic x Normal** | = 100% Normal/Melanistic |
| **Normal/Melanistic x Melanistic** | = 50% Normal/Melanistic<br>+ 50% Melanistic |
| **Normal/Melanistic<br>    x Normal/Melanistic** | = 25% Normal<br>+ 50% Normal/Melanistic<br>+ 25% Melanistic |
| **Melanistic x Melanistic** | = 100% Melanistic |

Melanistic mutations will combine effectively with most mutations except those that greatly reduce the grey family pigments. Grey family pigment mutations like Cinnamon create attractive mutations, but combinations with light Dilutes would produce only subtle combinations. As mentioned previously, the combination with the Lutino mutation is unlikely to result in any apparent change, although this can only be determined through experimentation. It is possible that the increase in grey family pigment will show through as a light grey suffusion on the Lutino highlighting the leaking tap feature of the Lutino mutation. Combination with the distribution mutations has not been explored to date. The results could also be interesting.

## Red-fronted and Red Suffusion

There are many species of parrots that have individuals with increased red pigment. Not all represent the same change, with many appearing to be a response to ill health or possibly a lack of direct sunlight. These birds known as Red Suffused have red feathering scattered through the plumage or as barring. Many of these birds are also expressing the Lutino gene and there may be a genetic link in some cases. However, none of this type has been established or shown to reproduce itself reliably. That may change in the future, but who knows the future?

A second less common form of spreading red pigment occurs in the Turquoise Parrot and the Scarlet-chested Parrot. This is generally referred to as the Red-fronted or Red-bellied mutation.

### Addendum

*There is also an established Red-fronted mutation in Swift Parrots and true genetic forms are being established in Princess Parrots and other species.*

Most authors then immediately point out the significance of selection in these birds and label them selective traits almost as a dismissal.

Whilst the importance of selection in producing good specimens of these mutations is undeniable, it should be remembered that genetics is still at work and this colour mutation is still worth recognising. You cannot breed a Red-fronted bird unless you have the gene that allows production of red pigment in these areas. This master gene is dominant to Normal (yellow plumage in these areas) and allows the multitude of selection genes to be accumulated so as to increase the spread of red pigment. If you mate two non-Red-fronted birds together, only Yellow-bellied birds are produced. However, yellow bellies can be produced from Red-fronted birds if they carry the master gene for yellow belly (the Normal gene).

*Red-fronted Turquoise Parrot.*

Because there are many selection genes involved in determining the spread of red pigment in these birds, it is difficult to predict the amount of red that will be passed on to a youngster, except to state that 'the redder the parents, the more likely a chick will carry more red'.

Red-fronted mutations combine well with almost every other mutation, except those which alter yellow family pigments (ie Blue and Parblue.) Yet the Parblue mutation can produce a 'Salmon-fronted' combination that does have some attraction although it is difficult to develop. Beautiful combinations result from combining this mutation with the Opaline mutation and the Yellow mutation in unison.

*Red-fronted Scarlet-chested Parrot.*

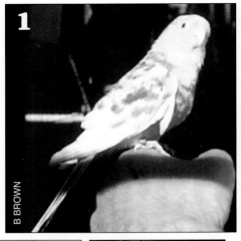

B BROWN

P BENDER

R LOW

ABK

1. *Red Suffused Red-rumped Parrot – attempts have been made to establish this as a genuine mutation.*
2. *Red Suffused Superb Parrot.*
3. *Red Suffused Peachfaced Lovebird – a common non-genetic colour modification.*
4. *Red Suffused African Grey Parrot.*
5. *Red-fronted Swift Parrot.*
6. *Red Suffused Princess Parrot – some strains appear to be genetic.*

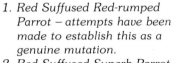

ANON

R ERHART

# Orangeface

The Orangeface mutation in the Peachfaced Lovebird is well established in countries other than Australia. Jim Hayward coined the name 'Tangerine' for this mutation, but it has not been taken up by the Lovebird Fancy. The mutation appears to control the conversion of yellow and orange pigments into pink or red pigments. Therefore, the rose-coloured face of the Peachfaced Lovebird is altered to orange and the spots on the tail also become orange. Any change to yellow pigment is very subtle, with no visible change being noted in the body colour of Orangeface Lutino combinations.

Some lovebird authors report a change in body colour associated with Orangeface Green birds, but not when in combination with other mutations such as the Parblue. They have suggested that there is a structural change associated with this mutation, but I find it unlikely that a gene controlling yellow family pigments would have effects on structure as well.

The mutation has been shown to be co-dominant in inheritance, because split birds are noticeably different from Normal faced birds, but are also clearly different from the desirable Orangeface colour. Whilst being identifiable, these Single Factor Orangeface birds have not been given a distinguishing name and are generally referred to as 'split Orangeface'. When in combination with other mutations, these 'splits' are very difficult to detect and most authorities prefer to classify the mutation as recessive.

At present no other species is recognised as having this mutation, however there may be another example of this mutation already in existence. The Dusky Lory naturally occurs in two colour 'phases' – red phase and yellow phase. The yellow phase is dominant to the red phase and I am suggesting that the yellow phase represents a naturally occurring Orangeface mutation in this species.

Mating expectations for the Orangeface mutation are as follows:

| | |
|---|---|
| **Orangeface (DF) x Normal** | = 100% split Orangeface (SF) |
| **split Orangeface (SF) x Orangeface (DF)** | = 50% Orangeface (DF) + 50% split Orangeface (SF) |
| **split Orangeface (SF) x split Orangeface (SF)** | = 25% Normal + 50% split Orangeface (SF) + 25% Orangeface (DF) |
| **split Orangeface (SF) x Normal** | = 50% split Orangeface (SF) + 50% Normal |
| **Orangeface (DF) x Orangeface (DF)** | = 100% Orangeface (DF) |

R ERHART

*Above: Orangeface Peachfaced Lovebirds (L to R) – comparison of Single Factor, Normal and Double Factor.*
*Far left: Red Phase Dusky Lory.*
*Left: Yellow Phase Dusky Lory.*

## Yellowface

Yellowface Cockatiel.

The mutation known as Yellowface in the Cockatiel is a sex-linked mutation that is probably species-specific. It controls development of the orange cheek spot present in the Normal Cockatiel. When the gene is damaged, the spot does not form. If and until other examples occur in other species, it is hard to speculate whether it is a pigment distribution gene controlling a marking (which seems likely) or whether it may in fact control the conversion of yellow pigment into orange pigment.

Its inheritance is sex-linked, which means that some interesting genetic results may occur regarding linkage with other sex-linked mutations. At this time, I have no information which deals with this aspect of the mutation. The mutation would combine best with almost any mutation, except those altering yellow family pigments (ie Blue and Parblue mutations).

Mating results for the Yellowface mutation are as follows:

| | |
|---|---|
| **Yellowface cock x Normal hen** | = Normal/Yellowface cocks<br>+ Yellowface hens |
| **Normal cock x Yellowface hen** | = Normal/Yellowface cocks<br>+ Normal hens |
| **Normal/Yellowface cock<br>x Normal hen** | = Normal and Normal/Yellowface cocks<br>+ Normal and Yellowface hens |
| **Normal/Yellowface cock<br>x Yellowface hen** | = Normal/Yellowface and Yellowface cocks<br>+ Normal and Yellowface hens |
| **Yellowface cock x Yellowface hen** | = Yellowface cocks and hens |

## Slate

Slate Blue Budgerigar – the primary mutation is a green base bird which is seldom bred as the Blue combination shows the characteristic colour change best.

This is another rare species-specific mutation (at this stage). It occurs in the Budgerigar and is a sex-linked mutation with an effect similar to a partial grey effect. When combined with the Blue mutation, a blue-grey colour is produced, which is distinctly different from any other mutation. It achieves this by altering the structure of the feather, thereby interfering with the light distortion effect in a manner different from the other structural mutations.

It is important to recognise this mutation, because it is common for lovebird breeders to call the Mauve combination in the Peachfaced Lovebird by the name 'Slate'. This habit will cause tremendous confusion if the true Slate mutation occurs in other species. Perhaps it never will, but it has a good chance.

Like all sex-linked mutations, it exhibits gene linkage with other sex-linked mutations. Mating results for the Slate mutation are as follows:

| | |
|---|---|
| **Slate cock x Normal hen** | = Normal/Slate cocks<br>+ Slate hens |
| **Normal cock x Slate hen** | = Normal/Slate cocks<br>+ Normal hens |
| **Normal/Slate cock x Normal hen** | = Normal and Normal/Slate cocks<br>+ Normal and Slate hens |
| **Normal/Slate cock x Slate hen** | = Normal/Slate and Slate cocks<br>+ Normal and Slate hens |
| **Slate cock x Slate hen** | = Slate cocks and hens |

It combines best with the Blue mutation and pigment distribution type mutations such as Opaline or Pied.

# KEY TO NAMING MUTATIONS

The following is a step-by-step key to identifying the correct name for any new mutation. Each question must be answered before moving on as directed. If an answer is not known, then you cannot correctly identify the mutation with 100% certainty, and assigning a name to the mutation is premature. It will become obvious that many mutations cannot be correctly named until other mutations appear in the species to allow appropriate test matings.

1.  What form is the genetic inheritance?
    **Recessive.** Go to 19.
    **Dominant/Co-dominant.** Go to 9.
    **Sex-linked.** Go to 2.

2.  Is the pattern or distribution of pigments altered?
    **Yes.** Go to 3.
    **No.** Go to 4.

3.  Are grey family pigments reduced in the plumage and removed from the down? Are yellow family pigments enhanced? Is the white underwing stripe retained in adults and enhanced on both sides of the wing?
    **Yes.** It is an **Opaline.**
    **No.** You may have a new type of mutation.

4.  Are all grey family pigments removed from the bird?
    **Yes.** It is a **Sex-linked Lutino.**
    **No.** Go to 5.

5.  Does the mutation belong to the sex-linked Lutino family? (Is it a multiple allele of Lutino?)
    **Yes.** It is a **Sex-linked Lime.**
    **No.** Go to 6.

6.  Are grey family pigments changed fully to brown shades?
    **Yes.** It is a **Cinnamon.**
    **No.** Go to 7.

7.  Does the mutation appear to alter structural colour of the bird, changing bright green to dull 'olive' green or bright blue to a 'blue-grey' colour?
    **Yes.** You may have a **Slate.** (It requires feather analysis.)
    **No.** Go to 8.

8.  Are orange pigments lost whilst yellow pigments are retained?
    **Yes.** You have a **Yellowface.**
    **No.** Your mutation is not currently recognised.

9.  Is the plumage pattern broken with patches of grey family pigment loss?
    **Yes.** Go to 10.
    **No.** Go to 12.

10. Are the grey family pigments removed fully from some feathers in patches?
    **Yes.** You have a **Dominant Pied.** (There are at least two forms.)
    **No.** Go to 11.

11. Are the grey family pigments removed in part from foreground areas in Single Factor and almost totally from all areas of all feathers in Dark Factor?
**Yes.** You have a **Spangle.**
**No.** Your mutation is not currently recognised.

12. Is the grey family pigment colour of the mutation reduced from normal?
**Yes.** You have a **Dominant Dilute.**
**No.** Go to 13.

13. Is pink and red pigment production stopped at the orange pigment stage?
**Yes.** You have an **Orangeface.**
**No.** Go to 14.

14. Does the mutation alter structural colour?
**Yes.** Go to 15.
**No.** Go to 34.

15. Is blue structural colour prevented totally in a full dominant fashion?
**Yes.** You have a **Dominant Grey mutation.**
**No.** Go to 16.

16. Does the mutation appear to darken the colour of the plumage?
**Yes.** Go to 17.
**No.** Your mutation is not currently recognised.

17. Does the mutation have a gene linkage with the Blue mutation?
**Yes.** You have an **Olive (Dark Factor) mutation;** the inheritance should be co-dominant with Dark Green as the intermediate.
**No.** Go to 18.

18. Does the mutation combine with Blue to produce a violet colour when in Double Factor?
**Yes.** You have a **Violet mutation.**
**No.** Your mutation is not currently recognised.

19. Is the plumage pattern broken with patches of grey family pigment loss?
**Yes.** Go to 20.
**No.** Go to 22.

20. Does the mutation remove virtually all grey family pigments, whilst a single gene produces either a Normal or sometimes light pied markings?
**Yes.** You have a **Black-eyed Clear** with variable penetrance.
**No.** Go to 21.

21. Does the mutation cause a loss of sexual dimorphism?
**Yes.** You have an **ADM Pied mutation.**
**No.** You have a **Recessive Pied.**

22. Is there a reduction in the amount of yellow family pigments within the plumage?
**Yes.** Go to 23.
**No.** Go to 24.

23. Are all yellow family pigments totally removed? (Test mate to a Lutino to prove this.)
**Yes.** You have a **Blue mutation.**
**No.** You have a **Parblue mutation.** (There can be more than one Parblue mutation in a species.)

24. Are all grey family pigments removed from the bird?
    **Yes.** You have a **Recessive Lutino.**
    **No.** Go to 25.

25. Does the mutation belong to the Recessive Lutino family? (Is it a multiple allele of Lutino?)
    **Yes.** You have a **Recessive Lime.**
    **No.** Go to 26.

26. Is production of grey family pigments altered to produce a brown or grey-brown pigment?
    **Yes.** Go to 27.
    **No.** Go to 28.

27. Does the adult bird retain red eyes?
    **Yes.** You have a **Fallow mutation.** There can be more than one form in each species.
    **No.** You may have a **Brown mutation.** This is very rare in parrots.

28. Does the mutation increase the amount and distribution of grey family pigments through the plumage?
    **Yes.** You have a **Melanistic mutation.** These are rare, but there are at least three different types.
    **No.** Go to 29.

29. Does the mutation alter structural colour?
    **Yes.** Go to 30.
    **No.** Go to 31.

30. Is structural colour totally eliminated, with no traces being left behind?
    **Yes.** You have a **Recessive Grey**, which is very rare.
    **No.** Your mutation is not currently recognised.

31. Are grey family pigments reduced in strength within the plumage?
    **Yes.** Go to 32.
    **No.** Your mutation is not currently recognised.

32. Is the degree of pigment reduction only slight?
    **Yes.** You have a mutation known as either **Faded** or **Isabel.**
    **No.** Go to 33.

33. Your mutation fits a broad category that includes the terms **Dilute**, **Yellow** and (in Europe) **Pastel**. It involves reduced deposition of otherwise normal grey family pigments to varying degrees. More than one locus may produce this effect. Mutations with approximately 50% reduction are generally known as **Dilutes** (Pastel in Europe). Those with stronger reduction, resulting in yellowish plumage are generally known as **Suffused**. Yellow is also commonly used but should be reserved for the Black-eyed Clear mutation. The exact genetic relationship between various types needs to be explored to determine the exact classification for your mutation.

34. Are the yellow family pigments in the facial area reduced in strength without altering yellow family pigments in other plumage areas?
    **Yes.** You have a mutation known as **Pale-headed.**
    **No.** Your mutation is not currently recognised.

**PART TWO**

*TurquoiseGrey Cleartail*
*Indian Ringnecked Parrot cock.*

# COMBINATIONS OF MUTATIONS

Most colour mutations can be combined, with a new visual effect resulting from the combination. Some authors refer to colour combinations as 'secondary' or 'tertiary mutations' but this terminology should be avoided because it can mislead readers into believing that single genes create these combinations. These effects can be very interesting to explore and help give an insight into what mutations actually do. Some colour combinations are not recommended, because the effect of one mutation hides the other mutation. Generally this refers to combinations involving a mutation which alters grey family pigments and the Lutino mutation because the Lutino prevents the production of grey family pigments, leaving nothing for the second mutation to work upon. There is an exception to this rule with the Cinnamon Lutino combination which will be discussed further under that heading.

Generally speaking, the best combinations involve combining mutations of different classes. Yellow family pigment mutations (Blue or Parblue) combine best with grey family pigment mutations (Lutino, Cinnamon, Dilute, Faded and Fallow). Yellow family pigment mutations also combine better than most with the structural altering mutations (Greygreen, Olive and Violet). Pieds combine best with darker mutations to show the pied contrast clearly. Opaline has proven very versatile in combination with any other mutation so far. Only a three-way combination with both Blue and Lutino seems pointless at this time.

Naming of combinations is a contentious issue. Some names have repeatedly been used incorrectly. In many instances a simple combination of the two primary mutation names is best, eg Lutino Opaline. Worldwide there is a strong move away from separate names for combinations and this is not a bad thing. There are, however, recognised combination names and I have used them here, giving precedence to those established first in species like the lovebird and the Budgerigar. Many breeders will always wish to use a special name for various combinations and it is important that everyone understands the correct definition of these names. Where a name is commonly misused I will discuss why.

When giving advice on matings to produce combinations, I try as much as possible to use those that produce young of known genetic make-up. Whilst it is not always possible to mate the required birds together (for financial or other reasons) you will find that there is great benefit in knowing what all your young are genetically, whether for sale or future matings. Sometimes short cuts may be possible to achieve the desired combination in fewer generations, but this will be at the expense of lower numbers of desired young and many wasted birds being produced. I have also concentrated on the best possible matings because (to put it simply) 'this book is not big enough' to include every possible mating for every possible mutation and combination!

## Albino – Blue Lutino

In parrots, the true Albino is always a combination of two mutations, the Blue and the Lutino. No single gene controls both yellow and grey family pigments, so no single mutation can exist to give Albino. This combination hardly needs description, as everyone would be aware that an Albino has pink eyes, is white and devoid of any pigment. The Blue gene removes the yellow family pigments and the Lutino gene removes the grey family pigments.

To breed Albino, you are generally combining a recessive gene with a sex-linked gene. Therefore it is best to start with a Lutino cock (the sex-linked mutation) and a Blue hen. This will produce Normal/Blue/Lutino cocks and Lutino/Blue hens.

At least two Lutino/Blue hens should be mated to Blue cocks to produce Blue/Lutino cock youngsters. Normal/Blue/Lutino cocks are also produced as well as Green/Blue and Blue hens, but none of these are useful. Some people are tempted to use the double split cocks but this slows down the results significantly. Whilst mating

Albino Red-rumped Parrot.     Albino Crimson Rosella.     Albino Cockatiel.

these double split cocks to the Lutino/Blue hens will result in small numbers of Albino, the percentage is very low and all other young have unknown genetic make-up, which makes further development difficult.

*To illustrate this point, consider the following list of outcomes for this mating:*

**Normal/Blue/Lutino cock x Lutino/Blue hen**
*= Normal/Lutino and Normal/Blue/Lutino cocks*
*+ Normal and Normal/Blue hens*
*+ Lutino and Lutino/Blue cocks and hens*
*+ Blue/Lutino cocks and Blue hens*
*+ Albino cocks and hens*

*From the mating outcomes, you can see that although different young are produced, many are useless to further breeding efforts and the ratio of Albinos produced is 1:8. This seems sufficient to many breeders, but the large numbers of unidentifiable young make it messy.*

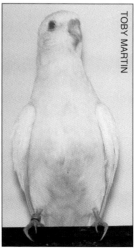

Above: Albino Indian Ringnecked Parrot.
Right: Albino Budgerigar.
Far right: Albino Scarlet-chested Parrot.

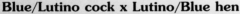

*The following Albino colours are all based on Recessive Lutino, instead of the more common sex-linked Lutino. Matings in this section do not apply to these colours. Use matings for White instead.*
1. Albino Princess Parrot.
2. Albino Quaker Parrot.
3. Albino Fischer's Lovebird.
4. Albino Masked Lovebird.

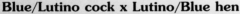

Next, the Blue/Lutino cocks are mated back to their Lutino/Blue aunts. This is preferable to being mated to their mothers and prevents excessive inbreeding. From this mating all young produced have known genetic make-up and 25% will be the desired Albino combination in both sexes.

**Blue/Lutino cock x Lutino/Blue hen**
= Normal/Blue/Lutino cocks and Normal/Blue hens
+ Blue/Lutino cocks and Blue hens
+ Lutino/Blue cocks and hens
+ Albino cocks and hens

Of these eight possible outcomes, only the Normal cocks and hens and the Blue hens have no further use. Albinos can be produced by many other matings as well, but the one described above is the most direct method.

Once Albinos are produced, mating them back to either Blue/Lutino cocks or Lutino/Blue cocks or hens can increase numbers. The possible outcomes are listed below:

**Blue/Lutino cock x Albino hen**
= Blue/Lutino cocks and Blue hens
+ Albino cocks and hens

**Lutino/Blue cock x Albino hen**
= Lutino/Blue cocks and hens
+ Albino cocks and hens

**Albino cock x Lutino/Blue hen**
= Lutino/Blue cocks and hens
+ Albino cocks and hens

## Creamino – Parblue Lutino

The Creamino is the combination of Parblue and Lutino genes. Parblues vary in the amount of yellow carried, as do Creaminos. They can be viewed as a subtle blend in appearance between Lutino and Albino. The Lutino gene removes all grey family pigments and the Parblue gene removes some of the yellow family pigments. The combination involves a recessive gene and a sex-linked gene.

To produce Creamino a number of paths may be taken. In species without true Blue (such as the Peachfaced Lovebird) a path mimicking that used for Albino is the only option. Lutino cocks are mated to Parblue hens, then Lutino/Parblue hen young are kept and mated back to Parblue cocks and finally the third generation Parblue/Lutino cocks are mated back to the Lutino/Parblue aunts. The outcomes for this mating are as follows:

H KREMER

**Parblue/Lutino cock x Lutino/Parblue hen**
= Normal/Parblue/Lutino cocks and
   Normal/Parblue hens
+ Parblue/Lutino cocks and Parblue hens
+ Lutino/Parblue cocks and hens
+ Creamino cocks and hens

Once again, there are eight possibilities with only three of no further use.

In species with both Parblues and Blues (eg Indian Ringnecked Parrots, Red-rumped Parrots), other options exist because these two mutations form a genetic family (the Parblue is dominant to Blue whilst still being recessive to Green). The most direct path is to mate an Albino cock with a Parblue hen. The outcome depends on whether the Parblue is split Blue (ParblueBlue) (see page 32) or not. In these species, most will be split Blue so the results are as follows:

**Albino cock x ParblueBlue hen**
= ParblueBlue/Lutino cocks
+ Blue/Lutino cocks
+ CreaminoBlue hens
+ Albino hens

G ROMAN

**Albino cock x Parblue hen**
= ParblueBlue/Lutino cocks
+ CreaminoBlue hens

J SUIKERBUIK

*Top: Creamino Crimson Rosella.*
*Centre: Creamino Indian Ringnecked Parrot.*
*Bottom: Creamino Scarlet-chested Parrot.*

Creamino Lineolated Parrot.

Creamino Peachfaced Lovebird.

It can be seen that it is preferable to use a pure Parblue hen which may be nearly impossible to obtain due to the common practice of mating Parblue to Blue in most species. To obtain Creamino cocks, the ParblueBlue/Lutino cock young can be mated to Albino hens, thus avoiding any inbreeding. The outcome is as follows:

**ParblueBlue/Lutino cock x Albino hen**
= Blue/Lutino cocks and Blue hens
+ ParblueBlue/Lutino cocks and ParblueBlue hens
+ Albino cocks and hens
+ CreaminoBlue cocks and hens

or

**ParblueBlue/Lutino cock x CreaminoBlue hen**
= Blue/Lutino cocks and Blue hens
+ ParblueBlue/Lutino cocks and ParblueBlue hens
+ Parblue/Lutino cocks and Parblue hens
+ Albino cocks and hens
+ CreaminoBlue cocks and hens
+ Creamino cocks and hens

Creamino Cockatiel – known incorrectly as 'Pastelface' Lutino.

This latter mating will produce Creamino of two shades as the CreaminoBlue is normally less yellow than the pure Creamino (in the same way that the ParblueBlue is less green than the pure Parblue). The preferred shade will depend on the breeder's preference and the species involved.

## Cinnamon Blue – Ivory

This combination is probably the most commonly misnamed combination in aviculture. In Australia, the lovebird fraternity set the precedent by establishing the name Ivory for Cinnamon Blue combinations. Unfortunately, a number of authors from Europe have incorrectly labelled these birds Silver and it has been adopted extensively in other places. I suspect that the mistake has been caused by translation difficulties, as I cannot believe that a bird that is light brown and blue could be called Silver, a colour that is light grey. The name Silver must be reserved for combinations that dilute grey family pigments, not those which convert them to brown. In Indian Ringnecked Parrots, the name Sky Blue has also been used. Unfortunately this also causes confusion as this name is used for the Blue mutation in the Budgerigar. Europeans also refer to the Lime Blue Scarlet-chested Parrot by the name Sky Blue. Therefore Sky Blue is not a suitable name either.

*Cinnamon(wing) Blue Budgerigar.*

*Cinnamon Blue Scarlet-chested Parrot – incorrectly known as 'Silver'.*

The appearance of the Cinnamon Blue will vary from species to species like most combinations. In some species with extensive bright green in the Normal bird, pale blue is the predominant colour. In other species with grey-green colouration and other areas lacking in structural colour, the browns and fawns predominate.

*Cinnamon Blue Red-rumped Parrot – incorrectly known as 'Silver'.*

To produce the combination, the breeder needs to combine a sex-linked mutation with a recessive mutation. The process therefore follows a parallel path to that used for the Albino. A Cinnamon cock should be chosen to mate with a Blue hen for the first generation. This will produce Normal/Cinnamon/Blue cocks and Cinnamon/Blue hens.

Using the method described for Albino, we take at least two Cinnamon/Blue hens and mate them to Blue cocks to produce Blue/Cinnamon cocks. These are mated back to their aunts to give the following possible outcomes:

### Blue/Cinnamon cock x Cinnamon/Blue hen
= Normal/Blue/Cinnamon cocks and Normal/Blue hens
+ Blue/Cinnamon cocks and Blue hens
+ Cinnamon/Blue cocks and hens
+ Ivory cocks and hens

One in four of these young is an Ivory and five in eight are useful for further breeding. Of course, once Ivory birds have been bred, they can be mated to either Blue/Cinnamon or Cinnamon/Blue cocks or Cinnamon/Blue hens to produce further Ivory birds at a rate of 50%. The results for these three matings are as follows:

### Blue/Cinnamon cock x Ivory hen
= Blue/Cinnamon cocks and Blue hens
+ Ivory cocks and hens

### Cinnamon/Blue cock x Ivory hen
= Cinnamon/Blue cocks and hens
+ Ivory cocks and hens

### Ivory cock x Cinnamon/Blue hen
= Cinnamon/Blue cocks and hens
+ Ivory cocks and hens

*Cinnamon Aqua Peachfaced Lovebird – this is the colour for which the name Ivory was originally used.*

H KREMER

B NELSON

G ROMAN

E ANTONIN

1. *Cinnamon Blue Crimson Rosella.*
2. *Cinnamon Blue Quaker Parrot.*
3. *Cinnamon Blue (Whiteface) Cockatiel.*
4. *'Cinnamon' Blue Twenty-eight Parrot –
   may eventually prove to be a Lime Blue.*
5. *Cinnamon Blue Indian Ringnecked
   Parrot – incorrectly known as 'Sky Blue'.*
6. *Cinnamon Blue Western Rosella.*

E STEPHENS

N LANSOM

# Grey – Greygreen Blue

The Grey colour is not a primary mutation, but the combination of the Blue gene and the Greygreen gene. The Blue gene removes all yellow from the bird and the Greygreen gene prevents structural colour, thereby nullifying the blue colour. As a result, the natural colour of the bird's grey family pigment is seen for the first time.

To produce Grey, you need to combine a recessive Blue mutation with a dominant Greygreen mutation. The sex of the birds used is unimportant (as long as you have a true pair). A dominant mutation like Greygreen can come in Double or Single Factor, with Double Factor being an advantage to use. However, they are often hard to obtain unless you breed your own as most breeders try to maximise their numbers by always breeding Greygreen to non Greygreen. Therefore I will assume that only Single Factor birds are being used for the following matings:

**Greygreen (SF) x Blue**
= Greygreen (SF)/Blue cocks and hens
+ Green/Blue cocks and hens

Next you mate the following:

**Greygreen (SF)/Blue x Blue**
= Green/Blue cocks and hens
+ Greygreen (SF)/Blue cocks and hens
+ Blue cocks and hens
+ Grey (SF) cocks and hens

Alternatively you can mate:

**Greygreen (SF)/Blue x Greygreen (SF)/Blue**
= Green and Green/Blue cocks and hens
+ Greygreen (SF) and Greygreen (SF)/Blue cocks and hens
+ Greygreen (DF) and Greygreen (DF)/Blue cocks and hens
+ Blue and Grey (SF) and Grey (DF) cocks and hens

As you can see, there is a greater range of genetic make-ups in the offspring, making effective identification of splits impossible. The percentage of Grey birds produced is also slightly lower. Therefore the previous mating is preferable.

The Grey combination is very useful for combining further with mutations that alter the grey family pigments, thereby allowing visualisation of the actual effect of the third mutation, eg Cinnamon, Fallow, Lime, Dilute (Yellow) and Faded. In some cases it is only then that the true nature of these other mutations can be realised.

Grey Scarlet-chested Parrot.

Grey Budgerigar.

Grey Indian Ringnecked Parrot.

# Fawn – Cinnamon Grey

Fawn is the correct name for a White Ground Cinnamon, remembering that White Ground indicates that a bird is lacking yellow pigment. The name was originally established by canary breeders and has since been used in other species whose ground colour is naturally white. In some parrot species such as Budgerigars, the compound name Cinnamonwing Grey is preferred. Unfortunately, a European author has used the name Silver for brown-coloured Indian Ringnecked Parrots. Perhaps translation is again the problem because it is impossible to see how light brown can be called Silver (a term meaning light grey).

The Cinnamon gene replaces grey family pigment with brown pigment. The Grey part of the name refers to two genes – the Blue gene and the Greygreen gene (ie the Fawn is a Cinnamon Blue Greygreen). The Blue gene removes yellow family pigments making the bird White Ground. The Greygreen gene prevents structural colour being produced thereby nullifying the blue colours. The result is a fawn-coloured bird.

A MATHEWS

*Cinnamon Double Dark Factor Turquoise (Mauve) Peachfaced Lovebird – this is the closest colour to Fawn currently possible in this species.*

To produce the Fawn colour, these three genes must be combined. To achieve this, a number of different starting points are possible with little difference in the rate of achievement. You are combining a dominant gene with a recessive gene and a sex-linked gene. Therefore, it is best to use a cock showing the Cinnamon mutation and if possible, a Double Factor Grey gene. Using a Double Factor Grey gene to start with reduces wastage in the first generation only. Possible pairings to start with include:

**Cinnamon cock x Grey (DF) hen**
**Cinnamon Greygreen (DF) cock x Blue hen**
**Ivory cock x Greygreen (DF) hen**

These three matings produce identical young:

= Greygreen (SF)/Cinnamon/Blue cocks
+ Cinnamon Greygreen (SF)/Blue hens

If Double Factor Grey genes are unavailable, the following pairings may be used:

**Cinnamon cock x Grey (SF) hen**
**Cinnamon Greygreen (SF) cock x Blue hen**
**Ivory cock x Greygreen (SF) hen**

These three matings also produce identical young:

= Green/Cinnamon/Blue cocks
+ Cinnamon/Blue hens
+ Greygreen (SF)/Cinnamon/Blue cocks
+ Cinnamon Greygreen (SF)/Blue hens

At least two Cinnamon Greygreen (SF)/Blue hens should be kept and mated to Blue cocks for the following outcomes. (If Blue/Cinnamon cocks or Ivory cocks are available from another source then you can skip this step.)

### Blue cock x Cinnamon Greygreen (SF)/Blue hen
= Green/Blue/Cinnamon cocks and Green/Blue hens
+ Greygreen (SF)/Blue/Cinnamon cocks and Greygreen (SF)/Blue hens
+ Blue/Cinnamon cocks and Blue hens
+ Grey (SF)/Cinnamon cocks and Grey (SF) hens

Either the Blue/Cinnamon cocks or the Grey (SF)/Cinnamon cocks should then be mated back to their aunts for the following outcomes: (Ivory cocks can also be used for this stage.)

### Blue/Cinnamon cock x Cinnamon Greygreen (SF)/Blue hen
= Green/Blue/Cinnamon cocks and Green/Blue hens
+ Cinnamon/Blue cocks and hens
+ Blue/Cinnamon cocks and Blue hens
+ Ivory cocks and hens
+ Greygreen (SF)/Blue/Cinnamon cocks and Greygreen (SF)/Blue hens
+ Cinnamon Greygreen (SF)/Blue cocks and hens
+ Grey (SF)/Cinnamon cocks and Grey (SF) hens
+ Fawn (SF) cocks and hens

### Grey (SF)/Cinnamon cock x Cinnamon Greygreen (SF)/Blue hen
= Green/Blue/Cinnamon cocks and Green/Blue hens
+ Cinnamon/Blue cocks and hens
+ Blue/Cinnamon cocks and Blue hens
+ Ivory cocks and hens
+ Greygreen (SF)/Blue/Cinnamon cocks and Greygreen (SF)/Blue hens
+ Cinnamon Greygreen (SF)/Blue cocks and hens
+ Grey (SF)/Cinnamon cocks and Grey (SF) hens
+ Fawn (SF) cocks and hens
+ Greygreen (DF)/Blue/Cinnamon cocks and Greygreen (DF)/Blue hens
+ Cinnamon Greygreen (DF)/Blue cocks and hens
+ Grey (DF)/Cinnamon cocks and Grey hens
+ Fawn (DF) cocks and hens

### Ivory cock x Cinnamon Greygreen (SF)/Blue hen
= Cinnamon/Blue cocks and hens
+ Ivory cocks and hens
+ Cinnamon Greygreen (SF)/Blue cocks and hens
+ Fawn (SF) cocks and hens

Once the Fawns are produced, various other matings are available to increase Fawn young. Some useful matings are as follows:

### Blue/Cinnamon cock x Fawn (SF) hen
= Blue/Cinnamon cocks and Blue hens
+ Ivory cocks and hens
+ Grey (SF)/Cinnamon cocks and Grey (SF) hens
+ Fawn (SF) cocks and hens

*Fawn Scarlet-chested Parrot.*

**Grey (SF)/Cinnamon cock x Fawn (SF) hen**
= Blue/Cinnamon cocks and hens
+ Ivory cocks and hens
+ Grey (SF)/Cinnamon cocks and Grey (SF) hens
+ Fawn (SF) cocks and hens
+ Grey (DF)/Cinnamon cocks and Grey (DF) hens
+ Fawn (DF) cocks and hens

**Ivory cock x Fawn (SF) hen**
= Ivory cocks and hens
+ Fawn (SF) cocks and hens

**Cinnamon/Blue cock x Fawn (SF) hen**
= Cinnamon/Blue cocks and hens
+ Ivory cocks and hens
+ Cinnamon Greygreen (SF)/Blue cocks and hens
+ Fawn (SF) cocks and hens

*Fawn (Cinnamonwing Grey) Budgerigar.*

**Cinnamon Greygreen (SF)/Blue cock x Fawn (SF) hen**
= Cinnamon/Blue cocks and hens
+ Ivory cocks and hens
+ Cinnamon Greygreen (SF)/Blue cocks and hens
+ Fawn (SF) cocks and hens
+ Cinnamon Greygreen (DF)/Blue cocks and hens
+ Fawn (DF) cocks and hens

**Fawn (SF) cock x Cinnamon/Blue hen**
= Cinnamon/Blue cocks and hens
+ Ivory cocks and hens
+ Cinnamon Greygreen (SF)/Blue cocks and hens
+ Fawn (SF) cocks and hens

**Fawn (SF) cock x Cinnamon Greygreen (SF)/Blue hen**
= Cinnamon/Blue cocks and hens
+ Ivory cocks and hens
+ Cinnamon Greygreen (SF)/Blue cocks and hens
+ Fawn (SF) cocks and hens
+ Cinnamon Greygreen (DF)/Blue cocks and hens
+ Fawn (DF) cocks and hens

**Fawn (SF) cock x Ivory hen**
= Ivory cocks and hens
+ Fawn (SF) cocks and hens

**Fawn (SF) cock x Fawn (SF) hen**
= Ivory cocks and hens
+ Fawn (SF) cocks and hens
+ Fawn (DF) cocks and hens

**Fawn (DF) x Fawn (SF)**
= Fawn (SF) cocks and hens
+ Fawn (DF) cocks and hens

**Fawn (DF) x Fawn (DF)**
= 100% Fawn (DF) cocks and hens !!

*Fawn Indian Ringnecked Parrot – incorrectly known as 'Silver'.*

# White – Yellow Blue

Historically, breeders have known the lightest forms of Dilute as 'Yellow' and its combination with Blue as 'White'. Strictly speaking, the colours produced by the Dilute gene are never pure yellow or white. It is the Black-eyed Clear gene that produces the true yellow and white colours. Having said that, the inheritance of the Dilute gene and the Black-eyed Clear gene are identical and therefore the following mating results apply equally to both.

Because White is the combination of two recessive genes it will take longer to achieve than the Albino combination. However, the sex of the birds used in each pairing is irrelevant.

Mating a Blue to a Yellow will give all Normal/Blue/Yellow young. As these need to be mated together it is best to start the first mating with two pairs and for the second mating cross birds from each pair. This mating of two double split birds is known as a **dihybrid cross**. It produces the following outcomes:

**Normal/Blue/Yellow x Normal/Blue/Yellow**
= Normal, Normal/Blue and Normal/Yellow
+ Normal/Blue/Yellow
+ Blue and Blue/Yellow
+ Yellow and Yellow/Blue
+ White

Normal young may have four different genetic make-ups. These should not be considered for further breeding as too many test matings must be performed to determine their value. Over 50% of young will be Normal, so the waste will be high. The odds of producing White offspring are only 1:16. To rely on this mating alone could take a while to produce a significant number of White young.

It is therefore important to test mate the Blue and Yellow offspring to find which are split for the other mutation and then use these Blue/Yellow and Yellow/Blue to increase the likelihood of producing a White. The process of test mating will also produce more splits suitable for further breeding. If a Blue from the above mating is mated to a Yellow, with any Yellow young being produced, we then know that the Blue is split Yellow and that the Yellow young are split Blue. Conversely, if the Yellow young from the above mating are mated to Blue, and if new Blue young are produced, we know that the Yellow is split Blue and that the Blue young are split Yellow. Therefore by this stage, good numbers of Blue/Yellow and Yellow/Blue should be available to mate together using the least inbred pairings. The fourth generation matings should be comprised of these birds with the expected results as follows:

**Blue/Yellow x Yellow/Blue**
= Normal/Blue/Yellow
+ Blue/Yellow
+ Yellow/Blue
+ White

From this pairing, 25% should be White. This has the added benefit that all the young produced will have a known genetic make-up, making selection for future breeding easier. Of course, once Whites are produced, they can be mated back to either Blue/Yellow or Yellow/Blue resulting in 50% White young. However, keep in mind any possibility of inbreeding.

**Blue/Yellow x White**
= Blue/Yellow + White

**Yellow/Blue x White**
= Yellow/Blue + White

## Silver – Dilute Blue, Dilute Grey or Faded Grey

Silver should be correctly used for combinations where the grey family pigments are diluted to silver and become visible to the eye. To achieve this, the yellow family pigments must be removed with a Blue gene and if possible, the structural colour removed using a Grey gene so that the raw grey pigment can be seen. Finally we use a gene that 'dilutes' the grey family pigments to a lighter shade.

Two common genes perform this function – the Faded gene and the Dilute (Yellow) gene. Faded combinations produce dark Silver and Dilute combinations produce light Silver. Deciding which is the more desirable combination depends on personal preference and varies with each species. I would remind the reader that the Dilute gene varies between species and in some species the combination with the Blue gene is almost White. In others, however, a much deeper Silver is produced. Many breeders prefer to call the lighter forms 'White', although it is better to refer to all as Silver.

I am grouping these two distinct combinations together because their appearance is similar and their inheritance patterns are the same. However, it is vitally important that Faded and Dilute not be indiscriminately mated together as the outcome is not desirable and will cause the breeder much future confusion and problems. Fortunately, the only time a breeder might be tempted to combine Faded and Dilute together is in species without a Lutino gene – to try and produce a more pure yellow bird. Apart from these instances, the combination is not recommended.

In all the breeding results I am about to discuss, I will use the Dilute gene. However, if the breeder wishes to use Faded to achieve a dark Silver, then this gene can be substituted into the matings tables following to replace the Dilute gene.

The Silver combination involves two recessive genes (the Blue gene and the Dilute gene) and where possible a dominant gene (the Grey gene). Sometimes the Blue gene has been unavailable and the Parblue gene is used. In these cases the name Parblue can be substituted for Blue in the following matings without altering the outcomes. In some species the Dilute Parblue has been called Silver and the Dilute Blue has been called White.

The sex of the birds used in the following matings is irrelevant as no sex-linked mutations are involved. You start by mating a Blue with a Dilute which produces Normal/Blue/Dilute cocks and hens. These must be mated together to produce the following:

*Left: Greywing Blue Budgerigar.*
*Right: Dilute Blue Budgerigar.*
*Below: Clearwing Blue Budgerigar.*

### Normal/Blue/Dilute x Normal/Blue/Dilute
= Normal
+ Normal/Blue
+ Normal/Dilute
+ Normal/Blue/Dilute
+ Dilute and Dilute/Blue
+ Blue and Blue/Dilute
+ Silver

Only 1:16 young are Silver, which is insufficient to be satisfactory. The majority of young are Normals, of varied genetic make-up and are useless for further matings unless extensively test mated. Therefore, the Dilute and Blue young are best selected and test mated to find those suitable for the next stage.

Mate Dilute young from the above mating to Blues. If any Blue young are produced, then the Dilute parent must be Dilute/Blue and the Blue young will be Blue/Dilute. Conversely, the Blue young from the second generation above should be mated to Dilutes. If Dilute young are produced, these will be Dilute/Blue and the Blue parent must be Blue/Dilute. From both of these matings the Normal/Blue/Dilute young produced should be discarded.

Once sufficient Blue/Dilute and Dilute/Blue are identified, they should be mated together for the following outcomes:

*'Silver' Crimson Rosella – is a light Silver form produced by the combination of 'Yellow' and Blue.*

### Blue/Dilute x Dilute/Blue
= Normal/Blue/Dilute
+ Blue/Dilute
+ Dilute/Blue
+ Silver

Silver is now being produced at the rate of 1:4 and all young produced are of known genetic make-up. With significant numbers of Silver now being produced, they can be mated to either Blue/Dilute or Dilute/Blue to produce even greater numbers.

### Silver x Dilute/Blue
= Dilute/Blue
+ Silver

### Silver x Blue/Dilute
= Blue/Dilute
+ Silver

At this point, the Grey gene should be used, if available, to produce an even more attractive Silver. The Grey combination (Greygreen Blue) should be chosen if possible, to mate with the Silvers above. Alternatively the Grey combination could have been used from the start instead of Blue in the above matings.

*Dilute Blue Crimson Rosella – is a dark Silver form.*

1. *Blue Suffused Indian Ringnecked Parrot.*
2. *The European 'Isabel' Blue Western Rosella appears to be a Silver colour.*
3. *Aqua Edged Dilute Peachfaced Lovebird – this colour was one of the first to be called Silver.*
4. *Faded Blue Princess Parrot – could be reasonably called Silver.*
5. *American 'White' Pacific Parrotlet.*

If the Silver has already been produced, the following mating can be used:

### Grey (SF) x Silver
= Blue/Dilute
+ Grey (SF)/Dilute

The Grey (SF)/Dilute produced are then used for matings further down the series. However, if you are starting from the top, using Grey instead of Blue for the first mating will produce the following:

Note: As we are now using the Greygreen gene, I will revert to using the term Green instead of using the term Normal. (See pages 29.)

### Grey (SF) x Dilute
= Green/Blue/Dilute
+ Greygreen (SF)/Blue/Dilute

### Greygreen (SF)/Blue/Dilute x Green/Blue/Dilute
= Green, Green/Blue, Green/Dilute and Green/Blue/Dilute
+ Greygreen (SF), Greygreen (SF)/Blue and Greygreen (SF)/Dilute
+ Greygreen (SF)/Blue/Dilute
+ Dilute and Dilute/Blue
+ Dilute Greygreen (SF) and Dilute Greygreen (SF)/Blue
+ Blue and Blue/Dilute
+ Grey (SF) and Grey (SF)/Dilute
+ Silver and Silver Grey (SF)

### Greygreen (SF)/Blue/Dilute x Greygreen (SF)/Blue/Dilute
= Green, Green/Blue, Green/Dilute and Green/Blue/Dilute
+ Greygreen (SF), Greygreen (SF)/Blue and Greygreen (SF)/Dilute
+ Greygreen (SF)/Blue/Dilute
+ Greygreen (DF), Greygreen (DF)/Blue and Greygreen (DF)/Dilute
+ Greygreen (DF)/Blue/Dilute
+ Dilute and Dilute/Blue
+ Dilute Greygreen (SF) and Dilute Greygreen (SF)/Blue
+ Dilute Greygreen (DF) and Dilute Greygreen (DF)/Blue
+ Blue and Blue/Dilute
+ Grey (SF) and Grey (SF)/Dilute
+ Grey (DF) and Grey (DF)/Dilute
+ Silver and Silver Grey (SF) and Silver Grey (DF)

Once again, test matings are needed to determine which are the Blue/Dilute, Dilute/Blue, Grey/Dilute and Dilute Greygreen/Blue from the previous two pairs. Once this is achieved, they can then be combined for the following matings:

### Grey (SF)/Dilute x Dilute/Blue
= Green/Blue/Dilute and Greygreen (SF)/Blue/Dilute
+ Dilute/Blue and Dilute Greygreen (SF)/Blue
+ Blue/Dilute and Grey (SF)/Dilute
+ Silver and Silver Grey (SF)

### Grey (SF)/Dilute x Dilute Greygreen (SF)/Blue
= Green/Blue/Dilute and Greygreen (SF)/Blue/Dilute
+ Greygreen (DF)/Blue/Dilute and Dilute Greygreen (DF)/Blue
+ Dilute/Blue and Dilute Greygreen (SF)/Blue
+ Blue/Dilute, Grey (SF)/Dilute and Grey (DF)/Dilute
+ Silver, Silver Grey (SF) and Silver Grey (DF)

### Dilute Greygreen (SF)/Blue x Blue/Dilute
= Green/Blue/Dilute and Greygreen (SF)/Blue/Dilute
+ Dilute/Blue and Dilute Greygreen (SF)/Blue
+ Blue/Dilute and Grey (SF)/Dilute
+ Silver and Silver Grey (SF)

Above: The Double Dark Factor Turquoise (Mauve) Edged Dilute Peachfaced Lovebird is the closest to a Silver colour that can be produced in this species.
Left: Dilute Grey Budgerigar.
Far left: Greywing Grey Budgerigar is a classic Silver colour.

**Grey (SF)/Dilute x Silver**
= Blue/Dilute and Grey (SF)/Dilute
+ Silver and Silver Grey (SF)

**Dilute Greygreen (SF)/Blue x Silver**
= Dilute/Blue and Dilute Greygreen (SF)/Blue
+ Silver and Silver Grey (SF)

**Silver Grey (SF) x Silver**
= Silver and Silver Grey (SF)

**Silver Grey (SF) x Blue/Dilute**
= Blue/Dilute and Grey (SF)/Dilute
+ Silver and Silver Grey (SF)

**Silver Grey (SF) x Dilute/Blue**
= Dilute/Blue and Dilute Greygreen (SF)/Blue
+ Silver and Silver Grey (SF)

**Silver Grey (SF) x Silver Grey (SF)**
= Silver and Silver Grey (SF) and Silver Grey (DF)

G ROMAN

*Dilute Blue Cockatiel – the true Silver colour is known by breeders as 'Whiteface Pastel Silver'.*

## Cream – Silver Cinnamon – Dilute Cinnamon Greygreen Blue

Cream is an established name in other species of birds, when referring to the Silver form of Cinnamon, or more precisely the Silver form of Fawn. Unfortunately in Europe, the name Cream has been recently applied to the Cinnamon Lime Parblue combination in the Scarlet-chested Parrot. Yet again we are faced with a name being randomly assigned and causing even more confusion. It could also be easily confused with the name Creamino which is applied to the Parblue Lutino combination. At the risk of creating further confusion, I am introducing parrot breeders to the correct use of the name Cream (adopted from other species), to try and prevent its being used for the wrong colour combinations.

The Dilute gene (within the Silver combination) acts to reduce the brown pigments of the Fawn to a lighter shade of cream. In some species which already have light pigments, the Fawn is very light and the Cream combination will result in an almost white bird. However, in species with rich colours (eg Indian Ringnecked Parrots and Cockatiels) the combination could be very attractive.

I use the phrase 'could be', because the four genes involved do not occur together in many species at present. The four genes are Cinnamon, Blue, Greygreen and Dilute (Yellow). They do occur in Cockatiels – the Dilute gene being called Silver, the Blue gene being called Whiteface and the Greygreen gene being the natural state of the Cockatiel.

In the Indian Ringnecked Parrot the combination is possible, however the necessary Dilute gene (which is known as Yellow Suffused), has not been imported into Australia. It would also be possible with the Budgerigar, but few breeders of this species are interested in such colour combinations.

Other species lack the Grey gene, but can still combine the other three. They include Peachfaced Lovebirds (use Parblue instead of Blue) and Red-rumped Parrots (Blue, Cinnamon and Faded).

For a four-way combination, you should already have two-way and three-way combinations, so you should start with these. We are combining a sex-linked mutation with two recessive genes and a dominant gene so the sex of the birds chosen is important. Start with an Ivory (Cinnamon Blue) cock or a Fawn cock and mate it to either a Silver hen or a Silver Grey hen. Outcomes are as follows:

**Ivory cock x Silver hen**
= Blue/Cinnamon/Dilute cocks
+ Ivory/Dilute hens

**Ivory cock x Silver Grey (SF) hen**
= Blue/Cinnamon/Dilute and Grey (SF)/Cinnamon/Dilute cocks
+ Ivory/Dilute and Fawn (SF)/Dilute hens

**Fawn (SF) cock x Silver hen**
= Blue/Cinnamon/Dilute and Grey (SF)/Cinnamon/Dilute cocks
+ Ivory/Dilute and Fawn (SF)/Dilute hens

**Fawn (SF) cock x Silver Grey (SF) hen**
= Blue/Cinnamon/Dilute and Grey (SF)/Cinnamon/Dilute cocks
+ Grey (DF)/Cinnamon/Dilute cocks
+ Ivory/Dilute and Fawn (SF)/Dilute hens
+ Fawn (DF)/Dilute hens

The Ivory/Dilute and Fawn/Dilute hens are the desired offspring. Select these and mate them to Silver and Silver Grey cocks.

**Silver cock x Ivory/Dilute hen**
= Blue/Cinnamon/Dilute and Silver/Cinnamon cocks
+ Blue/Dilute and Silver hens

**Silver cock x Fawn (SF)/Dilute hen**
= Blue/Cinnamon/Dilute and Silver/Cinnamon cocks
+ Grey (SF)/Cinnamon/Dilute and Silver Grey (SF)/Cinnamon cocks
+ Blue/Dilute and Silver hens
+ Grey (SF)/Dilute and Silver Grey (SF) hens

**Silver Grey (SF) cock x Ivory/Dilute hen**
= Blue/Cinnamon/Dilute and Silver/Cinnamon cocks
+ Grey (SF)/Cinnamon/Dilute and Silver Grey (SF)/Cinnamon cocks
+ Blue/Dilute and Silver hens
+ Grey (SF)/Dilute and Silver Grey (SF) hens

**Silver Grey (SF) cock x Fawn (SF)/Dilute hen**
= Blue/Cinnamon/Dilute and Silver/Cinnamon cocks
+ Grey (SF)/Cinnamon/Dilute and Silver Grey (SF)/Cinnamon cocks
+ Grey (DF)/Cinnamon/Dilute and Silver Grey (DF)/Cinnamon cocks
+ Blue/Dilute and Silver hens
+ Grey (SF)/Dilute and Silver Grey (SF) hens
+ Grey (DF)/Dilute and Silver Grey (DF) hens

T DULIERE

*Cinnamon Pastel Eastern Rosella.*
*This colour is one step towards*
*Cream. It needs to be combined*
*with Blue and Greygreen to*
*complete the process.*

The Silver/Cinnamon and the Silver Grey/Cinnamon cocks are then mated back to the Ivory/Dilute and Fawn/Dilute hens giving the following outcomes:

**Silver/Cinnamon cock x Ivory/Dilute hen**
= Blue/Cinnamon/Dilute cocks and Blue/Dilute hens
+ Silver/Cinnamon cocks and Silver hens
+ Ivory/Dilute cocks and hens
+ Cream cocks and hens

**Silver/Cinnamon cock x Fawn (SF)/Dilute hen**
= Blue/Cinnamon/Dilute cocks and Blue/Dilute hens
+ Grey (SF)/Cinnamon/Dilute cocks and Grey (SF)/Dilute hens
+ Silver/Cinnamon cocks and Silver hens
+ Silver Grey (SF)/Cinnamon cocks and Silver Grey (SF) hens
+ Ivory/Dilute cocks and hens
+ Fawn (SF)/Dilute cocks and hens
+ Cream cocks and hens
+ Cream Grey (SF) cocks and hens

**Silver Grey (SF)/Cinnamon cock x Ivory/Dilute hen**
= Blue/Cinnamon/Dilute cocks and Blue/Dilute hens
+ Grey (SF)/Cinnamon/Dilute cocks and Grey (SF)/Dilute hens
+ Silver/Cinnamon cocks and Silver hens
+ Silver Grey (SF)/Cinnamon cocks and Silver Grey (SF) hens
+ Ivory/Dilute cocks and hens
+ Fawn (SF)/Dilute cocks and hens
+ Cream cocks and hens
+ Cream Grey (SF) cocks and hens

**Silver Grey (SF)/Cinnamon cock x Fawn (SF)/Dilute hen**
= Blue/Cinnamon/Dilute cocks and Blue/Dilute hens
+ Grey (SF)/Cinnamon/Dilute cocks and Grey (SF)/Dilute hens
+ Grey (DF)/Cinnamon/Dilute cocks and Grey (DF)/Dilute hens
+ Silver/Cinnamon cocks and Silver hens
+ Silver Grey (SF)/Cinnamon cocks and Silver Grey (SF) hens
+ Silver Grey (DF)/Cinnamon cocks and Silver Grey (DF) hens
+ Ivory/Dilute cocks and hens
+ Fawn (SF)/Dilute cocks and hens
+ Fawn (DF)/Dilute cocks and hens
+ Cream cocks and hens
+ Cream Grey (SF) cocks and hens
+ Cream Grey (DF) cocks and hens

**Silver Grey (DF)/Cinnamon cock x Ivory/Dilute hen**
= Grey (SF)/Cinnamon/Dilute cocks and Grey (SF)/Dilute hens
+ Silver Grey (SF)/Cinnamon cocks and Silver Grey (SF) hens
+ Fawn (SF)/Dilute cocks and hens
+ Cream Grey (SF) cocks and hens

**Silver Grey (DF)/Cinnamon cock x Fawn (SF)/Dilute hen**
= Grey (SF)/Cinnamon/Dilute cocks and Grey (SF)/Dilute hens
+ Grey (DF)/Cinnamon/Dilute cocks and Grey (DF)/Dilute hens
+ Silver Grey (SF)/Cinnamon cocks and Silver Grey (SF) hens
+ Silver Grey (DF)/Cinnamon cocks and Silver Grey (DF) hens

+ Fawn (SF)/Dilute cocks and hens
+ Fawn (DF)/Dilute cocks and hens
+ Cream Grey (SF) cocks and hens
+ Cream Grey (DF) cocks and hens

Cream and Cream Grey can be mated to either Silver/Cinnamon cocks, Ivory/Dilute cocks, Silver Grey/Cinnamon cocks, Fawn/Dilute cocks, Ivory/Dilute hens or Fawn/Dilute hens. All these matings give 50% Cream or Cream Grey but there are too many different matings to list all here.

## Mustard – Cinnamon Olive or Cinnamon Greygreen

D VAN DEN ABEELE

*Cinnamon Olive Peachfaced Lovebird – commonly known as Mustard.*

The name Mustard was coined by the lovebird fraternity for the combination of the Olive gene and the Cinnamon gene. As the effects of the Olive gene and the Greygreen gene are very similar, the name could possibly be used for the Cinnamon Greygreen combination as well. The action of both the Olive and Greygreen genes is to eliminate or reduce the green structural colour from the bird, allowing the yellow pigment to become more visible and blend with the cinnamon brown pigments to produce a rich yellow-brown colour.

To produce the Cinnamon Olive combination, a sex-linked mutation must be combined with a co-dominant mutation. Therefore it is best to breed a Cinnamon cock with an Olive hen to give the following result:

**Cinnamon cock x Olive hen**
= Dark Green/Cinnamon cocks
+ Cinnamon Dark Green hens

From here many possible matings are available to produce Mustards, but keep in mind that inbreeding should be avoided.

**Dark Green/Cinnamon cock x Olive hen**
= Dark Green cocks and hens
+ Dark Green/Cinnamon cocks and Cinnamon Dark Green hens
+ Olive cocks and hens
+ Olive/Cinnamon cocks and Mustard hens

**Dark Green/Cinnamon cock x Cinnamon hen**
= Green/Cinnamon cocks and Green hens
+ Cinnamon cocks and hens
+ Dark Green/Cinnamon cocks and Dark Green hens
+ Cinnamon Dark Green cocks and hens

**Dark Green/Cinnamon cock x Cinnamon Dark Green hen**
= Green/Cinnamon cocks and Green hens
+ Cinnamon cocks and hens
+ Dark Green/Cinnamon cocks and Dark Green hens
+ Cinnamon Dark Green cocks and hens
+ Olive/Cinnamon cocks and Olive hens
+ Mustard cocks and hens

### Dark Green/Cinnamon cock x Mustard hen
= Dark Green/Cinnamon cocks and Dark Green hens
+ Cinnamon Dark Green cocks and hens
+ Olive/Cinnamon cocks and Olive hens
+ Mustard cocks and hens

### Cinnamon Dark Green cock x Olive hen
= Dark Green/Cinnamon and Olive/Cinnamon cocks
+ Cinnamon Dark Green and Mustard hens

### Cinnamon Dark Green cock x Cinnamon Dark Green hen
= Cinnamon cocks and hens
+ Cinnamon Dark Green cocks and hens
+ Mustard cocks and hens

### Cinnamon Dark Green cock x Mustard hen
= Cinnamon Dark Green cocks and hens
+ Mustard cocks and hens

### Olive/Cinnamon cock x Cinnamon Dark Green hen
= Dark Green/Cinnamon cocks and Dark Green hens
+ Cinnamon Dark Green cocks and hens
+ Olive/Cinnamon cocks and Olive hens
+ Mustard cocks and hens

### Mustard cock x Cinnamon Dark Green hen
= Cinnamon Dark Green cocks and hens
+ Mustard cocks and hens

The Greygreen gene based Mustard is even easier to produce than the Olive Mustard is. It is the combination of a sex-linked mutation and a dominant mutation. It is therefore best to start with a Cinnamon cock bred with a Greygreen hen to give the following outcome:

### Cinnamon cock x Greygreen (SF) hen
= Green/Cinnamon and Greygreen (SF)/Cinnamon cocks
+ Cinnamon and Mustard (Greygreen (SF) hens

From here a number of different matings are available to produce further Mustard young.

### Green/Cinnamon cock x Mustard (Greygreen (SF)) hen
= Green/Cinnamon cocks and Green hens
+ Greygreen (SF)/Cinnamon cocks and Greygreen (SF) hens
+ Cinnamon cocks and hens
+ Mustard (Greygreen (SF)) cocks and hens

### Cinnamon cock x Mustard (Greygreen (SF)) hen
= Cinnamon cocks and hens
+ Mustard (Greygreen (SF)) cocks and hens

### Greygreen (SF)/Cinnamon cock x Cinnamon hen
= Green/Cinnamon cocks and Green hens
+ Greygreen (SF)/Cinnamon cocks and Greygreen (SF) hens
+ Cinnamon cocks and hens
+ Mustard (Greygreen (SF)) cocks and hens

Cinnamon Greygreen Indian Ringnecked Parrot – incorrectly known as 'Gold Olive'.

Cinnamon(wing) Greygreen Budgerigar.

**Mustard (Greygreen (SF)) cock x Cinnamon hen**
= Cinnamon cocks and hens
+ Mustard (Greygreen (SF)) cocks and hens

**Greygreen (SF)/Cinnamon cock x Mustard (Greygreen (SF)) hen**
= Green/Cinnamon cocks and Green hens
+ Greygreen (SF)/Cinnamon cocks and Greygreen (SF) hens
+ Greygreen (DF)/Cinnamon cocks and Greygreen (DF) hens
+ Cinnamon cocks and hens
+ Mustard (Greygreen (SF)) cocks and hens
+ Mustard (Greygreen (DF)) cocks and hens

**Mustard (Greygreen (SF)) cock x Mustard (Greygreen (SF)) hen**
= Cinnamon cocks and hens
+ Mustard (Greygreen (SF)) cocks and hens
+ Mustard (Greygreen (DF)) cocks and hens

## Golden Yellow – Cinnamon Lime

Golden Yellow is a combination name initiated in Europe for the Cinnamon Lime (European Isabel) combination in the Scarlet-chested Parrot. This bird became very popular, possibly due to the lack of either a true Yellow gene or a Lutino gene. Now that the Lutino gene has been established, will the desire for Golden Yellow continue? This combination is also possible in Cockatiels (Cinnamon and Platinum), Red-rumped Parrots (Cinnamon and Platinum or Lime), Budgerigars (Cinnamonwing and Lime [Texas Clearbody]), Peachfaced Lovebirds (Cinnamon and Lime [Australian Cinnamon]) and Indian Ringnecked Parrots (Cinnamon and Lime [Lacewing]).

Unfortunately in Indian Ringnecked

Golden Yellow Scarlet-chested Parrot.

Parrots we also have the complication of the Cinnamon Greygreen combination being called Gold Olive. This combination would be best grouped with the Cinnamon Olive and called Mustard.

The Golden Yellow is not an easy combination to produce because both genes used are sex-linked. This means that both are also linked to one another as well. This linkage reduces the rate at which the two genes combine. However, once combined it reduces the rate at which they separate. This rate is known for Budgerigars as only 3%, a very low rate of recombination. It has not been calculated for other species to date. There is a good chance that it will be this low for most species, but not necessarily so.

To breed the combination, Normal/Cinnamon/Lime cocks are required. These can be bred from pairing the two mutations together either way. The Cinnamon or Lime hens produced from this first mating are of no further use. When these Normal/Cinnamon/Lime cocks are mated to any hen, a small percentage of young will be Golden Yellow hens. Some mating expectations are as follows:

**1. Normal/Cinnamon/Lime cock x Normal hen**
= 48.5% Normal/Cinnamon and Normal/Lime cocks
+ 1.5% Normal and Normal/Cinnamon-Lime cocks
+ 48.5% Cinnamon and Lime hens
+ 1.5% Normal and Golden Yellow hens

**2. Normal/Cinnamon/Lime cock x Cinnamon hen**
= 48.5% Normal/Cinnamon/Lime and Cinnamon cocks
+ 1.5% Normal/Cinnamon and Cinnamon/Lime cocks
+ 48.5% Cinnamon and Lime hens
+ 1.5% Normal and Golden Yellow hens

**3. Normal/Cinnamon/Lime cock x Lime hen**
= 48.5% Normal/Cinnamon/Lime and Lime cocks
+ 1.5%  Normal/Lime and Lime/Cinnamon cocks
+ 48.5% Cinnamon and Lime hens
+ 1.5% Normal and Golden Yellow hens

From these mating results you can see that only a very small number of Golden Yellows are produced – 0.75% of all young or 1.5% of hens produced. Remember that these percentages refer to Budgerigar pairings and are correct for the combination of Cinnamon and Texas Clearbody in that species. In other species the percentages are unlikely to be lower, but are possibly higher in some species. To increase the chances of breeding a Golden Yellow, use matings 2 and 3 above and then test mate the Cinnamon cocks from mating 2 against Lime hens and the Lime cocks from mating 3 against Cinnamon hens. If you are very lucky and the cock carries the second gene, the recombination has already occurred and you have a valuable bird. However the percentage for this to occur is the same as for the hens.

If the Cinnamon cocks (from mating 2) are pure Cinnamon, then the outcome from mating to a Lime hen will be Normal/Cinnamon/Lime cocks and Cinnamon hens. If, however, it is a Cinnamon/Lime, the outcome will be as follows:

**Cinnamon/Lime cock x Lime hen**
= Normal/Cinnamon/Lime and Lime/Cinnamon cocks
+ Cinnamon and Golden Yellow hens

This is quite a different outcome from mating pure Cinnamon cocks or even double split cocks to Lime hens – 25% Golden Yellow hens are produced as well as useful Lime/Cinnamon cocks.

Conversely, if the Lime cocks (from mating 3) are pure Lime, then the outcome from mating to a Cinnamon hen will be Normal/Cinnamon/Lime cocks and Lime hens. Whereas if they are Lime/Cinnamon cocks, the outcome will be as follows:

**Lime/Cinnamon cock x Cinnamon hen**
= Normal/Cinnamon/Lime and Cinnamon/Lime cocks
+ Lime and Golden Yellow hens

There are two important factors to consider: the importance of identifying the Lime/Cinnamon and Cinnamon/Lime cocks and the mating of cocks of one colour to hens of the other colour. By doing this all young are of known genetic make-up, with half the young useful for further matings. Once Golden Yellow hens are available, they should be mated to either Lime/Cinnamon or Cinnamon/Lime cocks for the following outcomes:

**Cinnamon/Lime cock x Golden Yellow hen**
= Cinnamon/Lime cocks and Cinnamon hens
+ Golden Yellow cocks and hens

**Lime/Cinnamon cock x Golden Yellow hen**
= Lime/Cinnamon cocks and Lime hens
+ Golden Yellow cocks and hens

Another interesting point is that a double split cock bred from a Normal cock and a Golden Yellow hen is different from the double split cocks bred above. These cocks will be Normal/Cinnamon-Lime, with the two genes still combined. If this cock is mated to a Normal hen, the outcome is as follows:

**Normal/Cinnamon-Lime cock x Normal hen**
= 48.5% Normal and Normal/Cinnamon-Lime cocks
+ 1.5% Normal/Cinnamon and Normal/Lime cocks
+ 48.5% Normal and Golden Yellow hens
+ 1.5% Cinnamon and Lime hens

Compare the percentage outcomes from this mating to those from mating 1.

## Blue Golden Yellow – Lime Ivory?

In Europe, the Golden Yellow Scarlet-chested Parrot has been combined with the 'White-fronted' Blue mutation to produce a new combination which has been called Ivory. This name has not been used correctly, although the Ivory combination is part of this three gene combination. The combination is in fact the Lime version of Ivory. Maybe it can be called Lime Ivory, hence the question mark after the heading name.

The Blue gene removes all traces of yellow family pigment from the Golden Yellow combination, leaving a white bird with light cream pigments throughout the body and wings.

*Lime Ivory Scarlet-chested Parrot – generally referred to as Ivory, but not the same colour as that originally defined as Ivory.*

TOBY MARTIN

To produce this combination, it is best to mate a Golden Yellow cock to a Blue hen to produce the following outcome:

**Golden Yellow cock x Blue hen**
= Normal/Blue/Cinnamon-Lime cocks
+ Golden Yellow/Blue hens

The Golden Yellow/Blue hens should be mated to Blue cocks for the following outcome:

**Blue cock x Golden Yellow/Blue hen**
= Normal/Blue/Cinnamon-Lime and Blue/Cinnamon-Lime cocks
+ Normal/Blue and Blue hens

The Blue/Cinnamon-Lime cocks are chosen to be mated back to Golden Yellow/Blue hens.

**Blue/Cinnamon-Lime cock x Golden Yellow/Blue hen**
**97% of young will comprise the following group:**
= Normal/Blue/Cinnamon-Lime and Blue/Cinnamon-Lime cocks
+ Golden Yellow/Blue and Lime Ivory cocks
+ Normal/Blue and Blue and Golden Yellow/Blue hens
+ Lime Ivory hens
**3% of young will comprise those below (due to recombination):**
+ Lime/Cinnamon/Blue and Cinnamon/Lime/Blue cocks
+ Lime Blue/Cinnamon and Ivory/Lime cocks
+ Cinnamon/Blue and Lime/Blue hens
+ Lime Blue and Ivory hens

The best young to choose for further breeding are the Golden Yellow/Blue cocks and hens mated to Lime Ivory cocks and hens.

**Golden Yellow/Blue cock x Lime Ivory hen**

or

**Lime Ivory cock x Golden Yellow/Blue hen**
= Golden Yellow/Blue cocks and hens
+ Lime Ivory cocks and hens

# Fallow Blue

Fallow is another mutation that combines well with the Blue gene. Because the Fallow gene reduces the bird's grey pigments to light fawns, it combines with Blue to produce soft, light blues often with fawn wings and, of course, the red eyes which are characteristic of Fallow and its combinations. There is no standard name for the Fallow Blue combination.

The combination involves two recessive mutations, so the sex of the birds used is irrelevant. The process is similar to that used to produce either Whites or Silvers, except that Fallow is used instead of the Dilute (Yellow) gene.

*(Australian) Bronze Fallow Blue Budgerigar.*

1. *(Australian) Bronze Fallow Blue Cockatiel –*
   *generally known as 'Whiteface Fallow'.*
2. *Ashen Fallow Blue Cockatiel – known incorrectly*
   *as 'Whiteface Recessive Silver' in Europe and the*
   *USA. This bird also has evidence of Pied in its*
   *genetic make-up.*
3. *Pale Fallow (Type 2) Aqua Peachfaced Lovebird.*
4. *Dun Fallow Blue Pacific Parrotlet.*
5. *(English) Dun Fallow Grey Budgerigar.*

### Fallow x Blue
= Normal/Fallow/Blue

### Normal/Fallow/Blue x Normal/Fallow/Blue
= Normal, Normal/Fallow, Normal/Blue and Normal/Fallow/Blue
+ Fallow and Fallow/Blue
+ Blue and Blue/Fallow
+ Fallow Blue

As was the case with those similar combinations, only 1:16 young are the desired Fallow Blue combination. Therefore it is important to identify Fallow/Blue and Blue/Fallow offspring for further matings. Mate the Fallow progeny to Blue and the Blue progeny to Fallow. Any Blues from the first type mating will be Blue/Fallow and any Fallow from the second type mating will be Fallow/Blue. When sufficient numbers have been identified, mate them together for the following outcomes:

### Blue/Fallow x Fallow/Blue
= Normal/Fallow/Blue
+ Fallow/Blue
+ Blue/Fallow
+ Fallow Blue

Fallow Blue comprises 25% of outcomes from this mating. Then, once sufficient numbers of Fallow Blue are produced, other matings become available as follows:

### Blue/Fallow x Fallow Blue
= Blue/Fallow
+ Fallow Blue

### Fallow/Blue x Fallow Blue
= Fallow/Blue
+ Fallow Blue

### Fallow Blue x Fallow Blue
= 100% Fallow Blue

R CUSICK

*Clearhead Fallow Blue Indian Ringnecked Parrot – has been known by various incorrect names.*

B BRANSTON

*Ashen Fallow Blue Scarlet-chested Parrot.*

## Other Fallow Combinations

*The following are a few beautiful combinations involving Fallow that are not individually covered in this book.*

P TOMAS

*Bronze Fallow Violet Budgerigar.*

G ROMAN

*Olive (Type 2) Fallow Turquoise Parrot.*

K BENTON

*Clearhead Fallow Greygreen Indian Ringnecked Parrot.*

## Cinnamon Lutino – Lacewing

This is an unusual combination because, by definition, the Lutino gene is supposed to remove all grey family pigments. Yet, when it is combined with the Cinnamon gene in Budgerigars, shades of light fawn appear on the wings in the exact position that a wildtype Budgerigar has the black scalloping on its wings. This combination was given the name Lacewing because of its appearance and because breeders initially did not realise what it was.

To combine the Cinnamon and Lutino genes is extremely difficult as the rate of recombination is only 3%. That means that 33 hens must be bred from a Normal/Cinnamon/Lutino cock before a single recombination will occur. Even then it may be the wrong one and result in a pure Normal hen instead of the desired Lacewing hen. There is little wonder that Budgerigar breeders took so long to determine the true nature of the combination.

With the realisation that the Lacewing was a Cinnamon Lutino, breeders of other species have started exploring the possibility that the Lacewing combination could exist in their species as well. Will a parrot without black markings produce a visually different colour? There is a colour in Cockatiels that suggests that it could be a Cinnamon Lutino. It is a very light coloured bird, almost Lutino but with a faint cream suffusion throughout. If the Cinnamon Lutino is visually different, this is what we would expect it to look like. However, I have performed some preliminary studies on this colour that appear to raise more questions than answers. A Cinnamon Lutino cock should throw 100% Cinnamon Lutino hens the same colour as the cock. In various matings using three different cocks, I have produced 80% Lutino and only 20% appearing like the father.

J SCULL

*Lacewing Budgerigar – the Cinnamon Lutino combination.*

1. The 'Lacewing' Elegant Parrot from Europe needs more investigation to determine its true identity.
2. Indian Ringnecked Parrot – the true Cinnamon Lutino (Lacewing) is known incorrectly as one type of 'Yellowhead Cinnamon'.
3. Fawn markings on the mantle of this Eastern Rosella may indicate that it is a Cinnamon Lutino.
4. Lacewing Peachfaced Lovebird – this colour is often mixed amongst pure Lutino birds.
5. Bred from Lutino lines, this Australian Elegant Parrot may prove to be a Lacewing.
6. Lacewing Cockatiel – is this a true Cinnamon Lutino?

B PEARSON

G ROMAN

G ROMAN

R ERHART

G ROMAN

A Cinnamon Lutino cock mated to a Cinnamon hen should produce only Cinnamon cocks. I have also produced Normal Grey Cockatiels from this mating. These results lead to the conclusion that the bird concerned is not a Cinnamon Lutino, although these birds seem to have at least one Cinnamon gene and two Lutino genes present. Maybe there is some sort of gene interaction between these two genes and possibly a third gene (Opaline or an unidentified modifier?). Only further investigation will elicit the truth. (See Part Three, page 271.)

In Indian Ringnecked Parrots, a mutation has been called 'Lacewing', which is, in fact, a Lime mutation. This misnaming is doubly unfortunate as the true Lacewing may also have been produced in the form known as 'Yellowhead Cinnamon'. Added to this, we have the LutinoLime that produces a colour almost identical to the 'Yellowhead Cinnamon'. This confusing situation will occur much more frequently in all parrots as more new mutations and combinations are produced unless we become far more careful in our choice of names. The high monetary value placed on these birds has, at this stage, prevented enough investigation to elicit the truth.

At this point in time, we are unable to be certain if the Lacewing is simply a one-off freak in the Budgerigar only, or whether it will appear in other species as well. It could be interesting to try and produce a Lacewing in the Eastern Rosella. Both the required genes exist and we also have a barring pattern similar to the Budgerigar on the back of the Eastern Rosella.

### Addendum

*There are in fact Eastern Rosellas that fit the description for Cinnamon Lutino. They have not been fully tested to prove that they have the correct genetic make-up, but evidence suggests that they are bona fide. Testing of certain strains of Indian Ringnecked Parrots with the 'Yellowhead Cinnamon' appearance is also indicating that a true Lacewing does exist in this species as well.*

The matings required to achieve this are as follows:

**Lutino cock x Cinnamon hen**

or

**Cinnamon Cock x Lutino hen**
= Normal/Cinnamon/Lutino cocks
+ Lutino hens (first pairing) or Cinnamon hens (second pairing)

**1. Normal/Cinnamon/Lutino cock x Normal hen**
= 48.5% Normal/Cinnamon and Normal/Lutino cocks
+ 1.5% Normal and Normal/Cinnamon-Lutino cocks
+ 48.5% Cinnamon and Lutino hens
+ 1.5% Normal and Lacewing hens

**2. Normal/Cinnamon/Lutino cock x Lutino hen**
= 48.5% Normal/Cinnamon/Lutino and Lutino cocks
+ 1.5% Normal/Lutino and Lutino/Cinnamon cocks
+ 48.5% Cinnamon and Lutino hens
+ 1.5% Normal and Lacewing hens

**3. Normal/Cinnamon/Lutino cock x Cinnamon hen**
= 48.5% Normal/Cinnamon/Lutino and Cinnamon cocks
+ 1.5% Normal/Cinnamon and Cinnamon/Lutino cocks
+ 48.5% Cinnamon and Lutino hens
+ 1.5% Normal and Lacewing hens

As you can see from these results, the level of wastage to produce this combination is very high. If the Lutino/Cinnamon cocks from mating 2 and the Cinnamon/Lutino cocks from mating 3 can be discovered using test matings, then the numbers of combined birds will escalate dramatically. To test these birds, mate the Lutino to Cinnamon and vice versa. The results for split birds are as follows. (Of course, if the birds are not split, only cocks of Normal colour and hens the same colour as the father will be produced.)

**Lutino/Cinnamon cock x Cinnamon hen**
= Normal/Cinnamon/Lutino and Cinnamon/Lutino cocks
+ Lutino and Lacewing hens

**Cinnamon/Lutino cock x Lutino hen**
= Normal/Cinnamon/Lutino and
   Lutino/Cinnamon cocks
+ Cinnamon and Lacewing hens

Once the Cinnamon/Lutino and Lutino/Cinnamon cocks are identified, the process of producing more Lacewings becomes easier using the following matings:

**Cinnamon/Lutino cock x Lacewing hen**
= Cinnamon/Lutino and Lacewing cocks
+ Cinnamon and Lacewing hens

**Lutino/Cinnamon cock x Lacewing hen**
= Lutino/Cinnamon and Lacewing cocks
+ Lutino and Lacewing hens

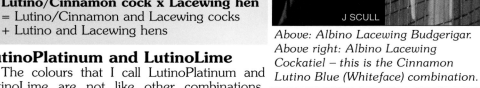

J SCULL

*Above: Albino Lacewing Budgerigar.*
*Above right: Albino Lacewing*
*Cockatiel – this is the Cinnamon*
*Lutino Blue (Whiteface) combination.*

## LutinoPlatinum and LutinoLime

The colours that I call LutinoPlatinum and LutinoLime are not like other combinations. Normally, a bird exhibiting two recessive mutations in combination must have two genes of each mutation. For ordinary sex-linked mutations in cocks this rule still applies, whereas in hens only one gene for each is required because she has only one X chromosome. The section which carries these positions is missing from the shorter Y chromosome. However, in the combination being discussed, cocks have only one gene for each mutation and it is simply not possible for hens to exist in this combination. This is because the three genes, Lutino, Platinum and Lime form one family of genes, and they all occupy the same position on the one chromosome. As these genes lie on the X chromosome, there are two positions for these genes in cocks but the hen has only one position, as the Y chromosome in hens has no position.

When a cock inherits a Lutino gene from only one parent, the bird has one Lutino gene on one X chromosome and the same position on the other X chromosome is occupied by a Normal (Green) gene (from the other parent). Therefore the bird appears as a Normal but is split for Lutino. In hens where no second position occurs, the bird must be a Lutino. In a cock that inherits a Lutino gene from one parent and a Platinum (or Lime) gene from the other, there are no Normal genes, so the bird becomes a blend between Lutino and Platinum (or Lime). Hens, however, cannot inherit a gene from each parent because the Y chromosome must be inherited from their mother and so they appear the same colour as their father. For this reason I use the combined name LutinoPlatinum (and LutinoLime) without a space between the two names, to alert the reader that this is not a standard combination. (For more information refer to page 32.)

G ROMAN

3

M ANDERSON

R ERHART

5

ABK

1. LutinoPlatinum Red-rumped Parrot.
2. An Indian Ringnecked Parrot with this appearance could be either a LutinoLime or a Cinnamon Lutino (true Lacewing). Breeders know it incorrectly as 'Yellowhead Cinnamon', a name that must be eliminated.
3. LutinoPlatinum Cockatiel.
4. LutinoLime Fischer's Lovebird – in this species these colours are recessive, therefore the mating results in this section do not apply.
5. LutinoLime Peachfaced Lovebird.

Matings involving LutinoPlatinum are as follows:

**Lutino cock x Platinum hen**
= LutinoPlatinum cocks and Lutino hens

**Platinum cock x Lutino hen**
= LutinoPlatinum cocks and Platinum hens

**Normal/Lutino cock x Platinum hen**
= Normal/Platinum and LutinoPlatinum cocks
+ Normal and Lutino hens

**Normal/Platinum cock x Lutino hen**
= Normal/Lutino and LutinoPlatinum cocks
+ Normal and Platinum hens

**LutinoPlatinum cock x Normal hen**
= Normal/Lutino and Normal/Platinum cocks
+ Lutino and Platinum hens

**LutinoPlatinum cock x Platinum hen**
= Platinum and LutinoPlatinum cocks
+ Lutino and Platinum hens

**LutinoPlatinum cock x Lutino hen**
= Lutino and LutinoPlatinum cocks
+ Lutino and Platinum hens

LutinoLime occurs in the same manner except the name Lime is substituted for Platinum.

## Lime Blue and Platinum Blue

Once again I will treat the combinations involving either Lime or Platinum together because of the close relationship of the two mutations. These combinations have been bred in the Budgerigar (Blue Texas Clearbody), the Cockatiel (Platinum Whiteface), the Scarlet-chested Parrot (Sky Blue), the Indian Ringnecked Parrot (Blue Lacewing), and the Red-rumped Parrot (Platinum Blue). Once again we see the crazy results of random naming. Species-specific names like Whiteface and Texas Clearbody are fine, but the undisciplined use of the names Sky Blue and Lacewing in two species means that for the five species with this combination we have five different names and much confusion!

The Lime and Platinum genes reduce the amount of grey family pigments present in the plumage and therefore lighten the blue structural colours. The Blue gene removes all yellow family pigments, preventing green structural colours and allowing the blue to show through. In the Cockatiel, which lacks structural colour, we see the true colour of the underlying grey pigments.

To produce the combination, the breeder must combine a sex-linked mutation with a recessive mutation.

P TOMAS

*Lime ('Texas Clearbody')*
*Blue Budgerigar.*

G ROMAN

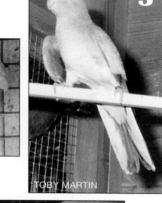

TOBY MARTIN

G ROMAN

G ROMAN

1. AlbinoPlatinum Red-rumped Parrot cock –
   this is a LutinoPlatinum Blue combination.
2. Platinum Blue Red-rumped Parrot hen.
3. Lime Blue Scarlet-chested Parrot – has been
   incorrectly called 'Sky Blue'.
4. Lime Blue Indian Ringnecked Parrots –
   incorrectly known as Blue 'Lacewing'.
5. LutinoPlatinum (Whiteface) Blue Cockatiel.
6. Platinum (Whiteface) Blue Cockatiel.
7. Lime (Pallid) Aqua Peachfaced Lovebird –
   is known by numerous incorrect names.

The process parallels that used for Albino, substituting either Lime or Platinum for Lutino and substituting Lime Blue or Platinum Blue for Albino in the matings on page 114. In addition we have extra possible matings due to the relationships between Lime and Platinum with the Lutino gene. Some of these follow:

**Lime cock x Albino hen**
= LutinoLime/Blue cocks and Lime/Blue hens

**Normal/Lime/Blue cock x Albino hen**
= Normal/Lutino/Blue and Blue/Lutino cocks
+ LutinoLime/Blue and AlbinoLime cocks
+ Normal/Blue and Blue hens
+ Lime/Blue and Lime Blue hens

**LutinoLime/Blue cock x Blue hen**
= Normal/Lutino/Blue and Normal/Lime/Blue cocks
+ Blue/Lutino and Blue/Lime cocks
+ Lutino/Blue and Lime/Blue hens
+ Albino and Lime Blue hens

**LutinoLime/Blue cock x Albino hen**
= Lutino/Blue and LutinoLime/Blue cocks
+ Albino and AlbinoLime cocks
+ Lutino/Blue and Lime/Blue hens
+ Albino and Lime Blue hens

**AlbinoLime Blue cock x Lime Blue hen**
= AlbinoLime and Lime Blue cocks
+ Albino and Lime Blue hens

*Lime (Pallid) Blue Quaker Parrot – Pallid is the European name for Lime mutations.*

The name AlbinoLime refers to the LutinoLime Blue combination.
If you are breeding Platinum, swap the name Platinum for Lime in all instances.

***The following colours are based upon Recessive Lutino and therefore matings from this section do not apply.***

*LutinoLime Blue Masked Lovebird (foreground).*

*Lime Blue Masked Lovebird.*

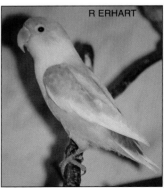

*LutinoLime Blue Fischer's Lovebird.*

## Platinum Grey and Lime Grey

If a Greygreen gene is available, combining it with the Platinum Blue or Lime Blue will show the true shade of grey pigment for the Lime or Platinum gene. These combinations are all probably best known as Platinum Grey because this is the shade of colour produced. At present this colour is possible in Budgerigars and Indian Ringnecked Parrots (Grey Lacewing), however the Cockatiel is also a natural Grey.

### Addendum

*The recent establishment of a Greygreen Red-rumped Parrot means that this combination is possible in that species as well.*

To breed this combination, a sex-linked gene has to be combined with a recessive gene and a dominant gene. This process parallels that used for producing the Fawn combination. Start with a Lime Blue cock mated to a Grey hen to produce the following:

**Lime Blue cock x Grey hen**
= Blue/Lime and Grey/Lime cocks
+ Lime Blue and Lime Grey hens

**Grey/Lime cock x Lime Blue hen**
= Blue/Lime and Grey/Lime cocks
+ Lime Blue and Lime Grey cocks
+ Blue, Grey, Lime Blue and Lime Grey hens

**Lime Blue cock x Lime Grey hen**
= Lime Blue cocks and hens
+ Lime Grey cocks and hens

G ROMAN

D MERVILDE

G ROMAN

*Above: Lime Greygreen Budgerigar – commonly known as Greygreen 'Texas Clearbody'.*
*Right: Lime Grey Indian Ringnecked Parrot – known incorrectly as Grey 'Lacewing'.*

*Lime Greygreen Indian Ringnecked Parrot – known incorrectly as Greygreen 'Lacewing'.*

*TurquoiseBlue Suffused Indian Ringnecked Parrots.*

## Parblue Combinations

The Parblue gene acts upon the yellow family pigments in the bird, reducing their production, but not totally preventing them as the Blue gene does. Parblue is an abbreviation for Partial Blue and that is exactly what it is. As a result, it is a versatile gene that can be combined with mutations from any of the other major groups (with those altering grey family pigment production or structural colour or with pigment distribution genes like Opaline or Pied). A number of combinations have been given special names such as Creamino. However others like 'Rainbow' have not been fully defined and are being used for different combinations in different species. As stated many times already, uniformity of naming is imperative and therefore I have chosen not to use the name 'Rainbow'.

*Above: Ashen Fallow Aqua (Parblue) Scarlet-chested Parrot – known in Australia as 'Isabel' Parblue.*
*Below: Ashen Fallow Seagreen Scarlet-chested Parrot – known in Australia as 'Isabel' Seagreen.*

Because the Parblue gene does not fully remove yellow family pigments, unique subtle shades of yellow-cream and green-blue are produced. Exploring these colours in combination with other genes to remove certain layers of colour can be an exciting exercise. It is interesting to note that in species where the true Blue gene arrived first, Parblues are more highly valued than in species where the Parblue came first, or exists by itself. This appears to be a typical case of breeders preferring what they do not have.

I have discussed separately some of the common Parblue combinations such as Creamino. However, space prevents my discussing every possibility in detail.

To put it simply, every combination that is possible involving the Blue gene, can be recreated using the Parblue gene, resulting in new variations to explore. As the Parblue gene is closely related to the Blue gene, the genetic results can be determined by simply substituting the Parblue name for the Blue name in any of the matings involving Blue.

The interesting point to note about Parblue, is that it forms a genetic family with the Blue gene, and as such a Parblue split for Blue has only one Parblue gene and one Blue gene. This ParblueBlue is generally less green and more blue than a pure Parblue. (There are some special exceptions where the ParblueBlue is more green than the Parblue.) Therefore, even more variations are possible to explore changes in colour with Parblue combinations. It also means that if the Blue gene exists in a species, short cuts to a Parblue combination exist by using the Blue form of the combination to start with.

G ROMAN

G ROMAN

G ROMAN

R CUSICK

J DEEGAN

G ROMAN

J POSTEMA

1. Cinnamon TurquoiseBlue Indian Ringnecked Parrot.
2. TurquoiseGrey (L) and Lime TurquoiseGrey (R) Indian Ringnecked Parrots.
3. Lime TurquoiseGrey Indian Ringnecked Parrot.
4. Parblue Dominant Silver Cockatiel – known incorrectly as 'Pastelface' Dominant Silver.
5. TurquoiseCobalt Indian Ringnecked Parrot.
6. Lime TurquoiseBlue Indian Ringnecked Parrot.
7. Parblue Cinnamon Cockatiel – known incorrectly as 'Pastelface' Cinnamon.

H KREMER

H KREMER

ABK

ABK

1. Cinnamon Parblue (Orange) Crimson Rosella.
2. Dilute Parblue (Orange) Crimson Rosella.
3. Aqua Black-eyed (Australian) Yellow Peachfaced Lovebird
   – this colour was called 'Primrose'.
4. Double Dark Factor Turquoise Dilute Peachfaced Lovebird.
5. Dark Factor Turquoise Dilute Peachfaced Lovebird.
6. Lime Turquoise Dilute Peachfaced Lovebird.
7. Turquoise Black-eyed (Australian) Yellow Peachfaced
   Lovebird.

R SMITH

R SMITH

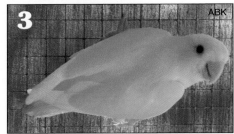

ABK

Creamface Cobalt Budgerigar.

Creamface Violet Budgerigar.

Above: Lime ('Texas Clearbody') Creamface Opaline Budgerigar.

I have highlighted this aspect in both the Creamino and the Parblue Opaline sections. Both of these involve combining the Parblue with a sex-linked mutation. I will briefly outline here some short cut matings for combining Parblue with a recessive mutation. With two recessive genes, the sexes involved are irrelevant and the outcomes are identical for both sexes.

**Parblue x Silver (Dilute Blue)**
= ParblueBlue/Dilute

**ParblueBlue x Silver**
= ParblueBlue/Dilute and Blue/Dilute

**ParblueBlue/Dilute x Silver**
= ParblueBlue/Dilute and Blue/Dilute
+ Dilute ParblueBlue and Silver

**ParblueBlue/Dilute x Dilute ParblueBlue**
= Blue/Dilute and Silver
+ ParblueBlue/Dilute and Dilute ParblueBlue
+ Parblue/Dilute and Dilute Parblue

Dark Factor Parblue (L) and Dark Factor ParblueBlue (R) Budgerigars known to breeders as 'Goldenface Cobalt'.

Similar matings can be used to combine Parblue with any pre-existing Blue combination.

## Cobalt and Mauve – Dark Blue and Olive Blue

When the Olive gene is combined with the Blue gene, we obtain new shades of blue colours known as Cobalt (for the intermediate colour) and Mauve (for the Olive version of Blue). In some species, the Olive gene when combined with the Blue gene results in a very deep blue-grey colour called Mauve (eg Budgerigars). However, in other species the Olive Blue is almost indistinguishable from a Grey bird and has been commonly called Slate (eg Peachfaced Lovebirds). In these latter cases, all structural colour is lost by the Olive Blue. I avoid calling it Grey as I believe that the true Grey gene that is fully dominant may one day appear in these species. It is also important not to confuse these 'Slate' birds with the true Slate mutation that so far only exists in Budgerigars. It will one day appear in other species without doubt. Therefore it is best to refer to them always as Mauve.

Cobalt Indian Ringnecked Parrot.

1. Dark Factor Applegreen Peachfaced Lovebird (foreground).
2. Dark Factor (Cobalt) Turquoise Peachfaced Lovebird.
3. Dark Factor (Cobalt) Aqua Peachfaced Lovebird.
4. Double Dark Factor (Mauve) Turquoise Peachfaced Lovebirds should never be called 'Slate'.
5. Mauve Masked Lovebird.
6. Cobalt Masked Lovebird.
7. Double Dark Factor (Olive) Applegreen Peachfaced Lovebird.

At first appearance, combining a recessive gene with a dominant gene should be simple. However, the Blue gene and the Olive gene both occur on the one chromosome and (in the Budgerigar at least) are closely linked together – and only recombine with a frequency of 14%. This means that it requires a fair degree of patience to combine the two genes and that a Cobalt is far more valuable to further breeding than a Dark Green/Blue (Type 1).

As neither mutation is sex-linked, the sex of the parents is irrelevant and the outcomes for both sexes are the same. For this reason the sexes are not recorded in the following matings:

M CHRISTIAN

*Cobalt Budgerigar.*

P TOMAS

*Mauve Budgerigar.*

### 1. Olive x Blue
= Dark Green/Blue (Type 1)

### 2. Dark Green/Blue (Type 1) x Blue
= 86% Dark Green/Blue (Type 1) and Blue
+ 14% Green/Blue and Cobalt

This is the best mating to start producing Cobalt. You simply have to have patience until the Cobalt appears. The following mating will tempt some people but it causes many complicated outcomes with lower Cobalt production.

### 3. Dark Green/Blue (Type 1) x Dark Green/Blue (Type 1)
= 74% Blue, Dark Green/Blue (Type 1) and Olive
+ 24% Green/Blue, Dark Green, Cobalt and Olive/Blue
+ 2% Green, Dark Green/Blue (Type 2) and Mauve

As you can see, the outcomes are varied and identifying the best birds for further matings is impossible without test matings and wasted time.

J CHOU
J CHOU

*Above: Turquoise (L) and Cobalt (Turquoise) Lineolated Parrots.*
*Right: (L to R) Cobalt (Turquoise), Turquoise, Lutino and Mauve (Turquoise) Lineolated Parrots.*

E ANTONIN

E ANTONIN

*Above: Mauve Western Rosella.*
*Left: Mauve Mallee Ringnecked Parrot.*

*Above: Cobalt Western Rosella.*
*Right: Cobalt Mallee Ringnecked Parrot.*

E ANTONIN

Y ARENDZE

*From left: Grey, Mauve and Cobalt Indian Ringnecked Parrots – a comparative photograph to show the difference between commonly confused colours.*

Therefore, stick to mating 2 above and once the Cobalt is produced, the following matings can be used:

**Cobalt x Cobalt**
= Blue, Cobalt and Mauve

**Cobalt x Blue**
= Blue and Cobalt

**Cobalt x Dark Green/Blue (Type 1)**
= 86% Blue, Cobalt, Dark Green/Blue (Type 1) and Olive/Blue
+ 14% Green/Blue, Dark Green/Blue (Type 2), Cobalt and Mauve

**Cobalt x Dark Green/Blue (Type 2)**
= 86% Green/Blue, Dark Green/Blue (Type 2), Cobalt and Mauve
+ 14% Blue, Cobalt, Dark Green/Blue (Type 1) and Olive/Blue

**Cobalt x Mauve**
= Cobalt and Mauve

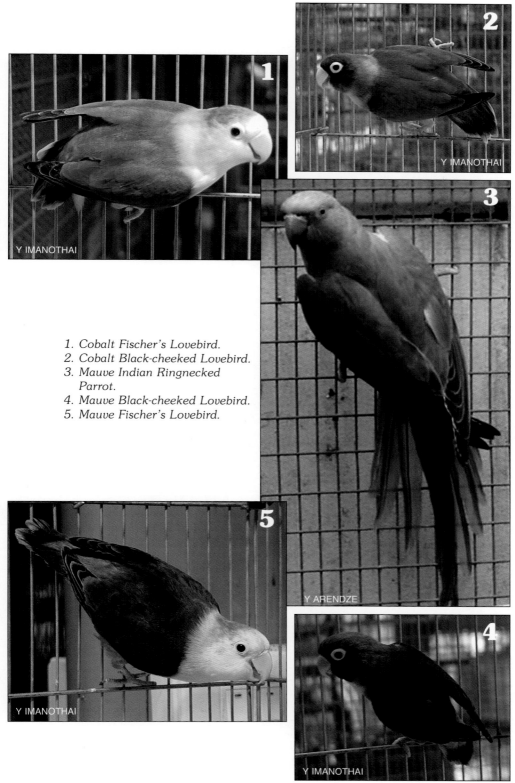

1. Cobalt Fischer's Lovebird.
2. Cobalt Black-cheeked Lovebird.
3. Mauve Indian Ringnecked Parrot.
4. Mauve Black-cheeked Lovebird.
5. Mauve Fischer's Lovebird.

Y IMANOTHAI

Y IMANOTHAI

Y ARENDZE

Y IMANOTHAI

Y IMANOTHAI

It is possible that in some species not all Olive genes are linked to Blue genes. In such a case, producing Cobalt and Mauve would be no more difficult than combining Blue and Greygreen to produce Grey. However, in that case the apparent Olive gene is more likely to be a Violet gene incorrectly identified. The terms Type 1 and Type 2 are genetic terms that are complicated to explain. (For a full explanation I refer you to page 274.)

## Dark Dilute and Olive Dilute

Combining the Olive gene with a Dilute (Yellow) gene produces darker forms of the latter. It tends to enhance blue and green colours, but can make yellow colours dirtier by bringing out any green tinges in them. If your desire is to produce as clear a yellow bird as possible, there are better combinations than this one. However, if you wish to enhance blue-coloured areas on a Dilute mutation, then this is a useful combination. It has been particularly good in the Turquoise Parrot as this bird has clear blue areas as well as the normal green body colour. The combination has not produced very distinctive birds in Budgerigars and Peachfaced Lovebirds where the Normal Green bird does not have large areas of blue colour. In the Budgerigar, combining the Olive with a darker Dilute gene (Greywing or Clearwing) rather than the lighter Suffused gene produces more attractive combinations.

P TOMAS

H SMITH

*Above: Dark Green Greywing Budgerigar.*
*Right: Dark Green Clearwing Budgerigar.*

G ROMAN

G ROMAN

*Olive Dilute Turquoise Parrot –*
*commonly known as Olive 'Yellow'.*

*Dark Dilute Turquoise Parrots – commonly known*
*as 'Jade Yellow'.*

To produce the combination, the breeder must combine the co-dominant Olive gene with the recessive Dilute gene. Therefore the sex of parents or young is irrelevant in the genetic outcomes. Start by mating an Olive to a Dilute to produce Dark Green/Dilute offspring. Then mate the following:

**Dark Green/Dilute x Dilute**
= Green/Dilute and Dilute
+ Dark Green/Dilute and Dark Dilute

**Dark Dilute x Olive**
= Dark Green/Dilute and Olive/Dilute

**Olive/ Dilute x Dilute**
= Dark Green/Dilute and Dark Dilute

**Dark Dilute x Olive/ Dilute**
= Dark Green/Dilute and Dark Dilute
+ Olive/Dilute and Olive Dilute

**Dark Green/ Dilute x Olive Dilute**
= Dark Green/Dilute and Dark Dilute
+ Olive/Dilute and Olive Dilute

**Dark Dilute x Olive Dilute**
= Dark Dilute and Olive Dilute

H SMITH

*Olive Clearwing Budgerigar.*

P TOMAS

*Cobalt Greywing Budgerigar.*

## Dilute Cobalt and Dilute Mauve

A Dilute Cobalt or Dilute Mauve is a three-way combination between a Dilute gene, the Blue gene and the Olive gene. Depending on the amount of blue structural colours in the wildtype bird, the compound name of Dilute Cobalt or Dilute Mauve is the most appropriate. The Dilute gene reduces the depth of colours while the Olive gene tends to darken them at the same time. Therefore there is some counteraction of effects, although the two genes work in completely different ways and the final outcome is variable between species. In the Turquoise Parrot the blue face is lightened by the Dilute (Yellow) gene but darkened by the Olive gene. The final outcome in the Dark Dilute is a face similar in colour to the Normal bird's face. However, the green colour of the body never returns. Therefore when the Blue gene occurs in this species, I would expect a Dilute Cobalt to have a strong face colour but a weaker blue body colour. It would be certainly worthwhile investigating further.

To produce this combination, the breeder must combine two recessive genes and a dominant gene. As the Blue and Olive genes are linked, it is best to use birds with these two genes already combined. Therefore mate a Dilute to a Cobalt or Mauve rather than mate an Olive Dilute to a Blue. Silver (Dilute Blue) can be used but does not increase the rate of success. The genes are not sex-linked, so the sex of parents and young is not considered.

**Dilute x Mauve**
= Dark Green/Blue/Dilute (Type 2)

**Dilute x Cobalt**
= Green/Blue/Dilute
+ Dark Green/Blue/Dilute (Type 2)

**Dark Green/Blue/Dilute (Type 2) x Dark Green/Blue/Dilute (Type 2)**
= 74% Green, Green/Dilute, Dilute, Dark Green/Blue (Type 2),
   Dark Green/Blue/Dilute (Type 2), Dilute Dark Green/Blue (Type 2),
   Mauve, Mauve/Dilute and Dilute Mauve
+ 24% Green/Blue, Green/Blue/Dilute, Dilute/Blue,
   Dark Green, Dark Green/Dilute, Dilute Dark Green,
   Cobalt, Cobalt/Dilute, Dilute Cobalt, Olive/Blue,
   Olive/Blue/Dilute and Dilute Olive/Blue
+ 2% Blue, Blue/Dilute, Silver, Dark Green/Blue (Type 1),
   Dark Green/Blue/Dilute (Type 1), Dilute Dark Green/Blue (Type 1),
   Olive, Olive/Dilute and Dilute Olive

From this mating, the Dilute Dark Green/Blue (Type 2), Mauve/Dilute, Dilute Mauve, Cobalt/Dilute, Dilute Cobalt and Dilute Olive/Blue should be selected for test mating and further breeding. You need test matings to find the Mauve/Dilute and Cobalt/Dilute birds. An alternative mating would be:

**Dark Green/Blue/Dilute (Type 2) x Silver**
= 86% Green/Blue/Dilute, Dilute/Blue,
   Cobalt/Dilute and Dilute Cobalt
+ 14% Dark Green/Blue/Dilute (Type 1), Dilute Dark Green/Blue (Type 1),
   Blue/Dilute and Silver

This mating gives much simpler results with more definite outcomes. You would select the Cobalt/Dilute and Dilute Cobalt for further matings. The number of possible matings at this stage is enormous, so I can only list a few.

**Cobalt/Dilute x Silver**
= Blue/Dilute, Silver, Cobalt/Dilute and Dilute Cobalt

**Cobalt/Dilute x Dilute Cobalt**
= Blue/Dilute, Silver, Cobalt/Dilute and Dilute Cobalt
+ Mauve/Dilute and Dilute Mauve

**Cobalt/Dilute x Dilute Mauve**
= Cobalt/Dilute, Silver, Mauve/Dilute and Dilute Mauve

**Dilute Cobalt x Silver**
= Silver and Dilute Cobalt

**Dilute Cobalt x Mauve/Dilute**
= Cobalt/Dilute, Silver, Mauve/Dilute and Dilute Mauve

**Mauve/Dilute x Silver**
= Cobalt/Dilute and Dilute Cobalt

*Cobalt Clearwing*
*Budgerigar.*

# Other Dark Factor Combinations

P ODEKERKEN

P ODEKERKEN

Y IMANOTHAI

1. *Lime Olive Fischer's Lovebird.*
2. *Lime (Pallid) TurquoiseCobalt (L) and Lime (Pallid) TurquoiseBlue (R) Indian Ringnecked Parrots.*
3. *Lime Cobalt and Lime Mauve (above) Fischer's Lovebirds.*
4. *Lime Mauve Masked Lovebird.*
5. *Lime (Pallid) Blue (L) and Lime (Pallid) Cobalt (R) Indian Ringnecked Parrots.*

# Cinnamon Dilute (Cinnamon Yellow)

In at least two species, the Cinnamon mutation has been combined with the Dilute ('Yellow') mutation to produce a clearer yellow colour. The Cinnamon mutation acts in a complementary manner to further reduce any traces of grey family pigments from the plumage of the Dilute. This has been used to advantage by Budgerigar breeders to produce the show standard 'Yellow'. In fact the practice started so far back in time that many modern breeders do not realise that their 'Yellow' birds carry Cinnamon genes. The proof is seen when they are mated to Cinnamon birds and produce Cinnamon sons.

Recently, the same combination has been produced in Turquoise Parrots in Europe. Once again the combination leads to a more pure yellow colour. However, the long term desirability of this combination could be questionable once either Lutino or Black-eyed Yellow is established in a species as both of these mutations produce even clearer yellow birds.

To produce the combination, start with a Cinnamon cock mated to a Dilute hen to produce Normal/Cinnamon/Dilute cocks and Cinnamon/Dilute hens. Then mate the Cinnamon/Dilute hens to Dilute cocks to give the following:

*Above: Cinnamon Dilute Turquoise Parrot.*
*Below: Cinnamon Dilute Budgerigar.*

**Dilute cock x Cinnamon/Dilute hen**
= Normal/Cinnamon/Dilute and Dilute/Cinnamon cocks
+ Normal/Dilute and Dilute hens

The Dilute/Cinnamon cocks should then be selected and mated to Cinnamon/Dilute hens to give the following outcomes:

**Dilute/Cinnamon cock x Cinnamon/Dilute hen**
= Normal/Cinnamon/Dilute and Dilute/Cinnamon cocks
+ Cinnamon/Dilute and Cinnamon Dilute cocks
+ Normal/Dilute and Dilute hens
+ Cinnamon/Dilute and Cinnamon Dilute hens

At this point further matings become possible including the following:

**Cinnamon/Dilute cock x Cinnamon/Dilute hen**
= Cinnamon, Cinnamon/Dilute and Cinnamon Dilute cocks and hens

**Cinnamon/Dilute cock x Cinnamon Dilute hen**
= Cinnamon/Dilute and Cinnamon Dilute cocks and hens

**Dilute/Cinnamon cock x Cinnamon Dilute hen**
= Dilute/Cinnamon and Cinnamon Dilute cocks
+ Dilute and Cinnamon Dilute hens

**Cinnamon Dilute cock x Cinnamon/Dilute hen**
= Cinnamon/Dilute and Cinnamon Dilute cocks and hens

**Cinnamon Dilute cock x Cinnamon Dilute hen**
= Cinnamon Dilute cocks and hens

# Cinnamon Dark Dilute

There are many combinations like this one that are not yet possible in most species and some would ask whether they are even worth trying. However, each combination is unique in each species, so unless they are tried we will never know. This combination is currently possible in the Budgerigar and the Peachfaced Lovebird as well as the Turquoise Parrot in Europe. I believe that the Turquoise Parrot combination would be the most interesting of the three species. The Cinnamon gene would create a brown hue to the Dark Dilute, probably further eliminating any green tinges to the plumage in the process.

Probably more attractive is the combination using a darker Dilute gene instead of a lighter Suffused gene, although in the Budgerigar, Cinnamonwing does not combine well with the darker Dilute genes, such as Greywing and Clearwing. Still the combination remains as an interesting exercise in combinations to be tried where possible.

To produce the combination, the breeder must combine a sex-linked mutation with a dominant mutation and a recessive mutation. Therefore the sex of the birds used is important. Mate a Cinnamon cock to an Olive Dilute hen or alternatively mate a Mustard cock to a Dilute hen. These matings will both produce identical outcomes:

### Cinnamon cock x Olive Dilute hen

or

### Mustard cock x Dilute hen
= Green/Cinnamon/Dilute and Dark Green/Cinnamon/Dilute cocks
+ Cinnamon/Dilute and Cinnamon Dark Green/Dilute hens

Select the Cinnamon Dark Green/Dilute hens and mate them to Olive Dilute cocks to give the following outcomes:

### Olive Dilute cock x Cinnamon Dark Green/Dilute hen
= Dark Green/Cinnamon/Dilute and Olive/Cinnamon/Dilute cocks
+ Dark Dilute/Cinnamon and Olive Dilute/Cinnamon cocks
+ Dark Green/Dilute, Olive/Dilute, Dark Dilute and Olive Dilute hens

Select the Dark Dilute/Cinnamon and Olive Dilute/Cinnamon cocks for matings back to Cinnamon Dark Green/Dilute hens to give the following:

### Dark Dilute/Cinnamon cock x Cinnamon Dark Green/Dilute hen
= Green/Cinnamon/Dilute and Dark Green/Cinnamon/Dilute cocks
+ Olive/Cinnamon/Dilute and Cinnamon Dark Green/Dilute cocks
+ Mustard/Dilute, Dilute/Cinnamon and Dark Dilute/Cinnamon cocks
+ Olive Dilute/Cinnamon, Cinnamon/Dilute and Cinnamon Dilute cocks
+ Cinnamon Dark Dilute and Cinnamon Olive Dilute cocks
+ Green/Dilute, Dark Green/Dilute, Olive/Dilute and Cinnamon/Dilute hens
+ Cinnamon Dark Green/Dilute, Mustard/Dilute and Dilute hens
+ Dark Dilute, Olive Dilute and Cinnamon Dilute hens
+ Cinnamon Dark Dilute and Cinnamon Olive Dilute hens

### Olive Dilute/Cinnamon cock x Cinnamon Dark Green/Dilute hen
= Dark Green/Cinnamon/Dilute and Olive/Cinnamon/Dilute cocks
+ Cinnamon Dark Green/Dilute and Dark Dilute/Cinnamon cocks
+ Olive Dilute/Cinnamon and Cinnamon Dark Dilute cocks
+ Mustard/Dilute and Cinnamon Olive Dilute cocks
+ Dark Green/Dilute, Olive/Dilute, Cinnamon Dark Green/Dilute
   and Mustard/Dilute hens
+ Dark Dilute, Olive Dilute and Cinnamon Dark Dilute hens
+ Cinnamon Olive Dilute hens

P TOMAS

N LIVANOS

*Above: Violet (SF) Blue Masked Lovebird – similar to but should never be called Cobalt.*
*Left: Violet (SF) Blue Budgerigar – this colour is very similar to a Cobalt.*

H-GRAF

*Violet (DF) Blue Masked Lovebird – very similar colour to the Violet (SF) Cobalt combination.*

## Violet Blue – Double Factor Violet Blue

It is not well known that the Violet gene when combined with the Blue gene will create a violet colour without the necessary presence of the Olive gene (see next section). This was first postulated by Taylor and Warner (1986) and has been recently 'rediscovered' or at least refreshed by an article by Peter Bergman which can be found at Clive Hesford's web site.

The Single Factor Violet Blue cannot be easily distinguished from a true Cobalt (Dark Blue) combination. There may be subtle differences but these no doubt vary between species. However, the true Violet colour is seen when in Double Factor. These birds are difficult to distinguish from the generally accepted 'Visual Violet' (Violet (SF) Cobalt).

Producing these Violet Blue birds is similar to producing a Mauve, except that there is no gene linkage to make things difficult. The sex of the birds in the following matings is irrelevant as no sex-linked mutations are involved. Start with the Violet Green mated to a Blue.

**Violet (SF) Green x Blue**
= Green/Blue and Violet (SF) Green/Blue

**Violet (DF) Green x Blue**
= Violet (SF) Green/Blue

**Violet (SF) Green/Blue x Blue**
= Green/Blue, Blue, Violet (SF) Green/Blue and Violet (SF) Blue

**Violet (SF) Green/Blue x Violet (SF) Green/Blue**
= Green, Green/Blue and Blue,
+ Violet (SF) Green, Violet (SF) Green/Blue and Violet (SF) Blue
+ Violet (DF) Green, Violet (DF) Green/Blue and Violet (DF) Blue

**Violet (SF) Green/Blue x Violet (SF) Blue**
= Green/Blue, Blue, Violet (SF) Green/Blue and Violet (SF) Blue
+ Violet (DF) Green/Blue and Violet (DF) Blue

1. *Violet (SF) Fischer's Lovebirds.*
2. *Violet (DF) Blue Indian Ringnecked Parrot – this combination produces the true violet colouration.*
3. *Violet (SF) Turquoise Peachfaced Lovebird – could easily be confused with a Dark Factor Turquoise (Cobalt).*
4. *Masked Lovebirds (L to R) Violet (DF) Blue, Violet (SF) Blue, Blue.*
5. *Violet (SF) Blue Indian Ringnecked Parrot – never call this colour Cobalt.*
6. *Violet (SF) Blue (L) and Violet (DF) Blue (R) Indian Ringnecked Parrots.*

**Violet (SF) Blue x Violet (DF) Green/Blue**
= Violet (SF) Green/Blue and Violet (SF) Blue
+ Violet (DF) Green/Blue and Violet (DF) Blue

**Violet (SF) Green/Blue x Violet (DF) Blue**
= Violet (SF) Green/Blue and Violet (SF) Blue
+ Violet (DF) Green/Blue and Violet (DF) Blue

**Violet (SF) Blue x Violet (DF) Blue**
= Violet (SF) Blue and Violet (DF) Blue

## Visual Violet – Violet Cobalt

It is generally accepted that the bird that is visually violet in colour, is in fact a three-way combination of genes. To achieve it you need the Violet gene, the Olive gene in Single Factor and the Blue gene. The Blue gene removes all yellow family pigments making the bird blue in colour. The other two genes combine to alter the shade of blue to a beautiful shade of violet. As mentioned previously, the Single Factor Violet gene, without the combination of the Olive gene, appears almost indistinguishable from the effects of a single Olive gene alone (ie Cobalt). The main distinction that can be made is that the Olive gene is linked to the Blue gene, whilst the Violet gene is not linked to the Blue gene. Also, violet colour can be produced simply through the Double Factor Violet and Blue combination (see previous section), whilst the Double Factor Olive and Blue combination produces the blue-grey colour called Mauve.

P TOMAS
*Visual Violet Budgerigar.*

To produce a Visual Violet (Violet Cobalt), the breeder must combine two dominant genes with a recessive gene, remembering that the Olive gene has linkage with the Blue gene. Therefore, although the sex of the birds is irrelevant, it is best to start with a Mauve and a Violet Green or better still, a Violet Blue if available.

R ERHART

R ERHART

*Above: The wing of a Visual Violet Peachfaced Lovebird.*
*Left: (L to R) Visual Violet, Violet Mauve and Visual Violet Peachfaced Lovebirds – the Violet Mauve combination is very close to Grey in colour.*

**Mauve x Violet Green**
= Dark Green/Blue (Type 2) and Violet Dark Green/Blue (Type 2)

**Mauve x Violet Blue**
= Cobalt and Visual Violet

**Mauve x Violet Dark Green/Blue (Type 2)**
= 86% Dark Green/Blue, Violet Dark Green/Blue (Type 2), Mauve and Violet Mauve
+ 14% Cobalt, Olive/Blue, Visual Violet and Olive Violet/Blue

**Violet Mauve x Blue**
= Cobalt and Visual Violet

**Violet Mauve x Cobalt**
= Cobalt and Visual Violet
+ Mauve and Violet Mauve

**Visual Violet x Visual Violet**
= Blue, Violet Blue and Violet (DF) Blue
+ Cobalt, Visual Violet and Violet (DF) Cobalt
+ Mauve, Violet Mauve and Violet (DF) Mauve

## Other Violet Combinations

*The following are some beautiful Violet combinations not discussed in this book.*

1. *Lime Violet (SF) Fischer's Lovebird.*
2. *Lime (Pallid) Turquoise Visual Violet Peachfaced Lovebird.*
3. *Cinnamon Turquoise Visual Violet Peachfaced Lovebird.*
4. *Lime Violet Masked Lovebird.*

Y IMANOTHAI

## More Violet Combinations

Violet (SF) LutinoLime Blue Masked Lovebird.

S HOUSE

Violet Lime ('Texas Clearbody') Budgerigar.

N LIVANOS

Violet (SF) Lime Blue Masked Lovebird.

## Faded (Isabel) Dilute

The Faded Dilute is another of the theoretical combinations that has limited appeal. The combining of two mutations that both reduce grey pigments results in an even clearer yellow bird. This is mainly a desire in species currently without a Lutino gene such as the Turquoise Parrot. Like the Golden Yellow (Cinnamon Lime) and the Cinnamon Dark Dilute mentioned previously, its long-term desirability will be questionable once the true Lutino appears.

If a breeder decides to produce this combination, culled birds should not be sold because they could easily destroy the populations of both Faded and Dilute mutations with the mixed genes, creating untold confusion for future breeders.

To produce the combination, the breeder must combine two recessive genes. The process is similar to producing White or Silver. To predict outcomes you can use matings from either of those two combinations and simply substitute Faded for Blue and Faded Dilute for White.

R ERHART

The Fallow Yellow Pacific Parrotlet is a similar colour to what we would expect for a Faded Dilute, but with a red eye.

## Blue Opaline

The Opaline gene combines well with most other genes because it alters pigment distribution rather than the types of pigment produced. The most interesting aspect of the Opaline gene is that its action varies in different species. Therefore it is always interesting to explore its combination with other genes in species where it occurs. The two main features, that are found across all species, are white down (grey family pigments are removed) and retained wing stripes in adult cocks. The presence of the Blue gene has no effect on either of these two features.

At present, this combination is possible in Budgerigars, Red-rumped Parrots and Cockatiels. The other three species with Opaline genes do not yet have an established Blue gene (eg Bourke's Parrots, Turquoise Parrots and Eastern Rosellas). The three species with this combination all look different except for the two consistent features previously mentioned. (Opaline Cockatiels do not show the white down as the Normal

*Blue Opaline Red-rumped Parrot.*

*Blue Opaline Budgerigar.*

bird has yellow rather than grey down. However, the Blue gene removes the yellow pigment and produces white down with this combination). I refer the reader to the photographs in this section.

To produce the combination, the breeder must combine a sex-linked mutation with a recessive mutation. Therefore, the sex of the birds to be paired is important. You should start with an Opaline cock and a Blue hen, which gives Normal/Opaline/Blue cocks and Opaline/Blue hens.

As mentioned with other combinations, the more pairs at each stage the better, and the less inbreeding will occur later in the process. Opaline/Blue hens are chosen and mated to Blue cocks for the following outcome:

**Blue cock x Opaline/Blue hen**
= Normal/Blue/Opaline cocks and Normal/Blue hens
+ Blue/Opaline cocks and Blue hens

Blue/Opaline cocks are chosen to mate back to Opaline/Blue hens giving the following outcome:

**Blue/Opaline cock x Opaline/Blue hen**
= Normal/Blue/Opaline cocks and Normal/Blue hens
+ Blue/Opaline cocks and Blue hens
+ Opaline/Blue cocks and hens
+ Blue Opaline cocks and hens

From this mating, only the Normal coloured cocks and hens and the Blue hens are of no further use. A number of various matings will now be available to increase Blue Opaline production at a faster rate. They include:

**Blue/Opaline cock x Blue Opaline hen**
= Blue/Opaline cocks and Blue hens
+ Blue Opaline cocks and hens

*Blue Opaline Cockatiel – this colour is generally called 'Whiteface Pearl'.*

**Opaline/Blue cock x Blue Opaline hen**
= Opaline/Blue cocks and hens
+ Blue Opaline cocks and hens

**Blue Opaline cock x Opaline/Blue hen**
= Opaline/Blue cocks and hens
+ Blue Opaline cocks and hens

**Blue Opaline cock x Blue Opaline hen**
= Blue Opaline cocks and hens

## Lutino Opaline

The Opaline gene, due to its variable nature in different species, can produce surprising effects in some species, some of which are visible even when combined with the Lutino gene which traditionally hides most other mutations concurrently present. In the Budgerigar, the combination is probably not detectable. However in Red-rumped Parrots, Cockatiels, Eastern Rosellas and Bourke's Parrots, the increased distribution of certain yellow family pigments is highlighted by the removal of the grey family pigments by the Lutino gene. With the grey family pigments gone, no structural colour can be seen and the yellows, reds, pinks or oranges are freely visible and often highlighted.

The main constant effects of the Opaline gene – the white down and the wing stripe – are no longer visible. This occurs because the Lutino has white down anyway (yellow in Cockatiels) and the wing stripe lacks contrast so it cannot be seen. Therefore to identify a Lutino Opaline in different species, you need to be familiar with the species-specific changes to yellow family pigments for the species you are looking at. The photographs in this section should be referred to for guidance.

To produce the combination, the breeder must link together two sex-linked genes. These two genes, as well as being linked to sex determination, will also be linked to one another. In some cases this linkage can be very tight (such as between Cinnamon and Lime). Fortunately in this case it is not as tight, with recombination occurring approximately 30% of the time. It does, however, still reduce production of the desired combination in some cases or can increase them in others.

It does not matter whether you start with an Opaline cock and a Lutino hen or a Lutino cock and an Opaline hen. Both matings produce double split cocks (the needed offspring) and one produces Opaline hens and the other Lutino hens.

The Normal/Lutino/Opaline cocks can be mated in three ways as follows:

**1. Normal/Lutino/Opaline cock x Normal hen**
= 35% Normal/Lutino and Normal/Opaline cocks
+ 15% Normal and Normal/Lutino-Opaline cocks
+ 35% Lutino and Opaline hens
+ 15% Normal and Lutino Opaline hens

**2. Normal/Lutino/Opaline cock x Lutino hen**
= 35% Normal/Lutino/Opaline and Lutino cocks
+ 15% Normal/Lutino and Lutino/Opaline cocks
+ 35% Lutino and Opaline hens
+ 15% Normal and Lutino Opaline hens

*Lutino Opaline Red-rumped Parrot.*

R WEBB

J POSTEMA

B PEARSON

3

D ANDERSEN

1. *Lutino Opaline (R) and LutinoLime Opaline (L) Peachfaced Lovebirds.*
2. *Lutino Opaline Bourke's Parrot.*
3. *Lutino Opaline (Pearl) Cockatiel.*
4. *Lutino Opaline Eastern Rosella.*

**3. Normal/Lutino/Opaline cock x Opaline hen**
    = 35% Normal/Lutino/Opaline and Opaline cocks
    + 15% Normal/Opaline and Opaline/Lutino cocks
    + 35% Lutino and Opaline hens
    + 15% Normal and Lutino Opaline hens

The percentage of Lutino Opaline hens from any of these matings is 7.5% overall or 15% of hens. This can be increased by identifying the Opaline/Lutino and the Lutino/Opaline cocks with test matings. To do this, you need to mate the Lutino cocks from mating 2 above to Opaline hens. If they are Lutino/Opaline, then the following outcomes will result:

**Lutino/Opaline cock x Opaline hen**
    = Normal/Lutino/Opaline and Opaline/Lutino cocks
    + Lutino and Lutino Opaline hens

Fifty percent of young should be visually Opaline or Lutino Opaline. If ten young are produced from the test mating without obtaining one of these birds, you can be reasonably confident that the cock is not split Opaline and should be culled from the program. Any Opaline cocks produced from this test mating are split Lutino and are therefore useful for further matings. Twenty-five percent of young are Lutino Opaline hens.

Opaline cocks from mating 3 above should be mated to Lutino hens. If they are split Lutino then the results are as follows:

**Opaline/Lutino cock x Lutino hen**
    = Normal/Lutino/Opaline and Lutino/Opaline cocks
    + Opaline and Lutino Opaline hens

Fifty percent of young should be visually Lutino or Lutino Opaline. If ten young are produced from the test mating without obtaining one of these birds, you can be reasonably confident that the cock is not split Lutino and should be culled from the program. Any Lutino cocks produced from this test mating are split Opaline and are quite useful for further matings. Twenty-five percent of young are once again Lutino Opaline hens.

At this point a number of options for further matings become available as follows:

**Lutino/Opaline cock x Lutino Opaline hen**
    = Lutino/Opaline and Lutino Opaline cocks
    + Lutino and Lutino Opaline hens

**Opaline/Lutino cock x Lutino Opaline hen**
    = Opaline/Lutino and Lutino Opaline cocks
    + Opaline and Lutino Opaline hens

**Green/Lutino/Opaline cock x Lutino Opaline hen**
    = 35% Lutino/Opaline and Opaline/Lutino cocks
    + 15% Normal/Lutino-Opaline and Lutino Opaline cocks
    + 35% Lutino and Opaline hens
    + 15% Normal and Lutino Opaline hens

**Normal/Lutino-Opaline cock x Lutino Opaline hen**
    = 35% Normal/Lutino-Opaline and Lutino Opaline cocks
    + 15% Lutino/Opaline and Opaline/Lutino cocks
    + 35% Normal and Lutino Opaline hens
    + 15% Lutino and Opaline hens

**Lutino Opaline cock x Lutino hen**
= Lutino/Opaline cocks
+ Lutino Opaline hens

**Lutino Opaline cock x Opaline hen**
= Opaline/Lutino cocks
+ Lutino Opaline hens

**Lutino Opaline cock x Lutino Opaline hen**
= Lutino Opaline cocks and hens

## Cinnamon Opaline

Once again, the combination of Cinnamon with Opaline is variable between species because of the variation involved with the Opaline gene. I refer the reader to the photographs in this section as a reference. The two main consistent features of the Opaline gene are unaffected by the combination with the Cinnamon gene. These features are the lack of grey pigment in the down (resulting in white down) and the retention and amplification of the wing stripe in both sexes.

To produce the Cinnamon Opaline combination, the breeder must combine two sex-linked mutations. Therefore the process is very similar to that for the Lutino Opaline combination just described. As with the previous combination, the problem of linkage exists to make the result a little more difficult. Fortunately the rate of recombination for Cinnamon and Opaline is about the same as for Lutino and Opaline, so it does not present a major obstacle.

*Below: Cinnamon Opaline Eastern Rosella (Aust.).*
*Right: Cinnamon Opaline Eastern Rosella (Europe).*
*Bottom: Cinnamon Opaline Western Rosella.*

*Above: Cinnamon Opaline Turquoise Parrot.*
TOBY MARTIN  *Left: Cinnamon Opaline Red-rumped Parrot.*

G GERAEDTS

You start by producing Normal/Opaline/Cinnamon cocks by mating a Cinnamon to an Opaline. The sex of the birds is irrelevant. The double split cocks are then mated in one of the following ways:

### 1. Normal/Cinnamon/Opaline cock x Normal hen
= 33% Normal/Cinnamon and Normal/Opaline cocks
+ 17% Normal and Normal/Cinnamon-Opaline cocks
+ 33% Cinnamon and Opaline hens
+ 17% Normal and Cinnamon Opaline hens

### 2. Normal/Cinnamon/Opaline cock x Cinnamon hen
= 33% Normal/Cinnamon/Opaline and Cinnamon cocks
+ 17% Normal/Cinnamon and Cinnamon/Opaline cocks
+ 33% Cinnamon and Opaline hens
+ 17% Normal and Cinnamon Opaline hens

### 3. Normal/Cinnamon/Opaline cock x Opaline hen
= 33% Normal/Cinnamon/Opaline and Opaline cocks
+ 17% Normal/Opaline and Opaline/Cinnamon cocks
+ 33% Cinnamon and Opaline hens
+ 17% Normal and Cinnamon Opaline hens

Cinnamon Opaline hens are produced at a rate of 17% of hens or 8.5% of all young. To increase the percentage of desirable young, it is important to identify the Cinnamon/Opaline cocks from mating 2 and the Opaline/Cinnamon cocks from mating 3. To do this you test mate the Cinnamon cocks from mating 2 with Opaline hens and the Opaline cocks from mating 3 with Cinnamon hens.

Any Cinnamon/Opaline cocks from mating 2 will give the following when test mated:

**Cinnamon/Opaline cock x Opaline hen**
= Normal/Cinnamon/Opaline and Opaline/Cinnamon cocks
+ Cinnamon and Cinnamon Opaline hens

Fifty percent of young should be visually Opaline or Cinnamon Opaline. If ten young are produced from the test mating without obtaining one of these birds you can be reasonably confident that the cock is not split Opaline and should be culled from the

Cinnamon Opaline (Pearl) Cockatiel.

Cinnamon(wing) Opaline Green Budgerigar.

program. Any Opaline cocks from this test mating are split Cinnamon and are therefore quite useful for further matings. Twenty-five percent of young are the desired Cinnamon Opaline hens.

Any Opaline/Cinnamon cocks from mating 3 will give the following outcome when test mated:

### Opaline/Cinnamon cock x Cinnamon hen
= Normal/Cinnamon/Opaline and Cinnamon/Opaline cocks
+ Opaline and Cinnamon Opaline hens

Fifty percent of young should be visually Cinnamon or Cinnamon Opaline. If ten young are produced from the test mating without obtaining one of these birds you can be reasonably confident that the cock is not split Cinnamon and should be culled from the program. Any Cinnamon cocks from this test mating are split Opaline and are therefore quite useful for further matings. Twenty-five percent of young are the desired Cinnamon Opaline hens.

At this stage a number of other matings become available to increase the number of desired young.

### Cinnamon/Opaline cock x Cinnamon Opaline hen
= Cinnamon/Opaline and Cinnamon Opaline cocks
+ Cinnamon and Cinnamon Opaline hens

### Opaline/Cinnamon cock x Cinnamon Opaline hen
= Opaline/Cinnamon and Cinnamon Opaline cocks
+ Opaline and Cinnamon Opaline hens

### Cinnamon Opaline cock x Cinnamon Opaline hen
= 100% Cinnamon Opaline cocks and hens

The following matings are not necessarily recommended for breeding Cinnamon Opaline but are worth considering to better understand the genetics of this combination more thoroughly.

### Normal cock x Cinnamon Opaline hen
= Normal/Cinnamon-Opaline cocks and Normal hens

**Normal/Cinnamon/Opaline cock x Cinnamon Opaline hen**
= 33% Cinnamon/Opaline and Opaline/Cinnamon cocks
+ 17% Normal/Cinnamon-Opaline and Cinnamon Opaline cocks
+ 33% Cinnamon and Opaline hens
+ 17% Normal and Cinnamon Opaline hens

**Normal/Cinnamon-Opaline cock x Cinnamon Opaline hen**
= 33% Normal/Cinnamon-Opaline and Cinnamon Opaline cocks
+ 17% Cinnamon/Opaline and Opaline/Cinnamon cocks
+ 33% Normal and Cinnamon Opaline hens
+ 17% Cinnamon and Opaline hens

## Fallow Opaline

In Australia to date, this combination has only been produced in two species, primarily because Fallows are not yet common for the other species with Opaline genes. The action of the Fallow gene is to change any grey pigment in the bird to a light fawn shade as well as producing the characteristic red eye colour. When combined with the Opaline gene, it softens any remaining grey family pigments, creating a much lighter coloured Opaline.

This combination can be produced in the Budgerigar and the Bourke's Parrot. In the Bourke's Parrot, whose main Fallow mutation is commonly called 'Cream' in Australia, the combination is known as Pink. Fallow does exist in Turquoise Parrots in Europe and breeders there have almost certainly combined it with Opaline. Fallows are being established in Cockatiels and Red-rumped Parrots in Australia (Fallow Cockatiels are more common elsewhere), so it will not be long before more examples of this combination are produced.

To produce the combination, the breeder must combine a sex-linked mutation with a recessive gene. Therefore it is best to start by mating an Opaline cock to a Fallow hen. This will produce Normal/Fallow/Opaline cocks and Opaline/Fallow hens.

*Above: Fallow Opaline Bourke's Parrot – generally known as 'Pink'.*
*Right: Faded 'European Isabel' Opaline Turquoise Parrot – the breeding expectations for this colour are the same as for a Fallow Opaline.*
*Far right: Parblue Fallow Opaline Cockatiel – known as 'Pastelface' Fallow 'Pearl' by breeders.*

The hens should be chosen and mated with Fallow cocks to give the following:

**Fallow cock x Opaline/Fallow hen**
= Normal/Fallow/Opaline and Fallow/Opaline cocks
+ Normal/Fallow and Fallow hens

The Fallow/Opaline cocks should be selected for mating to unrelated Opaline/Fallow hens to give the following:

**Fallow/Opaline cock x Opaline/Fallow hen**
= Normal/Fallow/Opaline cocks and Normal/Fallow hens
+ Fallow/Opaline cocks and Fallow hens
+ Opaline/Fallow cocks and hens
+ Fallow Opaline cocks and hens

This opens up a number of other possible matings, which include the following:

**Fallow/Opaline cock x Fallow Opaline hen**
= Fallow/Opaline cocks and Fallow hens
+ Fallow Opaline cocks and hens

**Opaline/Fallow cock x Fallow Opaline hen**
= Opaline/Fallow cocks and hens
+ Fallow Opaline cocks and hens

**Fallow Opaline cock x Opaline/Fallow hen**
= Opaline/Fallow cocks and hens
+ Fallow Opaline cocks and hens

**Fallow Opaline cock x Fallow Opaline hen**
= Fallow Opaline cocks and hens

# Platinum Opaline and Lime Opaline

This combination has been produced in the Cockatiel and remains a theoretical possibility in other species, with the two genes involved being present in Budgerigars and Red-rumped Parrots. In Red-rumped Parrots, both forms of the combination are possible as both Platinum and Lime occur.

As the Platinum and Lime genes belong to the Lutino gene family, the production of either Lime Opaline or Platinum Opaline mimics the process used for Lutino Opaline previously described in this book. These genes are also linked together, with the rate of recombination the same as for Lutino and Opaline – approximately 30%.

I will give breeding results for the Platinum Opaline combination, but if the name Lime is substituted for Platinum, the expectations apply for the Lime Opaline combination. Both genes involved are sex-linked. Therefore the sexes for the original pairing are not important.

*Green-cheeked Conure – I believe this colour may be a Lime Opaline combination. It is known by breeders as 'Yellow-sided Cinnamon'.*

R CUSICK

Either way Normal/Platinum/Opaline cocks are produced and are used for the next mating outcomes:

### 1. Normal/Platinum/Opaline cock x Normal hen
= 35% Normal/Platinum and Normal/Opaline cocks
+ 15% Normal and Normal/Platinum-Opaline cocks
+ 35% Platinum and Opaline hens
+ 15% Normal and Platinum Opaline hens

### 2. Normal/Platinum/Opaline cock x Platinum hen
= 35% Normal/Platinum/Opaline and Platinum cocks
+ 15% Normal/Platinum and Platinum/Opaline cocks
+ 35% Platinum and Opaline hens
+ 15% Normal and Platinum Opaline hens

### 3. Normal/Platinum/Opaline cock x Opaline hen
= 35% Normal/Platinum/Opaline and Opaline cocks
+ 15% Normal/Opaline and Opaline/Platinum cocks
+ 35% Platinum and Opaline hens
+ 15% Normal and Platinum Opaline hens

*Above: Lime Blue Opaline (L) and Lime Opaline Red-rumped Parrots.*
*Left: Platinum Opaline Red-rumped Parrot.*
*Below left: LutinoLime Opaline Peachfaced Lovebird.*
*Below right: Platinum Opaline Cockatiel.*

Mirroring what we did for Lutino Opaline, we test mate the Platinum cocks from mating 2 and the Opaline cocks from mating 3. The results are as follows:

**Platinum/Opaline cock x Opaline hen**
= Normal/Platinum/Opaline and Opaline/Platinum cocks
+ Platinum and Platinum Opaline hens

**Opaline/Platinum cock x Platinum hen**
= Normal/Platinum/Opaline and Platinum/Opaline cocks
+ Opaline and Platinum Opaline hens

The method used to interpret the test results is the same as that used for Lutino Opaline production. (See page 172.) Once again, this will open up the possibilities for further matings as follows:

**Platinum/Opaline cock x Platinum Opaline hen**
= Platinum/Opaline cocks and Platinum hens
+ Platinum Opaline cocks and hens

**Opaline/Platinum cock x Platinum Opaline hen**
= Opaline/Platinum cocks and Opaline hens
+ Platinum Opaline cocks and hens

**Platinum Opaline cock x Platinum Opaline hen**
= Platinum Opaline cocks and hens

**Platinum Opaline cock x Lutino Opaline hen**
= LutinoPlatinum Opaline cocks
+ Platinum Opaline hens

**Lutino Opaline cock x Platinum Opaline hen**
= LutinoPlatinum Opaline cocks
+ Lutino Opaline hens

Following are two matings involving a LutinoPlatinum Opaline cock. Remember that the LutinoPlatinum is not a standard combination of mutations. This bird has only one gene for each colour, thereby giving a blend between the two colours. The LutinoPlatinum Opaline has two Opaline genes, one Lutino gene and one Platinum gene.

**LutinoPlatinum Opaline cock x Lutino Opaline hen**
= Lutino Opaline and LutinoPlatinum Opaline cocks
+ Lutino Opaline and Platinum Opaline hens

**LutinoPlatinum Opaline cock x Platinum Opaline hen**
= LutinoPlatinum Opaline and Platinum Opaline cocks
+ Lutino Opaline and Platinum Opaline hens

*Following are more complicated mating results for those interested in understanding the nature of the Platinum, Lime, Lutino and Opaline genes. It is complex and difficult to explain without the use of genetic symbols. If it confuses too much, ignore it. It is not necessary to understand these results to breed the combinations.*

### Platinum cock x Lutino Opaline hen
= *LutinoPlatinum/Opaline (Type 1) cocks*
+ *Platinum hens*

### Platinum Opaline cock x Lutino hen
= *LutinoPlatinum/Opaline (Type 2) cocks*
+ *Platinum Opaline hens*

### Lutino Opaline cock x Platinum hen
= *LutinoPlatinum/Opaline (Type 1) cocks*
+ *Lutino Opaline hens*

### Lutino cock x Platinum Opaline hen
= *LutinoPlatinum/Opaline (Type 2) cocks*
+ *Lutino hens*

### LutinoPlatinum/Opaline cock (Type 2) x Platinum hen
= *35% LutinoPlatinum and Platinum/Opaline cocks*
+ *15% LutinoPlatinum/Opaline (Type 1) and Platinum cocks*
+ *35% Lutino and Platinum Opaline hens*
+ *15% Platinum and Lutino Opaline hens*

### LutinoPlatinum/Opaline cock (Type 1) x Platinum hen
= *35% LutinoPlatinum/Opaline (Type 1) and Platinum cocks*
+ *15% LutinoPlatinum and Platinum/Opaline cocks*
+ *35% Platinum and Lutino Opaline hens*
+ *15% Lutino and Platinum Opaline hens*

*From these results, the important thing to notice is that different percentages of young are produced depending on whether the Opaline gene is linked to either the Platinum or the Lutino gene. Type 1 is linked to the Lutino gene; Type 2 is linked to the Platinum gene.*

## Other Opaline Combinations
The presence of the Opaline gene in a species effectively doubles the number of possible combinations because it can be combined with any other gene or combination of genes to create a new effect. It would be impossible to cover every possible combination in the depth I have to date. Indeed you could fill a separate book just on Opaline combinations, both real and theoretical and Opaline exists in only six species at present! I will therefore cover as many as possible in this section with only minimal detail, but hopefully enough information for you to breed them if desired.

### Parblue Opaline
This combination is currently possible in Budgerigars, Cockatiels and Red-rumped Parrots. In Australia we can only produce the Budgerigar (Yellowface Opaline) and Cockatiel (Pastelface Pearl) versions at the present time. Parblue in the Red-rumped Parrot is only available overseas at present. The method required to produce this combination is the same as for Blue Opaline, with Parblue substituted for Blue in the matings.

*Aqua Opaline and Applegreen Opaline Peachfaced Lovebirds.*

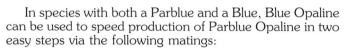

*Parblue Lutino (Creamino) Opaline Eastern Rosella – as more mutations appear, sometimes a new primary mutation (Parblue) appears in combination in the first instance and then needs to be separated out.*

*Parblue Opaline Cockatiel – called 'Pastelface Pearl' by breeders.*

In species with both a Parblue and a Blue, Blue Opaline can be used to speed production of Parblue Opaline in two easy steps via the following matings:

**Blue Opaline cock x ParblueBlue hen**
= Blue/Opaline and ParblueBlue/Opaline cocks
+ Blue Opaline and ParblueBlue Opaline hens

**Blue Opaline cock x ParblueBlue Opaline hen**
= Blue Opaline cocks and hens
+ ParblueBlue Opaline cocks and hens

**ParblueBlue Opaline cock x ParblueBlue Opaline hen**
= Blue Opaline cocks and hens
+ ParblueBlue Opaline cocks and hens
+ Parblue Opaline cocks and hens

Remember that a ParblueBlue is less green than a pure Parblue.

*Applegreen Opaline Peachfaced Lovebird.*

### Dilute Opaline
Dilute (Yellow) Opaline can be produced in the Budgerigar, Eastern Rosella, Cockatiel, Red-rumped Parrot and Turquoise Parrot at this time. The method for production is similar to that for Fallow Opaline, substituting Dilute for Fallow.

*Dilute (Yellow) Opaline Turquoise Parrot.*

*The Faded Opaline (Pearl) Cockatiel is similar to a Dilute Opaline in appearance.*

*Page 181*

Left: Dilute (Pastel) Opaline Eastern Rosella.
Right: Cinnamon Dilute (Pastel) Opaline Eastern Rosella.
Below: Dilute (Pastel) Opaline Eastern Rosella.

B PEARSON

T DULIERE

T DULIERE

## Olive Opaline and Dark Green Opaline

Olive and Dark Green versions of Opaline are possible only in Budgerigars and Turquoise Parrots at present. European aviculturists have produced this combination in Turquoise Parrots but as yet it has not been produced in Australia. This combination involves a sex-linked mutation and a co-dominant mutation. To produce it, you should start with an Opaline cock and an Olive hen. This will give Dark Green/Opaline cocks and Dark Green Opaline hens. Then the following matings can be used:

**Dark Green/Opaline cock x Dark Green Opaline hen**
= Green/Opaline and Opaline cocks
+ Dark Green/Opaline and Dark Green Opaline cocks
+ Olive/Opaline and Olive Opaline cocks
+ Green and Opaline hens
+ Dark Green and Dark Green Opaline hens
+ Olive and Olive Opaline hens

**Olive cock x Dark Green Opaline hen**
= Dark Green/Opaline and Olive/Opaline cocks
+ Dark Green and Olive hens

**Olive/Opaline cock x Dark Green Opaline hen**
= Dark Green/Opaline and Olive/Opaline cocks
+ Dark Green Opaline and Olive Opaline cocks
+ Dark Green and Olive hens
+ Dark Green Opaline and Olive Opaline hens

**Dark Green Opaline cock x Opaline hen**
= Opaline and Dark Green Opaline cocks
+ Dark Green Opaline cocks and hens

**Olive Opaline cock x Opaline hen**
= Dark Green Opaline cocks and hens

Olive Opaline Budgerigar.

### Dark Green Opaline cock x Dark Green Opaline hen

= Opaline cocks and hens
+ Dark Green Opaline cocks and hens
+ Olive Opaline cocks and hens

### Dark Green Opaline cock x Olive Opaline hen

= Dark Green Opaline cocks and hens
+ Olive Opaline cocks and hens

### Olive Opaline cock x Dark Green Opaline hen

= Dark Green Opaline cocks and hens
+ Olive Opaline cocks and hens

### Olive Opaline cock x Olive Opaline hen

= Olive Opaline cocks and hens

1. Dark Green Opaline Budgerigar.
2 & 3. (L to R) Green Opaline, Dark Green Opaline and Olive Opaline Peachfaced Lovebirds (front and rear views).
4. Olive Opaline Turquoise Parrot.

## Cobalt Opaline and Mauve Opaline

At present this combination is only possible in the Budgerigar, which is the only species with an Opaline, a Blue and an Olive gene. When it becomes possible in other species, the method employed will depend on which species, as other combinations will already be established. For instance, in the Red-rumped Parrot a Blue Opaline cock should be mated to an Olive hen (the new mutation), but in the Turquoise Parrot an Olive Opaline cock should be mated to a Blue hen (the new mutation in this species).

Cobalt Opaline Budgerigar.

There is one complication however: the Blue and Olive genes are linked on the one chromosome. Therefore, the percentage for combination is reduced. In Budgerigars the recombination frequency is 14% and I will use these figures for this section. The availability of either Cobalt or Mauve will greatly increase the rate at which the three-way combination can be produced. In fact, it is probably wise to combine the Olive gene with the Blue gene first, before trying to add other genes. The following results will hopefully highlight the trouble created by attempting to add the third gene before linking the Olive and Blue genes.

### Blue Opaline cock x Olive hen
= Dark Green/Blue/Opaline (Type 1) cocks
+ Dark Green Opaline/Blue (Type 1) hens

### Olive Opaline cock x Blue hen
= Dark Green/Blue/Opaline (Type 1) cocks
+ Dark Green Opaline/Blue (Type 1) hens

### Dark Green/Blue/Opaline (Type 1) cock x Blue Opaline hen
= 43% Dark Green/Blue/Opaline, Blue/Opaline, Dark Green Opaline/Blue
   or Blue Opaline cocks
+ 7% Green/Blue/Opaline, Cobalt/Opaline, Opaline/Blue or Cobalt Opaline cocks
+ 43% Dark Green/Blue, Blue, Dark Green Opaline/Blue or Blue Opaline hens
+ 7% Green/Blue, Cobalt, Opaline/Blue or Cobalt Opaline hens

### Dark Green/Blue/Opaline (Type 1) cock
### x Dark Green Opaline/Blue (Type 1) hen
= 37% Blue/Opaline, Dark Green/Blue/Opaline (Type 1), Olive/Opaline.
   Blue Opaline, Dark Green Opaline/Blue (Type 1) or Olive Opaline cocks
+ 12% Green/Blue/Opaline, Dark Green/Opaline, Cobalt/Opaline,
   Olive/Blue/Opaline, Opaline/Blue, Dark Green Opaline, Cobalt Opaline
   or Olive Opaline/Blue cocks
+ 1% Green/Opaline, Dark Green/Blue/Opaline (Type 2),
   Mauve/Opaline, Opaline, Dark Green Opaline/Blue (Type 2)
   or Mauve Opaline cocks
+ 37% Blue, Dark Green/Blue (Type 1), Olive, Blue Opaline,
   Dark Green Opaline/Blue (Type 1) or Olive Opaline hens
+ 12% Green/Blue, Dark Green, Cobalt, Olive/Blue, Opaline/Blue,
   Dark Green Opaline, Cobalt Opaline or Olive Opaline/Blue hens
+ 1% Green, Dark Green/Blue (Type 2), Mauve, Opaline,
   Dark Green Opaline/Blue (Type 2) or Mauve Opaline hens

Now, if you can understand that you should be writing this book. It took me over an hour to calculate all the outcomes and even then I had to correct it in the final proof!

All outcomes grouped after a percentage add together to give that percentage, but are not all equal in frequency. I have not calculated each outcome individually. For example, Mauve hens comprise 0.125% of outcomes and Dark Green/Blue/Opaline (Type 1) hens comprise 9.25% of total outcomes. However, the degree of detail given above shows the problem adequately. As you can see, for any particular colour produced, the genetics are not easy to document.

J SCULL

*Mauve Opaline Budgerigar.*

Therefore I recommend that the breeder start by combining the two linked genes – the Olive gene and the Blue gene. (Refer also to the section on Cobalt and Mauve mutations on page 153.) Once this is achieved, the Opaline gene can be introduced into the mix. Mate a Blue Opaline cock to a Mauve hen to begin.

**Blue Opaline cock x Mauve hen**
= Cobalt/Opaline cocks and Cobalt Opaline hens

**Blue Opaline cock x Cobalt Opaline hen**
= Blue Opaline cocks and hens
+ Cobalt Opaline cocks and hens

**Cobalt/Opaline cock x Mauve hen**
= Cobalt and Cobalt/Opaline cocks
+ Mauve and Mauve/Opaline hens

**Cobalt/Opaline cock x Blue Opaline hen**
= Blue/Opaline and Blue Opaline cocks
+ Cobalt/Opaline and Cobalt Opaline cocks
+ Blue and Blue Opaline hens
+ Cobalt and Cobalt Opaline hens

**Cobalt Opaline cock x Cobalt Opaline hen**
= Blue Opaline cocks and hens
+ Cobalt Opaline cocks and hens
+ Mauve Opaline cocks and hens

**Mauve Opaline cock x Cobalt Opaline hen**
= Cobalt Opaline cocks and hens
+ Mauve Opaline cocks and hens

**Cobalt Opaline cock x Mauve Opaline hen**
= Cobalt Opaline cocks and hens
+ Mauve Opaline cocks and hens

**Mauve Opaline cock x Blue Opaline hen**
= Cobalt Opaline cocks and hens

Now isn't that much easier!

### Visual Violet Opaline

To date, this combination can only be produced in the Budgerigar, but with time it may be possible in other species. Visual Violet requires the Violet gene in Single Factor, the Olive gene in Single Factor (ie Dark Green) and the Blue gene. Therefore with the Opaline added, we have a four-way combination. You would not attempt it without first having Visual Violet and Mauve Opaline combinations available for further matings. The Violet gene is dominant, as is the Olive gene, the Blue gene is recessive and finally we have a sex-linked gene in the form of Opaline. Quite a combination! Here are a few matings:

**Mauve Opaline cock x Visual Violet (Violet Cobalt) hen**
= Cobalt/Opaline and Mauve/Opaline cocks
+ Visual Violet/Opaline and Mauve Violet/Opaline cocks
+ Cobalt Opaline and Mauve Opaline hens
+ Visual Violet Opaline and Mauve Violet Opaline hens

**Visual Violet/Opaline cock x Mauve Opaline hen**
= Cobalt/Opaline and Mauve/Opaline cocks
+ Visual Violet/Opaline and Mauve Violet/Opaline cocks
+ Cobalt Opaline and Mauve Opaline cocks
+ Visual Violet Opaline and Mauve Violet Opaline cocks
+ Cobalt and Mauve hens
+ Cobalt Opaline and Mauve Opaline hens
+ Visual Violet and Mauve Violet hens
+ Visual Violet Opaline and Mauve Violet Opaline hens

*Visual Violet Opaline Budgerigar.*

**Visual Violet/Opaline cock x Cobalt Opaline hen**
= Blue/Opaline, Cobalt/Opaline and Mauve/Opaline cocks
+ Blue Violet/Opaline and Visual Violet/Opaline cocks
+ Blue Opaline, Cobalt Opaline and Mauve Opaline cocks
+ Blue Violet Opaline and Visual Violet Opaline cocks
+ Mauve Violet/Opaline cocks and Mauve Violet Opaline cocks
+ Blue, Cobalt and Mauve hens
+ Blue Opaline, Cobalt Opaline and Mauve Opaline hens
+ Blue Violet, Visual Violet and Mauve Violet hens
+ Blue Violet Opaline and Visual Violet Opaline hens
+ Mauve Violet Opaline hens

**Cobalt Opaline cock x Mauve Violet Opaline hen**
= Cobalt Opaline and Mauve Opaline cocks
+ Visual Violet Opaline and Mauve Violet Opaline cocks
+ Cobalt Opaline and Mauve Opaline hens
+ Visual Violet Opaline and Mauve Violet Opaline hens

**Mauve Opaline cock x Visual Violet Opaline hen**
= Cobalt Opaline and Mauve Opaline cocks
+ Visual Violet Opaline and Mauve Violet Opaline cocks
+ Cobalt Opaline and Mauve Opaline hens
+ Visual Violet Opaline and Mauve Violet Opaline hens

Double Factor (DF) Violet Blue also produces a violet colour. Therefore it would be simpler to produce a DF Violet Blue Opaline combination, but not as much fun!

### Grey Opaline

The three-way combination to produce a Grey Opaline is another combination currently restricted to Budgerigars but will be interesting when it occurs in other species.

### Addendum

*This combination is now possible in Red-rumped Parrots.*

You need to start with a Blue Opaline cock and a Grey (Greygreen Blue) hen. From there the process is straightforward, as the Grey gene is dominant.

**Blue Opaline cock x Grey hen**
= Blue/Opaline and Grey/Opaline cocks
+ Blue Opaline and Grey Opaline hens

**Grey/Opaline cock x Blue Opaline hen**
= Blue/Opaline and Grey/Opaline cocks
+ Blue Opaline and Grey Opaline cocks
+ Blue and Grey hens
+ Blue Opaline and Grey Opaline hens

*Grey Opaline Budgerigars.*

**Blue Opaline cock x Grey Opaline hen**
= Blue Opaline cocks and hens
+ Grey Opaline cocks and hens

### Cinnamon Blue Opaline – Ivory Opaline

This combination is currently creating interest in Red-rumped Parrots. It is also possible in Budgerigars and Cockatiels. Typical of Opaline combinations each species has its own unique appearance. The combination involves two sex-linked mutations and a recessive mutation. Therefore, although I have called it an Ivory Opaline, it is best to start with a Cinnamon Opaline cock. This can be mated to either an Ivory hen or a Blue Opaline hen.

*Above: Cinnamon Blue Opaline Red-rumped Parrot hen.*
*Left: Cinnamon Blue Opaline Red-rumped Parrot cock.*

*Cinnamon Blue Opaline Cockatiel – known as 'Whiteface Cinnamon Pearl'.*

*Cinnamon(wing) Blue Opaline Budgerigar.*

**Cinnamon Opaline cock x Blue Opaline hen**
= Opaline/Blue/Cinnamon cocks
+ Cinnamon Opaline/Blue hens

**Cinnamon Opaline cock x Ivory hen**
= Cinnamon/Blue/Opaline cocks
+ Cinnamon Opaline/Blue hens

**Ivory cock x Cinnamon Opaline/Blue hen**
= Cinnamon/Opaline/Blue and Ivory/Opaline cocks
+ Cinnamon/Blue and Ivory hens

**Blue Opaline cock x Cinnamon Opaline/Blue hen**
= Opaline/Blue/Cinnamon and Blue Opaline/Cinnamon cocks
+ Opaline/Blue and Blue Opaline hens

**Blue Opaline/Cinnamon cock x Cinnamon Opaline/Blue hen**
= Opaline/Blue/Cinnamon and Cinnamon Opaline/Blue cocks
+ Blue Opaline/Cinnamon and Ivory Opaline cocks
+ Opaline/Blue and Cinnamon Opaline/Blue hens
+ Blue Opaline and Ivory Opaline hens

**Ivory/Opaline cock x Cinnamon Opaline/Blue hen**
= Cinnamon/Blue/Opaline and Cinnamon Opaline/Blue cocks
+ Ivory/Opaline and Ivory Opaline cocks
+ Cinnamon/Blue and Cinnamon Opaline/Blue hens
+ Ivory and Ivory Opaline hens

**Cinnamon Opaline/Blue cock x Cinnamon Opaline/Blue hen**
= Cinnamon Opaline cocks and hens
+ Cinnamon Opaline/Blue cocks and hens
+ Ivory Opaline cocks and hens

**Cinnamon Opaline/Blue cock x Ivory Opaline hen**
= Cinnamon Opaline/Blue cocks and hens
+ Ivory Opaline cocks and hens

**Blue Opaline/Cinnamon cock x Ivory Opaline hen**
= Blue Opaline/Cinnamon and Ivory Opaline cocks
+ Blue Opaline and Ivory Opaline hens

**Ivory/Opaline cock x Ivory Opaline hen**
= Ivory/Opaline and Ivory Opaline cocks
+ Ivory and Ivory Opaline hens

### Creamino Opaline – Lutino Parblue Opaline
This combination is possible in Budgerigars, but with little exploration to date. It shows promise as a combination in other species such as the Cockatiel and the Red-rumped Parrot. Whilst the necessary mutations exist, they are not all present in Australia where we lack an established Paleface Cockatiel or a Parblue Red-rumped Parrot. These mutations are present in Europe and elsewhere, so will eventually be combined.

The combination involves two sex-linked genes and one recessive gene. The process imitates that used for the Ivory Opaline combination above. A Lutino Opaline cock is mated to a Creamino hen or a Parblue Opaline hen. In the above matings for Ivory Opaline, substitute Lutino for Cinnamon, Creamino for Ivory and Parblue for Blue.

### Cinnamon Lutino Opaline – Lacewing Opaline
This is one of those combinations which pose many questions for those of us interested in genetics. Some questions still need to be answered. Does this combination produce a visible difference to the Lutino gene on its own? Are they merely Lutino birds with pale cream suffusions?

To produce a three-way combination of sex-linked mutations is difficult and unpredictable in outcome. You need crossover to combine two, and then again to add the third, but you have to be certain that you

*Cinnamon Lutino Opaline (Pearl) Cockatiel.*

do not lose the original combination. Cinnamon and Lutino are the hardest to combine so you should start here first, by producing or buying a Cinnamon Lutino. This bird should be mated to an Opaline to produce triple split cocks – Green/Cinnamon-Lutino/Opaline. This should be mated to a Cinnamon Lutino hen for the following outcome:

**Green/Cinnamon-Lutino/Opaline cock x Cinnamon Lutino hen**
= 32.5% Green/Cinnamon-Lutino/Opaline and Cinnamon Lutino cocks
+ 16% Green/Cinnamon-Lutino and Cinnamon Lutino/Opaline cocks
+ 1.5% Cinnamon/Lutino, Cinnamon/Lutino/Opaline, Lutino/Cinnamon
  and Lutino/Cinnamon/Opaline cocks
+ 32.5% Opaline and Cinnamon Lutino hens
+ 16% Green and Cinnamon Lutino Opaline hens
+ 1.5% Cinnamon, Cinnamon Opaline, Lutino and Lutino Opaline hens

Test mate the Cinnamon Lutino cocks with matings to Opaline hens to find the ones split for Opaline, and then use them to produce the following:

**Cinnamon Lutino/Opaline cock x Opaline hen**
= Green/Cinnamon-Lutino and Opaline/Cinnamon-Lutino cocks
+ Cinnamon Lutino and Cinnamon Lutino Opaline hens

**Cinnamon Lutino/Opaline cock x Cinnamon Lutino Opaline hen**
= Cinnamon Lutino/Opaline and Cinnamon Lutino Opaline cocks
+ Cinnamon Lutino and Cinnamon Lutino Opaline hens

### Albino Opaline – Blue Lutino Opaline

We would expect this combination to look like a basic Albino. However, surprising things have happened when Lutino is combined with some mutations. In Cockatiels, birds that are believed to be Cinnamon Lutino Opaline Blue can be identified. These particular birds have basically a white plumage with a light cream suffusion. Are they Lacewing? Is the Opaline an important part of the puzzle?

### Silver Opaline – Dilute Blue Opaline

This combination is possible in Budgerigars, Cockatiels and Red-rumped Parrots. (Do not confuse this colour with the Cinnamon Blue Opaline. See page 187.) In Cockatiels they are known as Silver Whiteface Pearl. The Dilute gene reduces the grey pigments to a lighter, silver shade. The Blue gene removes all yellow pigment, making the effects of the Dilute gene more visible. Then in each species, the Opaline gene gives a unique appearance to all this.

It requires the breeder to combine two recessive mutations with a sex-linked mutation. Therefore it is best to start with either a Blue Opaline or a Dilute Opaline cock mated to a Silver (Dilute Blue) hen:

**Blue Opaline cock x Silver hen**
= Blue/Dilute/Opaline cocks and Blue Opaline/Dilute hens

**Dilute Opaline cock x Silver hen**
= Dilute/Blue/Opaline cocks and Dilute Opaline/Blue hens

**Blue/Dilute/Opaline cock x Silver hen**
= Blue/Dilute and Blue/Dilute/Opaline cocks
+ Silver and Silver/Opaline cocks
+ Blue/Dilute and Blue Opaline/Dilute hens
+ Silver and Silver Opaline hens

**Blue/Dilute/Opaline cock x Dilute Opaline/Blue hen**
= Green/Blue/Dilute/Opaline and Blue/Dilute/Opaline cocks
+ Dilute/Blue/Opaline and Silver/Opaline cocks
+ Opaline/Blue/Dilute and Blue Opaline/Dilute cocks
+ Dilute Opaline/Blue and Silver Opaline cocks
+ Green/Blue/Dilute, Blue/Dilute, Dilute/Blue and Silver hens
+ Opaline/Blue/Dilute and Blue Opaline/Dilute hens
+ Dilute Opaline/Blue and Silver Opaline hens

**Dilute/Blue/Opaline cock x Silver hen**
= Dilute/Blue and Dilute/Blue/Opaline cocks
+ Silver and Silver/Opaline cocks
+ Dilute/Blue and Dilute Opaline/Blue hens
+ Silver and Silver Opaline hens

### Dilute/Blue/Opaline cock x Blue Opaline/Dilute hen
= Green/Blue/Dilute/Opaline and Blue/Dilute/Opaline cocks
+ Dilute/Blue/Opaline and Silver/Opaline cocks
+ Opaline/Blue/Dilute and Blue Opaline/Dilute cocks
+ Dilute Opaline/Blue and Silver Opaline cocks
+ Green/Blue/Dilute, Blue/Dilute, Dilute/Blue and Silver hens
+ Opaline/Blue/Dilute and Blue Opaline/Dilute hens
+ Dilute Opaline/Blue and Silver Opaline hens

### Dilute Opaline/Blue cock x Blue Opaline/Dilute hen
= Opaline/Blue/Dilute and Blue Opaline/Dilute cocks and hens
+ Dilute Opaline/Blue and Silver Opaline cocks and hens

### Blue Opaline/Dilute cock x Dilute Opaline/Blue hen
= Opaline/Blue/Dilute and Blue Opaline/Dilute cocks
+ Dilute Opaline/Blue and Silver Opaline cocks
+ Opaline/Blue/Dilute and Blue Opaline/Dilute hens
+ Dilute Opaline/Blue and Silver Opaline hens

### Dilute Opaline/Blue cock x Silver Opaline hen
= Dilute Opaline/Blue and Silver Opaline cocks and hens

### Blue Opaline/Dilute cock x Silver Opaline hen
= Blue Opaline/Dilute cocks and hens
+ Silver Opaline cocks and hens

### Silver/Opaline cock x Silver Opaline hen
= Silver/Opaline and Silver Opaline cocks
+ Silver and Silver Opaline hens

### *Fawn Opaline – Cinnamon Greygreen Blue Opaline*
This four-way combination remains theoretical in all species except Budgerigars at this stage, although in Cockatiels (a species where the Grey gene is the natural state) the Cinnamon Whiteface Pearl is the equivalent of a Fawn Opaline. *This combination is now possible in Red-rumped Parrots.*

To produce it, mate an Ivory Opaline (Cinnamon Blue Opaline) cock to either a Fawn hen or a Grey Opaline hen. Some matings include:

*Cinnamon(wing) Greygreen Opaline Budgerigar – one step short of the Fawn Opaline colour.*

### Ivory Opaline cock x Grey hen
= Blue/Cinnamon-Opaline and Grey/Cinnamon-Opaline cocks
+ Ivory Opaline and Fawn Opaline hens

### Ivory Opaline cock x Fawn hen
= Ivory/Opaline and Fawn/Opaline cocks
+ Ivory Opaline and Fawn Opaline hens

### Ivory Opaline cock x Grey Opaline hen
= Blue Opaline/Cinnamon and Grey Opaline/Cinnamon cocks
+ Ivory Opaline and Fawn Opaline hens

**Grey Opaline/Cinnamon cock x Ivory Opaline hen**
= Blue Opaline/Cinnamon and Ivory Opaline cocks
+ Grey Opaline/Cinnamon and Fawn Opaline cocks
+ Blue Opaline and Ivory Opaline hens
+ Grey Opaline and Fawn Opaline hens

**Grey/Cinnamon-Opaline cock x Ivory Opaline hen**
= 33.5% Blue/Cinnamon-Opaline, Grey/Cinnamon-Opaline, Ivory Opaline
and Fawn Opaline cocks
+ 16.5% Ivory/Opaline, Fawn/Opaline, Blue Opaline/Cinnamon
and Grey Opaline/Cinnamon cocks
+ 33.5% Blue, Grey, Ivory Opaline and Fawn Opaline hens
+ 16.5% Ivory, Fawn, Blue Opaline and Grey Opaline hens

**Fawn/Opaline cock x Ivory Opaline hen**
= Ivory/Opaline, Fawn/Opaline, Ivory Opaline and Fawn Opaline cocks
+ Ivory, Fawn, Ivory Opaline and Fawn Opaline hens

**Fawn Opaline cock x Ivory Opaline hen**
= Ivory Opaline cocks and hens
+ Fawn Opaline cocks and hens

## Pied Combinations

Pied mutations can be combined with any other mutation or combination of mutations, effectively doubling possible combinations for the species. However, the impact of the Pied gene is greatest when combined with dark mutations, thereby reducing the desirability of combinations with mutations such as Dilute, Suffused, Lime, Fallow and even Cinnamon (in some species). Combination with the Lutino gene is totally pointless except perhaps for genetic study.

The action of Pied mutations is to cause intermittent deposition of the grey family pigments. This results in green areas becoming yellow and blue areas becoming white. One class of Pied mutation also prevents the expression of the sexual dimorphism of the species. This class therefore has unexpected, but predictable effects on colours other than just the grey family pigments. The effects are unique to the species concerned.

There are multiple different genes that cause pied effects; therefore the genetics of combinations involving Pieds vary depending on which Pied mutation is used. I will discuss matings for Pieds in two basic classes, Dominant Pieds and Recessive Pieds.

H KREMER

*Cinnamon Dilute Opaline Dominant Pied Eastern Rosella.*

J SCULL

*Cinnamon(wing) Blue Opaline Dominant Pied Budgerigar.*

Above: Cinnamon Blue Opaline Pied Cockatiel – generally known as Cinnamon 'Whiteface Pearl' Pied.
Below: Parblue Opaline Pied Cockatiel.

Platinum Pied Red-rumped Parrot.

Blue Opaline Pied Cockatiel – generally known as 'Whiteface Pearl' Pied.

## Dark Green Pied and Olive Pied

In my opinion, Pieds look best when their contrast is emphasised most. Therefore a mutation that deepens the colour of the bird such as the Olive gene creates an attractive Pied combination.

Producing the **Dark Green Recessive Pied** and the **Olive Recessive Pied** involves combining a co-dominant gene with a recessive gene. Therefore the sexes used are irrelevant. Starting with an Olive (if possible) and a Pied you will produce all Dark Green/Pied young. These should then be mated back to Pied for the following outcomes:

**Dark Green/Pied x Pied**
= Green/Pied and Pied
+ Dark Green/Pied and Dark Green Pied

**Dark Green/Pied x Dark Green Pied**
= Green/Pied and Pied
+ Dark Green/Pied and Dark Green Pied
+ Olive/Pied and Olive Pied

**Dark Green/Pied x Olive Pied**
= Dark Green/Pied and Dark Green Pied
+ Olive/Pied and Olive Pied

**Dark Green Pied x Olive/Pied**
= Dark Green/Pied and Dark Green Pied
+ Olive/Pied and Olive Pied

R CUSICK

ABK

Dark Green Recessive Pied Budgerigar.

Producing the **Dark Green Dominant Pied** and the **Olive Dominant Pied** involves combining a co-dominant gene and a dominant gene, which makes it one of the easiest tasks possible. The sex of the birds is once again irrelevant.

**Olive x Pied (SF)**
= Dark Green and Dark Green Pied (SF)

**Dark Green Pied (SF) x Olive**
= Dark Green and Dark Green Pied (SF)
+ Olive and Olive Pied (SF)

**Dark Green Pied (SF) x Dark Green Pied (SF)**
= Green, Pied (SF) and Pied (DF)
+ Dark Green, Dark Green Pied (SF) and
  Dark Green Pied (DF)
+ Olive, Olive Pied (SF) and Olive Pied (DF)

*Olive Dominant Pied Peachfaced Lovebird.*

**Olive Pied (SF) x Dark Green**
= Dark Green and Dark Green Pied (SF)
+ Olive and Olive Pied (SF)

### Greygreen Pied

The combination of the Grey gene with a Pied gene is also attractive, although adding a Blue gene as well to produce a Grey Pied is probably even more attractive.

For the **Greygreen Recessive Pied** combination, the breeder must combine a dominant gene with a recessive gene. If possible, use Double Factor (DF) Greygreen.

**Greygreen (DF) x Pied**
= Greygreen (SF)/Pied

**Greygreen (SF) x Pied**
= Green/Pied and Greygreen (SF)/Pied

**Greygreen (SF)/Pied x Pied**
= Green/Pied and Pied
+ Greygreen (SF)/Pied and Greygreen (SF) Pied

**Greygreen (SF) Pied x Greygreen (SF)/Pied**
= Green/Pied and Pied
+ Greygreen (SF)/Pied and Greygreen (SF) Pied
+ Greygreen (DF)/Pied and Greygreen (DF) Pied

*Above: Greygreen Recessive Pied Rainbow Lorikeet – this bird is actually a visual split. Above left: Greygreen Recessive Pied Budgerigar.*

For the **Greygreen Dominant Pied** combination, we are combining two dominant genes which is the easiest combination possible.

**Greygreen (DF) x Pied (DF)**
= Greygreen (SF) Pied (SF)

**Greygreen (SF) x Pied (SF)**
= Green, Pied (SF), Greygreen (SF) and Greygreen (SF) Pied (SF)

**Greygreen (DF) x Pied (SF)**
= Greygreen (SF) and Greygreen (SF) Pied (SF)

**Greygreen (SF) x Pied (DF)**
= Pied (SF) and Greygreen (SF) Pied (SF)

**Greygreen (SF) Pied (SF) x Greygreen (SF) Pied (SF)**
= Green, Pied (SF), Pied (DF), Greygreen (SF) and Greygreen (SF) Pied (SF)
+ Greygreen (SF) Pied (DF), Greygreen (DF) and Greygreen (DF) Pied (SF)
+ Greygreen (DF) Pied (DF)

*Greygreen Dominant Pied Budgerigar.*

### Blue Pied

In my opinion the Blue Pied combination is probably the most attractive of the Pied combinations. The action of the Blue gene, to remove all yellow family pigments from the plumage, results in pied areas becoming white instead of yellow as well as changing green areas into blue. The contrast of blue and white tends to highlight the breaks in colour created by the Pied gene, which is the feature that appeals to the human eye.

To produce a **Blue Recessive Pied** combination, the breeder must combine two recessive genes. As mentioned earlier, this is what is known as a dihybrid cross. Mating a Blue to a Pied produces only Green/Blue/Pied. These are mated together to produce the following:

**Green/Blue/Pied x Green/Blue/Pied**
= Green, Green/Blue, Green/Pied and Green/Blue/Pied
+ Blue, Blue/Pied, Pied and Pied/Blue
+ Blue Pied

*Blue Pied Indian Ringnecked Parrot.*

However Blue Pied comprise only 1:16 young so you need to test mate the Pied and the Blue young to find those split for the other gene which will then allow other matings to increase Blue Pied outcomes.

*Blue Pied Fischer's Lovebird.*

*Blue Dominant (Dutch) Pied Budgerigar.*

*Blue Pied Crimson Rosella.*

*Blue Pied Red-rumped Parrot.*

**Blue/Pied x Pied**
= Green/Pied/Blue and Pied/Blue

**Pied/Blue x Blue**
= Green/Blue/Pied and Blue/Pied

**Pied/Blue x Blue/Pied**
= Green/Blue/Pied, Blue/Pied, Pied/Blue and Blue Pied

**Pied/Blue x Blue Pied**
= Pied/Blue and Blue Pied

**Blue/Pied x Blue Pied**
= Blue/Pied and Blue Pied

Of course the **Blue Dominant Pied** is much simpler to produce. Use a Double Factor Pied if possible to give all Pied (SF)/Blue. Then mate these as follows:

**Pied (SF)/Blue x Blue**
= Green/Blue, Blue, Pied (SF)/Blue and Blue Pied (SF)

**Blue Pied (SF) x Blue**
= Blue and Blue Pied (SF)

**Blue Pied (SF) x Pied (SF)/Blue**
= Green/Blue, Blue, Pied (SF)/Blue and Blue Pied (SF)
+ Pied (DF)/Blue and Blue Pied (DF)

**Blue Pied (SF) x Blue Pied (SF)**
= Blue, Blue Pied (SF) and Blue Pied (DF)

*Blue (Whiteface) Pied Cockatiel.*

*Parblue Pied Cockatiel –
incorrectly called
'Pastelface' Pied.*

*Parblue (Yellowface)
Dominant Pied Budgerigar.*

*Turquoise Dominant Pied
Peachfaced Lovebird.*

*Aqua Dominant Pied
Peachfaced Lovebird.*

*Turquoise ADM Pied Red-
rumped Parrot – note the
yellow pigment across the
back of the bird which
distinguishes this bird from
the Blue Pied.*

## Parblue Pied

The Parblue Pied combination is definitely worth producing. The outcome is a bird part way between a Green Pied and a Blue Pied in colour. The process is the same as that for producing Blue Pied, unless Blue Pied is already available, in which case a short cut can be taken.

For the **Parblue Recessive Pied** the following matings are useful:

**Parblue x Blue Pied**
= ParblueBlue/Pied

**ParblueBlue/Pied x Blue Pied**
= Blue/Pied, Blue Pied, ParblueBlue/Pied and ParblueBlue Pied

**ParblueBlue Pied x Blue Pied**
= Blue Pied and ParblueBlue Pied

**ParblueBlue Pied x ParblueBlue Pied**
= Blue Pied, ParblueBlue Pied and Parblue Pied

For the **Parblue Dominant Pied** combination, the following matings can be used:

**Parblue x Blue Pied (SF)**
= ParblueBlue and ParblueBlue Pied (SF)

### ParblueBlue Pied (SF) x Blue Pied (SF)
= Blue, Blue Pied (SF) and Blue Pied (DF)
+ ParblueBlue, ParblueBlue Pied (SF) and ParblueBlue Pied (DF)

### ParblueBlue Pied (SF) x ParblueBlue Pied (SF)
= Blue, Blue Pied (SF) and Blue Pied (DF)
+ ParblueBlue, ParblueBlue Pied (SF) and ParblueBlue Pied (DF)
+ Parblue, Parblue Pied (SF) and Parblue Pied (DF)

### ParblueBlue Pied (SF) x Parblue Pied (DF)
= ParblueBlue Pied (SF) and ParblueBlue Pied (DF)
+ Parblue Pied (SF) and Parblue Pied (DF)

P TOMAS

### *Cobalt Pied and Mauve Pied*

Cobalt Pied and Mauve Pied are beautiful combinations that are well worth producing. As the Blue gene is linked to the Olive gene, it is best to use Mauve or Cobalt to start with, mated to Blue Pied if possible.

To produce a **Cobalt Recessive Pied** combination, the breeder can use the following matings:

*Cobalt Recessive Pied Budgerigar.*

### Mauve x Pied
= Dark Green/Blue/Pied (Type 2)

### Dark Green/Blue/Pied (Type 2) x Pied
= 86% Green/Pied, Pied, Dark Green/Blue/Pied (Type 2)
   and Dark Green Pied/Blue (Type 2)
+ 14% Green/Blue/Pied, Pied/Blue, Dark Green/Pied and Dark Green Pied

### Dark Green Pied/Blue (Type 2) x Mauve
= 86% Dark Green/Blue/Pied (Type 2) and Mauve/Pied
+ 14% Olive/Blue/Pied and Cobalt/Pied

### Mauve x Blue Pied
= Cobalt/Pied

### Cobalt/Pied x Blue Pied
= Blue/Pied, Blue Pied, Cobalt/Pied and Cobalt Pied

### Mauve/Pied x Blue Pied
= Cobalt/Pied and Cobalt Pied

### Cobalt Pied x Cobalt Pied
= Blue Pied, Cobalt Pied and Mauve Pied

ABK

J SCULL

Y IMANOTHAI

*Right: Cobalt Dominant Pied Budgerigar.*

*Far right (top): Double Dark Factor Turquoise (Mauve) Dominant Pied Peachfaced Lovebird.*

*Far right (bottom): Dark Factor Turquoise (Cobalt) Dominant Pied Peachfaced Lovebird.*

For the **Cobalt Dominant Pied**, the following matings are useful. Of course it is always best to start with a double factor Pied if possible.

**Mauve x Pied (DF)**
= Dark Green Pied (SF)/Blue (Type 2)

**Dark Green Pied (SF)/Blue (Type 2) x Mauve**
= 86% Dark Green/Blue (Type 2) and Dark Green Pied (SF)/Blue (Type 2)
+ Mauve and Mauve Pied (SF)
+ 14% Olive/Blue, Olive Pied (SF)/Blue, Cobalt and Cobalt Pied (SF)

**Mauve x Blue Pied (DF)**
= Cobalt Pied (SF)

**Cobalt Pied (SF) x Mauve**
= Cobalt, Cobalt Pied (SF), Mauve and Mauve Pied (SF)

### Grey Pied

The Grey Pied combination produces probably the ultimate in contrast for a Pied. At the time of writing this combination is only possible in the Budgerigar and the Indian Ringnecked Parrot. However, there is no doubt that other species will soon join the list. *This combination is now possible in Red-rumped Parrots.* This is a three-way combination involving the recessive Blue gene, the dominant Grey gene and one of the Pied genes. Of course the Cockatiel is a natural Grey gene, therefore the Whiteface Pied is the equivalent of the Grey Pied in other species.

To produce a **Grey Recessive Pied** it is best to use a Blue Pied and a Grey (Greygreen Blue) to start with.

**Grey (SF) x Blue Pied**
= Blue/Pied and Grey (SF)/Pied

**Grey (SF)/Pied x Blue Pied**
= Blue/Pied, Blue Pied, Grey (SF)/Pied and Grey (SF) Pied

**Grey (SF) Pied x Blue Pied**
= Blue Pied and Grey (SF) Pied

Grey Recessive Pied
Budgerigar.

Grey (Dominant Dutch)
Pied Budgerigar.

Grey (Dominant Australian)
Pied Budgerigar.

For the **Grey Dominant Pied**, the process is very simple if Blue Pieds are available.

**Grey (SF) x Blue Pied (SF)**
= Blue, Blue Pied (SF), Grey (SF) and Grey (SF) Pied (SF)

**Grey (SF) Pied (SF) x Blue Pied (SF)**
= Blue, Blue Pied (SF) and Blue Pied (DF)
+ Grey (SF), Grey (SF) Pied (SF) and Grey (SF) Pied (DF)

**Grey (SF) Pied (SF) x Grey (SF) Pied (SF)**
= Blue, Blue Pied (SF) and Blue Pied (DF)
+ Grey (SF), Grey (SF) Pied (SF) and Grey (SF) Pied (DF)
+ Grey (DF), Grey (DF) Pied (SF) and Grey (DF) Pied (DF)

### Visual Violet Pied

Visual Violet Pied is a four-way combination between the co-dominant Violet gene, the co-dominant Olive gene, the recessive Blue gene and one of the Pied genes. To produce it with any ease, it is essential that you start with a Visual Violet (Violet Cobalt) and a Blue Pied, or perhaps even a Cobalt Pied or Mauve Pied.

For the **Visual Violet Recessive Pied**, use the following matings:

Visual Violet (Recessive) Pied Budgerigar.

Turquoise Visual Violet Dominant Pied Peachfaced Lovebird.

**Visual Violet x Blue Pied**
= Blue/Pied, Cobalt/Pied, Violet Blue/Pied and Visual Violet/Pied

**Visual Violet x Cobalt Pied**
= Blue/Pied, Cobalt/Pied and Mauve/Pied
+ Violet Blue/Pied, Visual Violet/Pied and Violet Mauve/Pied

**Visual Violet x Mauve Pied**
= Cobalt/Pied, Mauve/Pied, Visual Violet/Pied and Violet Mauve/Pied

**Visual Violet/Pied x Blue Pied**
= Blue/Pied, Blue Pied, Cobalt/Pied, Cobalt Pied and Violet Blue/Pied
+ Visual Violet/Pied, Violet Blue Pied and Visual Violet Pied

**Visual Violet/Pied x Cobalt Pied**
= Blue/Pied, Blue Pied, Cobalt/Pied, Cobalt Pied and Mauve/Pied
+ Mauve Pied, Violet Blue/Pied, Visual Violet/Pied and Violet Mauve/Pied
+ Violet Blue Pied, Visual Violet Pied and Violet Mauve Pied

**Visual Violet/Pied x Mauve Pied**
= Cobalt/Pied, Cobalt Pied, Mauve/Pied, Mauve Pied and Visual Violet/Pied
+ Violet Mauve/Pied, Visual Violet Pied and Violet Mauve Pied

For the **Visual Violet Dominant Pied**, use the following matings:

### Visual Violet x Blue Pied (SF)
= Blue, Blue Pied (SF), Cobalt, Cobalt Pied (SF) and Violet Blue
+ Violet Blue Pied (SF), Visual Violet and Visual Violet Pied (SF)

### Visual Violet x Cobalt Pied (SF)
= Blue, Blue Pied (SF), Cobalt, Cobalt Pied (SF), Mauve and Mauve Pied (SF)
+ Violet Blue, Violet Blue Pied (SF), Visual Violet and Visual Violet Pied (SF)
+ Violet Mauve and Violet Mauve Pied (SF)

### Visual Violet x Mauve Pied (SF)
= Cobalt, Cobalt Pied (SF), Mauve, Mauve Pied (SF) and Visual Violet
+ Visual Violet Pied (SF), Violet Mauve and Violet Mauve Pied (SF)

### Visual Violet x Mauve Pied (DF)
= Cobalt Pied (SF) and Mauve Pied (SF)
+ Visual Violet Pied (SF) and Violet Mauve Pied (SF)

*Note: Remember that in all cases Single Factor Violets are being used.*

## Cinnamon Pied

The attractiveness of the Cinnamon Pied varies with each species, depending on the depth of colour of Cinnamon for each species. The combination is at its best when the species displays a rich cinnamon colour.

For the **Cinnamon Recessive Pied** combination, the breeder must combine a sex-linked mutation with a recessive mutation. Therefore it is best to mate a Cinnamon cock to a Pied hen. This will give Green/Cinnamon/Pied cocks and Cinnamon/Pied hens. These Cinnamon/Pied hens should be mated to Pied cocks to produce the following:

### Pied cock x Cinnamon/Pied hen
= Green/Cinnamon/Pied and Pied/Cinnamon cocks
+ Green/Pied and Pied hens

*Above: Cinnamon Pied Cockatiel.*
*Right: Cinnamon Recessive Pied Elegant Parrot.*
*Far right: Cinnamon Dominant Pied Elegant Parrot.*

*Turquoise Cinnamon Pied Peachfaced Lovebird.*

*Cinnamon Pied Red-rumped Parrot.*

*Cinnamon Pied Crimson Rosella.*

The Pied/Cinnamon cocks should be selected and mated to Cinnamon/Pied hens for the following:

### Pied/Cinnamon cock x Cinnamon/Pied hen
= Green/Cinnamon/Pied, Pied/Cinnamon, Cinnamon/Pied and Cinnamon Pied cocks
+ Green/Pied, Pied, Cinnamon/Pied and Cinnamon Pied hens

### Pied/Cinnamon cock x Cinnamon Pied hen
= Pied/Cinnamon and Cinnamon Pied cocks
+ Pied and Cinnamon Pied hens

For the **Cinnamon Dominant Pied** combination, the breeder is combining a sex-linked mutation with a dominant mutation, so it is best to use a Cinnamon cock and if possible a Double Factor Pied hen.

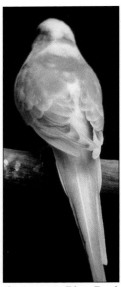

*Cinnamon Blue Pied Red-rumped Parrot.*

### Cinnamon cock x Pied (SF) hen
= Green/Cinnamon and Pied (SF)/Cinnamon cocks
+ Cinnamon and Cinnamon Pied (SF) hens

### Cinnamon cock x Pied (DF) hen
= Pied (SF)/Cinnamon cocks and Cinnamon Pied (SF) hens

### Pied (SF)/Cinnamon cock x Cinnamon hen
= Green/Cinnamon, Cinnamon, Pied (SF)/Cinnamon and Cinnamon Pied (SF) cocks
+ Green, Cinnamon, Pied (SF) and Cinnamon Pied (SF) hens

### Pied (SF)/Cinnamon cock x Cinnamon Pied (SF) hen
= Green/Cinnamon, Cinnamon and Pied (SF)/Cinnamon cocks
+ Cinnamon Pied (SF), Pied (DF)/Cinnamon and Cinnamon Pied (DF) cocks
+ Green, Cinnamon, Pied (SF) and Cinnamon Pied (SF) hens
+ Pied (DF) and Cinnamon Pied (DF) hens

ABK

G ROMAN

*Mauve Opaline Pied Budgerigar.*

*Opaline Pied Cockatiel.*

### Opaline Pied

There has been little experimentation with Opaline Pied combinations to date. As the Opaline gene removes much of the grey family pigments from the bird, there is less left for the Pied gene to work upon. Nevertheless breeders will want to try the combination.

As the Opaline is a sex-linked mutation, the matings used for Cinnamon Pied above can be used, by substituting the Opaline mutation for the Cinnamon mutation.

### Other Pieds

Many people will want to explore combinations of Pied with mutations other than those listed in this book. As stated previously, many people feel that the lighter colour mutations do not make appealing Pieds. However, others like to explore the subtleties of colours produced. As it is a physical impossibility to include every mating in this book, readers who want to breed Fallow Pied or Dilute Pieds, should use the matings for Blue Pied substituting the desired mutation for the Blue gene. (See page 195.) This will also apply to any other recessive gene combined with Pied.

If you wish to combine the Pied gene with a sex-linked mutation, such as a Lime Pied or Platinum Pied, then use the matings listed for Cinnamon Pied above.

## Spangle Combinations

At present the Spangle mutation only exists in the Budgerigar. However it may appear in other species such as rosellas that have the black scalloping on their backs.

P TOMAS

ABK

ABK

*Above: Violet Spangle Budgerigar.*
*Left: Spangle Blue Opaline Budgerigar.*
*Far left: Goldenface Blue Spangle Budgerigar.*

*Page 203*

D VAN DEN ABEELE    D VAN DEN ABEELE    Y IMANOTHAI

*Above: Dominant Edged (SF) Dark Green Fischer's Lovebird.*
*Above centre: Dominant Edged (DF) Dark Green Fischer's Lovebird.*
*Above right: Dominant Edged (SF) Olive Fischer's Lovebird (bird at top).*
*Right: Dominant Edged (DF) Violet Fischer's Lovebird.*

Y IMANOTHAI

When trying to combine Spangle with other mutations it is important to remember that it is a co-dominant mutation and that when the bird carries two genes, it becomes visually a Black-eyed Yellow. If these Double Factor birds are available, they are the best starting place for combining with other mutations. The best combinations are those involving the darker colours, mostly mutations which alter yellow family pigments or structural colours. (See also page 101.)

## Yellowface Combinations

Although the Yellowface is an established sex-linked Cockatiel mutation it is not yet common in Australia. It could be combined with any mutation except the Blue, as the Blue gene removes all yellow family pigments leaving nothing for the Yellowface gene to work upon.

To combine the mutation with any other mutation, find a combination in this book between the desired mutation and another sex-linked gene (such as Cinnamon or Lutino), then substitute in the Yellowface gene for the sex-linked gene.

This rule cannot apply to other sex-linked genes in combination with Yellowface, as a gene linkage will occur and crossover will be necessary to produce the combined mutations. The percentage of recombination is unknown at present and, as the gene does not exist in any other species, I cannot extrapolate. From the point of view of genetics, it is an interesting mutation to explore.

## Orangeface Combinations

The Orangeface is another single species mutation, which only exists in the Peachfaced Lovebird. Like the Yellowface in the Cockatiel, it can be combined with any other mutation except the Blue gene. It does combine with the Parblue gene with noticeable effect.

It is co-dominant in inheritance, with Single Factor birds detectable (and often considered splits). However, the Double Factor bird is required for the full colour to be produced. When combined with the Parblue mutation, the combination has a yellow face because the change in yellow family pigments caused by the Parblue

Y IMANOTHAI

*Orangeface Olive Pied Peachfaced Lovebird.*

R ERHART

R WEBB

L BRANDT

Y IMANOTHAI

R ERHART

Y IMANOTHAI

1. Orangeface Lutino Peachfaced Lovebird – note that the yellow body colour is unaffected.
2. Orangeface Double Dark Factor (Olive) Applegreen Peachfaced Lovebird.
3. Orangeface Olive Opaline Peachfaced Lovebird – this young bird has not moulted into full Opaline colour yet.
4. Orangeface Olive Peachfaced Lovebird.
5. Orangeface (Edged) Dilute Peachfaced Lovebird.
6. Orangeface Olive Lime (Pallid) (above) and Orangeface Olive Pied (below) Peachfaced Lovebirds.
7. Orangeface Aqua (Parblue) Peachfaced Lovebird – commonly called 'Yellowface Blue'.
8. Orangeface Dark Lime (Pallid) Peachfaced Lovebird.

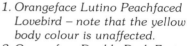

Y IMANOTHAI

Y IMANOTHAI

complements the change created by the Orangeface. In this combination detecting Single Factor birds is more difficult, reinforcing the idea that Orangeface is a recessive trait instead of co-dominant.

Creating Orangeface combinations is no different from combining any other co-dominant mutation with the one you wish. I give the following matings for Orangeface and Parblue as examples of some outcomes. Sexes are irrelevant in these matings.

**Parblue x Orangeface (DF)**
= split Orangeface (SF) Green/Parblue

**split Orangeface (SF) Green/Parblue x Parblue**
= Green/Parblue and Parblue
+ split Orangeface (SF) Green/Parblue and split Orangeface (SF) Parblue

**split Orangeface (SF) Green/Parblue x split Orangeface (SF) Parblue**
= Green/Parblue and Parblue
+ split Orangeface (SF) Green/Parblue and split Orangeface (SF) Parblue
+ Orangeface (DF) Green/Parblue and Orangeface (DF) Parblue

**split Orangeface (SF) Parblue x split Orangeface (SF) Parblue**
= Parblue, split Orangeface (SF) Parblue and Orangeface (DF) Parblue

**split Orangeface (SF) Parblue x Orangeface (DF) Parblue**
= split Orangeface (SF) Parblue and Orangeface (DF) Parblue

## Melanistic Combinations

Melanistic mutations are a new group to be explored and examples exist in only four species of parrots at this stage. Therefore possible combinations are currently limited. To date, the only combination produced has been the Cinnamon Black Eastern Rosella. *Melanistic mutations have now been combined with Greygreen in lorikeets and other colours in Budgerigars!*

However the Melanistic mutation would theoretically combine with any other mutation except the Lutino mutation, although breeders are even attempting this combination. Who knows, they may be proved to be justified in trying it. As every species is unique, the outcome for each combination always varies at least slightly for each species.

Lutino Melanistic Eastern Rosella – a surprising outcome for an unusual combination.

Melanistic (Blackface) Cobalt Budgerigar.

Melanistic (Blackface) Blue Budgerigar.

Currently, the Melanistic gene can be combined with Cinnamon, Opaline and Dilute in the Eastern Rosella and Dilute and Greygreen in the Rainbow Lorikeet. No doubt other mutations will appear in these two species. Melanistic genes may also appear in other species as well. The Melanistic gene in the Budgerigar could theoretically be combined with dozens of other mutations and combinations, some of which are only just being explored. Following are some matings for the possible combinations available at present.

### Cinnamon Melanistic – Cinnamon Black

Currently only possible in the Eastern Rosella and the Budgerigar, this combination involves a sex-linked mutation and a recessive mutation. It is an ideal combination in that the two genes complement each other. The Cinnamon gene alters grey pigment to brown pigment and changes black pigment to darker brown. The Melanistic gene increases the amount of grey pigment that can be worked upon by the Cinnamon gene.

P RANKINE

*Cinnamon Melanistic (R) and Cinnamon Opaline Melanistic (L) Eastern Rosellas.*

Mate a Cinnamon cock to a Melanistic hen to produce Normal/Cinnamon/Melanistic cocks and Cinnamon/Melanistic hens. Then mate a Melanistic cock to a Cinnamon/Melanistic hen to produce the following outcomes:

**Melanistic cock x Cinnamon/Melanistic hen**
= Normal/Cinnamon and Melanistic/Cinnamon cocks
+ Normal and Melanistic hens

**Melanistic/Cinnamon cock x Cinnamon/Melanistic hen**
= Normal/Cinnamon/Melanistic cocks and Normal/Melanistic hens
+ Cinnamon/Melanistic cocks and hens
+ Melanistic/Cinnamon cocks and Melanistic hens
+ Cinnamon Melanistic cocks and hens

**Melanistic/Cinnamon cock x Melanistic hen**
= Melanistic cocks and hens
+ Melanistic/Cinnamon cocks
+ Cinnamon Melanistic hens

**Cinnamon/Melanistic cock x Melanistic hen**
= Normal/Cinnamon/Melanistic and Melanistic/Cinnamon cocks
+ Cinnamon/Melanistic and Cinnamon Melanistic hens

**Cinnamon/Melanistic cock x Cinnamon/Melanistic hen**
= Cinnamon cocks and hens
+ Cinnamon/Melanistic cocks and hens
+ Cinnamon Melanistic cocks and hens

**Cinnamon/Melanistic cock x Cinnamon Melanistic hen**
= Cinnamon/Melanistic cocks and hens
+ Cinnamon Melanistic cocks and hens

**Melanistic/Cinnamon cock x Cinnamon Melanistic hen**
= Melanistic/Cinnamon cocks and Melanistic hens
+ Cinnamon Melanistic cocks and hens

### Dilute Melanistic

The Dilute Melanistic combination is currently possible in three species, the Budgerigar, the Rainbow Lorikeet and the Eastern Rosella, although the Dilute Eastern Rosella is rare in Australia. The Dilute is common in the Rainbow Lorikeet but has been incorrectly called Cinnamon.

The Dilute gene combines reasonably well with the Melanistic gene, reducing pigmented areas to a silvery colour. This is less noticeable in the Rainbow Lorikeet because of the nature of the Melanistic mutation in that species but will become visible when the Blue mutation recurs and can be included in the combination. The Greygreen mutation is another useful addition to this combination.

Producing the Dilute Melanistic involves combining two recessive mutations, therefore the process is a slow one. The sexes involved are irrelevant. Start by mating a Dilute to a Melanistic bird to produce double splits. These should be mated together for the following outcome:

**Normal/Dilute/Melanistic x Normal/Dilute/Melanistic**
= Normal, Normal/Dilute, Normal/Melanistic and Normal/Dilute/Melanistic
+ Dilute and Dilute/Melanistic
+ Melanistic and Melanistic/Dilute
+ Dilute Melanistic

As with other matings involving double splits, the desired outcome is only 1:16 of the youngsters produced and many young have little use for further matings. To increase the odds of producing the desired youngsters, test mate the Dilute and Melanistic young to find those split for the other mutation. Then use these birds in the following matings:

**Dilute/Melanistic x Melanistic/Dilute**
= Normal/Dilute/Melanistic, Dilute/Melanistic and Melanistic/Dilute
+ Dilute Melanistic

**Dilute/Melanistic x Dilute Melanistic**
= Dilute/Melanistic and Dilute Melanistic

**Melanistic/Dilute x Dilute Melanistic**
= Melanistic/Dilute and Dilute Melanistic

(For further information, read earlier sections on combining two recessive mutations, eg White. See page 125.)

### Greygreen Melanistic

This combination is possible in the Budgerigar and the Rainbow Lorikeet at present. In the Budgerigar it should produce a darker greygreen colour than the regular greygreen colour, along with the black face feature. In the Rainbow Lorikeet, as the Melanistic mutation extends areas of body colour only, the other areas of the bird will not vary from the Greygreen bird alone. In both species, the three-way combination including a Blue mutation

*Melanistic (Blackface) Grey Budgerigar – the next step after Greygreen is to add Blue and produce this colour.*

*Greygreen Melanistic Rainbow Lorikeet.*

would produce the most desirable combination, which is a fully dark grey bird.

To produce a Greygreen Melanistic combination, the breeder must combine a dominant mutation with a recessive mutation. Therefore the sex of each bird is irrelevant for mating results. Mating a Melanistic bird to a Greygreen bird will produce Green/Melanistic and Greygreen/Melanistic birds. Breed the Greygreen/Melanistic birds back to Melanistic birds for the next generation to give:

**Greygreen (SF)/Melanistic x Melanistic**
= Green/Melanistic, Melanistic and Greygreen (SF)/Melanistic
+ Greygreen (SF) Melanistic

**Greygreen (SF) Melanistic x Melanistic**
= Melanistic and Greygreen (SF) Melanistic

**Greygreen (SF) Melanistic x Greygreen (SF) Melanistic**
= Melanistic, Greygreen (SF) Melanistic and Greygreen (DF) Melanistic

**Greygreen (DF) Melanistic x Melanistic**
= 100% Greygreen (SF) Melanistic

### Opaline Melanistic

Currently possible in the Eastern Rosella and the Budgerigar, this combination will be interesting when attempted. In many species the Opaline mutation removes grey family pigments, from the head area in particular. Will it do this when combined with the Melanistic mutation in Eastern Rosellas? Only time will tell. What will happen to the Blackface in the Budgerigar? These will certainly be interesting combinations to pursue.

To begin, you should mate an Opaline cock to a Melanistic hen. This will produce Normal/ Opaline/ Melanistic cocks and Opaline/Melanistic hens. Select the Opaline/Melanistic hens and mate these to Melanistic cocks to produce the following results:

*Opaline Melanistic Eastern Rosella – an interesting result consistent with what might be imagined.*

### Melanistic cock x Opaline/Melanistic hen
= Normal/Opaline/Melanistic and Melanistic/Opaline cocks
+ Normal/Melanistic and Melanistic hens

Retain the Melanistic/Opaline cocks and use them for the following matings:

### Melanistic/Opaline cock x Melanistic hen
= Melanistic and Melanistic/Opaline cocks
+ Melanistic and Opaline Melanistic hens

### Melanistic/Opaline cock x Opaline/Melanistic hen
= Normal/Opaline/Melanistic, Opaline/Melanistic and Melanistic/Opaline cocks
+ Melanistic Opaline cocks
+ Normal/Melanistic, Opaline/Melanistic and Melanistic hens
+ Opaline Melanistic hens

### Melanistic/Opaline cock x Opaline hen
= Normal/Opaline/Melanistic and Opaline/Melanistic cocks
+ Normal/Melanistic and Opaline/Melanistic hens

### Opaline/Melanistic cock x Melanistic hen
= Normal/Opaline/Melanistic and Melanistic/Opaline cocks
+ Opaline/Melanistic and Opaline Melanistic hens

### Opaline/Melanistic cock x Opaline Melanistic hen
= Opaline/Melanistic and Opaline Melanistic cocks and hens

### Melanistic/Opaline cock x Opaline Melanistic hen
= Melanistic/Opaline cocks and Melanistic hens
+ Opaline Melanistic cocks and hens

### Opaline Melanistic cock x Opaline/Melanistic hen
= Opaline/Melanistic and Opaline Melanistic cocks and hens

### Opaline Melanistic cock x Opaline Melanistic hen
= 100% Opaline Melanistic cocks and hens

## Red-fronted Combinations

The Red-fronted mutation is well established in two species, the Turquoise Parrot and the Scarlet-chested Parrot. Similar colours are also appearing in a number of other species. It combines best with mutations that highlight or enhance yellow family pigments such as Dilute, Lutino and Opaline. It could also produce an attractive 'Salmon-fronted' Scarlet-chested Parrot if a good specimen was produced,

G GERAEDTS

*Above & right: Red-fronted Greygreen Opaline Turquoise Parrot cock.*

G GERAEDTS

by combining it with either of the Parblue mutations. However, because selection is so important for improving this mutation, combinations often do not receive enough work to attain an attractive result. Combination with mutations that have heavy grey family pigments, can hide the red colouration and result in less impact being attained, for example the Red-fronted Olive Turquoise Parrot.

To combine the Red-fronted with other mutations is not difficult because of its dominant nature. The problem is improving the results to an acceptable level. To do this, high quality Red-fronted birds must be used to begin with. For each subsequent generation, birds with the greatest spread of red must be selected.

For example, if you are trying to produce Red-fronted Dilute Turquoise Parrots, start by mating Red-fronted to Dilute and you will produce all Red-fronted/Dilute offspring, but with less red than the Red-fronted parent. This is because you have selected against a good spread of red by using the Dilute parent. If you then mate the offspring back to another Dilute bird, the outcome will be quite disappointing more often than not, as you have bred away from the Red-fronted for two successive generations. It would be better to mate two Red-fronted/Dilute birds together or try to obtain good Red-fronted Dilute birds to start with.

When mating the Red-fronted/Dilute together, some non Red-fronted birds will be produced as well as a range of quality in the Red-fronted offspring. Some of these young (25%) will be Dilute. If you breed enough and are patient, you can eventually breed high quality Red-fronted Dilute Turquoise Parrots after a number of generations.

The same principle applies to combining the mutation with any other mutation. Select the best Red-fronted bird to begin with, then mate back to the best whenever possible, avoiding the further use of non Red-fronted birds after the first generation and always using the offspring with the greatest spread of red.

*Red-fronted Dilute Turquoise Parrot cock.*

*Red-fronted Dilute Turquoise Parrot hen.*

*Above: Red-fronted Cinnamon Turquoise Parrot hen.*
*Left: Red-fronted Cinnamon Turquoise Parrot cock.*

*Red-fronted Opaline Dilute Turquoise Parrot hen.*

*Red-fronted Opaline Dilute Turquoise Parrot hen.*

# Miscellaneous Colour Combinations

D SMITH

J GOESSENS

D SMITH

D VAN DEN ABEELE

A MATHEWS

K SHEPHERD

G ROMAN

1. *Greygreen Suffused Indian Ringnecked Parrot.*
2. *TurquoiseBlue Suffused Indian Ringnecked Parrot.*
3. *Grey Suffused Indian Ringnecked Parrot.*
4. *Greygreen Dilute Rainbow Lorikeet.*
5. *Greygreen Dilute Scaly-breasted Lorikeet.*
6. *Recessive Lime Dark Green Masked Lovebird.*
7. *Double Dark Factor Turquoise (Mauve) Cinnamon Pied Peachfaced Lovebird.*

Above: Lime Turquoise
Red-rumped Parrot.

Right: Parblue
(Yellowface) Grey
Opaline Budgerigar.

Dark Factor Turquoise (Cobalt)
Cinnamon Peachfaced Lovebirds.

The following photographs are not standard Fischer's Lovebirds based on the nominate (wildtype) race. They have been called 'Sable' by some breeders, however I believe that they would be classified as Type 2 (domesticate race) Fischer's Lovebirds by the African Lovebird Society (ALBS) in the USA. Some experts view this 'race' as being created by the extensive hybridisation that has occurred within the White Eye-ring Lovebird group. The attractiveness of these colours are without question, however care must be taken so that the true nominate race is not lost to this colour form.

Violet Fischer's
Lovebird (Type 2).

Lime Fischer's Lovebird (Type 2).

Lime Mauve (L) and Lime Cobalt Fischer's
Lovebirds (Type 2).

Lime Olive Fischer's Lovebird (Type 2).

# PART
# THREE

*Aqua Khaki*
*Scarlet-chested Parrot cock.*

# SEALED SECTION
# WARNING! ENTER AT OWN RISK!

The following section is technical in nature and not required reading for bird keepers whose aim is simply to breed birds. This section is for the breeder who understands basic genetics and wishes to contemplate the more complex issues of colour morph and genetic theory with respect to parrots.

# EXPLANATION OF GENETIC TERMS

Throughout this part of the book I will use the correct genetic terms. This glossary will assist the inquisitive reader to understand these terms as simply as possible.

### Chromosome
The *chromosome* is a chain of DNA (deoxyribonucleic acid). Sections of the DNA sequences form what we call genes. Therefore the chromosome can be viewed as a chain of genes. Different species have different numbers of chromosomes, but in all cases there are two copies of each chromosome except for the sex chromosomes. The cock has two X chromosomes forming a pair, but the hen has only one X chromosome.

The second chromosome in this pair is the Y chromosome, which is very much smaller and can therefore carry only a few of the genes present on the X chromosome. This means that the hen only has one copy of sex-linked genes. Because the sex chromosomes in birds are the reverse of those in mammals, the correct designation for them is in fact Z (for the X) and W (for the Y). However, this designation is rarely used in aviculture.

### Homologous Chromosomes and Sister Chromatids
The term *homologous chromosomes* refers to the two chromosomes that form a pair. They are basically copies of each other in that each gene has an exact location (locus) along the length of each chromosome. However, each location may be occupied by either the wildtype gene or a different allele of that gene. Only homologous chromosomes can participate in a crossover. (See page 217.) Therefore only alleles of a specific locus may swap during the process of crossover.

The term *sister chromatids* refers to the two copies of a particular chromosome that form during meiosis, the process of genetic replication to form sex cells. Crossover occurs during the stage where homologous chromosomes are aligned with each other and sister chromatids have been produced. Crossover may occur between sister chromatids instead of homologous chromatids, however the result does not alter the genetic mix.

### Gene
The *gene* is the base unit of instruction within the chromosome. Each gene codes for a specific protein that has a specific action. Some genes code for transcription factors, which are proteins that control the activation of other genes somewhere within the bird's genetic make-up. This type of gene can be considered a control gene or a master gene.

Each gene has a unique function and only occurs at a specific locus on a chromosome.

### Locus, Loci (plural)
The term *locus* refers to the location or address where a particular gene occurs on a chromosome. Each gene has an exact locus that cannot be altered except through rare mutations. If a gene is moved from its locus, it will generally no longer function correctly.

### Allele

An *allele* is an alternative gene for a particular locus. If a locus has not mutated, then it is occupied by its wildtype gene. However once mutation has occurred, it is normal to refer to all possible genes for that location as alleles for that locus, ie the wildtype allele and its alternate (mutant) alleles.

### Multiple Alleles

The term *multiple alleles* is used when more than one mutant allele is known to exist. As multiple alleles occupy only a single locus, the bird may carry a maximum of only two of these alleles at any one time. This has relevance when understanding the outcome of combining mutations that are multiple alleles of one another.

In these cases, wildtype alleles are excluded by the presence of different mutant alleles occupying the locus on each homologous chromosome. Therefore, without the presence of a wildtype gene, normally recessive mutations appear to behave in a dominant fashion.

Two possible outcomes exist. One mutant allele may dominate the other or alternatively a blended outcome may occur. With some loci, the blended outcome can be quite surprising and may be mistaken for a new allele.

### Genotype

*Genotype* is the correct term for the genetic make-up of an organism. It is correctly given using the accepted symbols for any loci containing mutant alleles. It is always impossible to list all 'normal' alleles and their loci, so they are generally only listed if relevant to the discussion.

### Phenotype

The term *phenotype* refers to the physical appearance of the bird. Many different genotypes may have the same phenotype. For instance a Normal bird has a Normal phenotype but may be carrying various hidden alleles within its genotype. Certain mutant phenotypes may be created by more than one genotype. This may sometimes occur due to hidden recessive genes and also because different alleles from unrelated loci sometimes behave in a similar fashion.

### Colour Morph

*Colour morph* is the correct term for all mutant phenotypes. The word *morph* indicates a change, therefore colour morphs are alternative plumage colourations.

### Homozygous

The term *homozygous* refers to a feature of the bird's genotype in that the bird has two identical alleles for a particular locus. The bird could have two identical wildtype alleles or alternatively two identical mutant alleles. In either case the alleles are identical.

### Heterozygous

The term *heterozygous* also refers to a feature of the bird's genotype in that the bird has two different alleles for a particular locus. This could be one wildtype allele and one mutant allele, or two different mutant alleles.

### Wildtype Allele

This is the Normal gene for a particular locus on a chromosome.

### Autosome, Autosomal

An *autosome* is any chromosome other than the sex chromosomes. An *autosomal* mutation is a mutation of a locus lying upon one of the many autosomes.

### Recessive

*Recessive* refers to the form of genetic inheritance followed by a mutant allele.

It implies that the mutant allele is not expressed (ie it is suppressed) when heterozygous with a wildtype allele. By strict definition a recessive mutation can be either autosomal or sex-linked. Sex-linked mutations can be dominant or recessive, although almost all sex-linked mutations have proven recessive in nature.

## Dominant
A *dominant* allele is one that will express itself fully whether heterozygous or homozygous with no change in the phenotype of the bird. Dominant alleles can be either sex-linked or autosomal. For most loci, the wildtype allele is the dominant allele, however not all wildtype alleles are dominant.

## Co-dominant
*Co-dominant* is the form of inheritance whereby both the wildtype allele and the mutant allele express themselves equally. As a result, three different phenotypes occur in this situation: the homozygous wildtype phenotype, the heterozygous phenotype and the homozygous mutant phenotype. Co-dominance can also occur between two mutant alleles in a multiple allelic series, once again producing three distinct phenotypes. In fact it is the most common form of genetic interaction between multiple mutant alleles of loci controlling plumage colouration. It is also known as *incomplete dominance*.

## Semi-dominant Lethal
*Semi-dominant lethal* is a specialised type of co-dominance where the homozygous mutant phenotype is lethal and therefore does not exist. As a result only two phenotypes exist, the homozygous wildtype phenotype and the heterozygous phenotype.

## Crossover and Recombinant Frequency
*Crossover* is the means by which loci that are linked on the one chromosome are able to re-assort their combination of alleles, by transferring DNA sequences with their homologous chromosome. It occurs during the stage of meiosis where sister chromatids have formed and homologous chromosomes are aligned. These chromosomes join briefly during meiosis and can swap sections of their DNA sequence when they separate again. It may occur a number of times along the length of a chromosome, resulting in multiple crossover events. The rate of crossover is known as the *recombinant frequency* and as the occurrence is random along the length of the chromosome, the frequency increases with increased distance between loci. This distance is measured in map units, with one map unit correlating to a recombinant frequency of 1%. Collating recombinant frequencies can allow the scientist to map the relative positions of various loci, if enough data is available.

## Melanin
*Melanin* is a type of pigment that is naturally black in colour. It is deposited within feathers and other body parts by specialised cells called melanocytes. It is produced by these cells from proteins via a chemical pathway. Damage to an enzyme during this process may result in altered pigment colour (eg cinnamon or fallow causing brown melanin).

It may also appear as shades of grey depending on the quantity of pigment deposited and where it lies within the feather. When it is found in the outer cortex of the feather, it appears as its natural black colour. However, when it lies deeper in the medulla of the feather it appears grey. When combined with the cloudy cell structure, it produces the blue distortion effect (constructive interference).

## Melanocyte, Melanoblast
The *melanocyte* is the cell responsible for producing melanin pigment. Immature cells begin life in the neural crest of the embryo and are known as *melanoblasts*. They migrate throughout the skin and into other specialised areas such as the eye. Once at

their final destination, they mature and differentiate into mature melanocytes. Melanocytes are not present in feathers, only skin and feather follicles. They produce particles of melanin pigment known as melanosomes, which are then transferred into the feathers.

## Psittacin

Psittacin is the type of pigment that creates the yellows, oranges, reds and pinks that we see. Psittacin is modified from dietary carotenoid pigments taking probably only a few short steps. I make this statement because few mutations are known that alter psittacin production and deposition. If it were a more complex process like the production of melanins, then more steps would be at risk of mutation.

Yellow psittacin appears to be the base pigment that is then modified into the other colours if they are present in the plumage. A few known mutations prevent this modification, but no mutations exist that stop yellow production without preventing the other psittacin pigments as well.

Psittacin pigments are found primarily in the outer cortical layers of the feather.

Addendum
Psittacin pigment has finally been isolated and identified by scientists, confirming that it is different from carotenoid pigments found in the feathers of other avian species. The pigments producing red in the feathers of the Scarlet Macaw Ara macao have been identified as **linear polyenals** (Stradi et al, 2001). The biochemical pathway is yet to be determined, but will be unique amongst animal species. Dietary carotenoids are not involved in the production of these pigments. The researchers also believe that the polyenal molecules interact significantly with the feather keratin to create a particular colour. Their research is continuing.

## Tyndall Effect

The Tyndall effect is the name given to the phenomena that make the sky appear blue. It is also known as Raleigh scattering. It was previously thought that the blue and green colours of a bird's feathers were produced by a similar effect.

We now know that the light distortion effect is correctly caused by **constructive interference**. It is created through special structural features within the parrot's feathers.

## Albinism, Albino, Ino

Albinism was originally coined as a broad classification term for certain types of pigment loss. Albinism refers to the loss of melanin pigments from the body. It may be total, incomplete, imperfect or partial. These definitions were originally coined for mammals where the total form is known as albino. As parrots have a second pigment within their body known as psittacin which is unaffected by albinism, the term 'Lutino' has been coined to describe total albinism in these species. Because the name Albino implies 'white' for most people, we now prefer to use the name ino for the loci that produce a total albinistic bird.

Other forms of melanin changes such as fallow and cinnamon can in fact be defined as forms of imperfect albinism. This does not imply that they have anything to do with the Albino colour or the ino loci, only that the changes in pigment within the bird's body can be roughly grouped together under one scientific description. These descriptions date back to 1911 (Pearson et al) and can seem inappropriate for today's level of understanding. However, there is value in recognising that a colour morph is albinistic because it helps with identification purposes. It also correlates with loci that control melanin metabolism, making albinism an important subdivision for colour morphs. All albinistic colour morphs have qualitative changes to melanin granules, altering the colour, shape or size of the granules.

It has become apparent that ino animals cannot survive without at least a faint trace of melanin. These pigments do much more than just provide colour for our pleasure. They have indispensable functions in other areas of the body. Therefore an ino bird is never totally without feather pigment as with a leucistic bird.

## Leucism, Leucistic

Leucism is another classification term for colour mutations. The term *leucism* refers to the total absence of melanin pigments from feathers but not body parts. This latter feature distinguishes this classification of mutation from albinism and dilution. It is the technical term for a Black-eyed Clear mutation. Because melanin is still present within the body in normal quantities, the bird is able to function. *Leucistic* colour morphs correlate with loci that control melanocyte or melanoblast cellular functions, making their recognition important when contemplating how a new colour morph may be functioning.

## Partial Leucism

Partial leucistic birds have melanin totally removed from some but not all feathers. It may also have total melanin loss from only part of the feather. In the original definition it should not involve body parts other than feathers, but this has had to evolve since it has been realised that some leucistic mutations lose pigment from feet, bills and irises. Partial leucism is the scientific term for the action of Pied colour morphs and certain rare colours like Spangle and Grizzle.

## Dilution, Dilute

Dilution is another term used to describe certain pigment changes caused by colour mutations. Dilution is the process by which a less than normal quantity of melanin is deposited within feathers. The type of melanin is not altered, but the quantity is. Any change to quantity from almost fully normal through to virtually none can qualify as dilution. A mutation exhibiting dilution of melanin is called a Dilute. The process involved in creating these mutations is quite distinct from either leucism or albinism.

The original definition for dilution implied that all pigments within the body were equally diluted. However, the term was once again coined for mammals that only have melanin pigments, which are all controlled through common pathways. In parrots with psittacin pigment, no known mutation can affect both psittacin and melanin production as they have separate pathways. Therefore a mutation can be either a psittacin dilute or a melanin dilute. Psittacin dilutes are in fact partial blue alleles and are seldom described as dilutes, whereas melanin dilutes involve more than one loci and are the common group of mutations known by the name Dilute.

## Schizochroism

Schizochroism is a classification for certain types of colour mutations. It implies total loss of one pigment type without any effect on another pigment type. Total albinism could be considered a form of schizochroism, as could Blue mutations. Some species of birds have more than one form of melanin and loss of one form only could be described as another type of schizochroism. This term is rarely used except in scientific literature.

## Melanism, Melanistic

Melanism refers to greater than normal deposition of melanin pigments. More than one type of melanism is now known and certain physiological conditions can also mimic *melanistic* mutations creating a false expectation in the breeder.

Structural mutations like the Olive (Dark Factor) and the Grey are sometimes believed to increase melanin deposition like a melanistic mutation. Whilst some researchers have reported an apparent small increase in melanin, the primary action of these mutations is through alteration of the feather structure involved in constructive interference.

# THE SCIENTIFIC INVESTIGATION OF COLOUR MORPHS

## Classification Systems for Mutation Types

Scientifically, a number of systems exist which attempt to group colour mutations into categories or types. I used to work from these systems, however as my knowledge of mutations and the way they function have increased, I have come to accept all these systems as artificial and flawed. However, as the scientific community continues to use variations of these systems, I will discuss them briefly so that the aviculturist will be aware of these terms if ever confronted by them. Some terms do have some practical use in describing the difference between two mutations of similar appearance.

P ODEKERKEN

*'Cinnamon' Red-flanked Lorikeet – a new colour morph that has yet to be studied.*

One of the earliest systems for classifying colour mutations which alter melanin (Pearson *et al*, 1911), classified them into the following groupings:

- **Total albinism**: complete loss of melanin.
- **Incomplete albinism**: loss of melanin from eyes, skin or feathers but not all three.
- **Imperfect albinism**: partial loss of melanin but not total absence in any area.
- **Partial albinism**: complete or partial loss of melanin within localised areas.

Of these four classifications, most breeders would only recognise the first as a form of albinism. The other three categories would generally be given other names now.

Paul Buckley (1982) devised another system of classification which classifies naturally occurring colour morphs in wild species of birds. He defines types of colour morphs in the following way:

- **Albinism**: total loss of pigment from all body parts.
- **Leucism**: total loss of pigment from feathers but not from other body tissue. (This would be *incomplete albinism* in the Pearson system.)
- **Partial Leucism**: total loss of pigment from localised areas of plumage with no alteration in others. (This would be called *partial albinism* in the Pearson system.)
- **Dilution**: reduction in the amount of pigment deposited, but not total loss of pigment. (This would be *imperfect albinism* in the Pearson system.)
- **Schizochroism**: the absence of one pigment type without alteration to other pigments. (This is not classified in the Pearson system.)

If we consider these terms in relation to known parrot mutations, we discover that all categories need modification because no single mutation alters both melanin and psittacin pigment families. Therefore whilst Lutino is clearly the equivalent of the mammalian Albino, in Buckley's system it is classified not as albinism, but as a form of schizochroism. Black-eyed Clear (Black-eyed Yellow) is an example of leucism, except that it should be Black-eyed White to strictly fit the classification. Pied mutations fall into the partial leucism category, except that many (but not all) Pied mutations remove pigment from random toes and other body parts excluded by the original definition.

At first glance, dilutes appear to be commonly occurring and easily fitting the definition. However, all pigments are meant to be evenly diluted to fit the definition for dilution, when in fact different pigment types are never controlled synchronously. Dilutes therefore either dilute melanin or they dilute psittacin but never both.

Schizochroism has a number of examples. For instance the Blue mutation represents total loss of psittacin without the alteration of melanin pigments. It can also refer to loss of one form of melanin, yet retention of other forms. Buckley classifies Cinnamon mutations as a form of schizochroism, however this is based on the belief that brown melanin represents phaeomelanin and black melanin represents eumelanin. Currently other authors, including the respected Inte Onsman (Mutavi) from Holland, classify brown melanin as simply a precursory stage for black eumelanin. They categorise phaeomelanin as a red-brown melanin (called erythromelanin by Buckley) not occurring in parrots, but found in the cheek patches of Zebra Finches as well as other types of birds. Therefore the correct classification for the very common and well-defined Cinnamon mutation becomes a matter for conjecture, depending on how you classify the pigment types within the bird. All this needs to be decided well before tackling the issue of what the mutation actually does and how it should be classified.

Buckley describes a type of mutation (as grey schizochroism) where in theory a bird is unable to produce any brown phaeomelanin. However, with the current acceptance of brown melanin as a precursory stage for normal black eumelanin, it becomes obvious that you cannot have black (or grey) without prior production of brown melanin. This is in fact the true situation we see. 'Grey' schizochroism is a physical impossibility in parrots. In other species with red-brown melanin (ie Zebra Finches) a form of schizochroism does exist to separate the two melanin types. One mutation eliminates all red-brown from the bird and another mutation, operating from a totally different locus, prevents any production of eumelanin (both black and brown melanins in this case).

Dr Alessandro D'Angieri, author of *The Colored Atlas of Lovebirds*, attempts to apply Paul Buckley's system of classification to lovebird mutations. Unfortunately his interpretation of how various mutations function and how they fit into the Buckley system is inaccurate, with most mutations being placed into the wrong category. For instance, Dr D'Angieri classifies Cinnamon as a dilute and Fallow as schizochroism, yet Buckley clearly identifies the sex-linked cinnamon locus as schizochroism involving loss of eumelanin. This is a problem with artificial and man-made categories and mistakes can be made in using them.

Another shortcoming of these systems of classification is that there is no category for structural mutations such as Olive, Violet or Greygreen. And where do we place a pigment distribution gene such as the Opaline mutation?

It is obvious that these systems of classification have become cumbersome under the weight of knowledge now available on colour mutations in parrots. How can we accept two different mutations of the same locus being categorised as different types of mutations? (For example, Blue is schizochroism whilst Parblue would be defined as dilution, yet both are expressions of the same locus!)

We are becoming aware of how an increasing number of mutations behave. We are able to correctly assign many to identifiable loci whose function is known. Therefore, identifying

Z RANA

*Grey Cleartail Indian Ringnecked Parrot – the Cleartail mutation does not fit easily into any recognised colour morph classification, however there are indications that it may be a Fallow colour morph. Study is continuing.*

mutations by correctly recognising how they function and where they belong in the genetic structure is the logical path to follow. Although terms like 'dilution' and 'leucism' still have some place in identifying significant differences between the action of certain loci, we should strive to understand how the mutation is created, and not just try to classify the final outcome on visual terms.

### Other Naming Systems in Use

As this book was being written, respected Australian aviculturist Stan Sindel released a new book entitled *Australian Broad-tailed Parrots (The Platycercus and Barnardius Genera)*. This is his fifth book in a series on Australian parrots in which he discusses all aspects of these birds from taxonomy and ornithology to captive breeding management and colour mutations. Stan Sindel's experience in captive management of Australian parrots is unquestionable and his research into the historical background of the birds and their colour mutations is very thorough. However, the system he uses for naming colour mutations is not standard and I am therefore compelled to discuss the Sindel system of naming for colour mutations.

When reading some of the earlier books by Sindel, I was never happy with the system he was using, but until this most recent book he had not defined his system in any detail. I can now see that he has been quite thorough in trying to correctly identify phenotypes, naming them consistently across species. However he makes no use of pre-existing knowledge about gene function, nor does he consider genetic relationships when classifying various mutations.

Sindel, together with a few prominent USA authors, is responsible for the current popular use of the name 'Cinnamon' for a large number of mutations that are not true Cinnamon mutations. This leads to great confusion when reading his books because such a large number of colours are being called by variations of the name 'Cinnamon'. I will give him credit for consistency in using the same name variations across species, even if the names chosen have ignored those precedents set in the Budgerigar and other species.

Sindel uses the name 'Cinnamon' for all colours that are forms of imperfect albinism (Pearson *et al*, 1911). As I have discussed already, we are now well aware that colour morphs fitting this broad description can be placed into a number of well-defined categories, each of which is created by a distinctly different gene with differing functions. There are six cinnamon name variations defined in the Sindel system and he includes 'Fallow' mutations as forms of 'Cinnamon'. The easiest way to follow the Sindel system is to substitute the words 'imperfect albinism' whenever you read 'Cinnamon'.

As I have discussed in this book, Cinnamon is the name assigned to a specific mutation which is sex-linked recessive and whose action prevents conversion of brown into black melanin. Its use must be reserved for only this mutation rather than perpetuate the confusion currently being generated. Sindel calls true cinnamon mutations, 'Sex-linked Cinnamon'. However, because he relies solely on phenotype, a number of Lime (par-ino) mutations are incorrectly added to this group. The most notable case is the Lime Red-rumped Parrot, commonly misnamed 'UK Cinnamon' in Australia, but called 'Yellow' or 'Isabel' in Europe. 'Sex-linked Cinnamon Yellow' is another category used by Sindel, and the birds in this group are probably all Lime mutations. As discussed elsewhere, test matings with sex-linked Lutino mutations are needed to prove that these genes are multiple alleles of the same locus.

'Recessive Cinnamon' is used by Sindel for the group of mutations I have discussed as Faded in this book. Whether these birds represent just one mutation or a number of mutations still awaits thorough investigation. Two groupings made by Sindel are of uncertain nature, the mutations which he calls either 'Recessive Cinnamon Yellow' or 'Semi-advanced Cinnamon Yellow (recessive)'. Some of these mutations are possibly recessive Lime mutations, but others are probably forms of dilutes. Once again more investigation is needed.

*Greygreen Cleartail Indian Ringnecked Parrot.*

His last category is 'Advanced Cinnamon Yellow (recessive)', and all the birds he calls by this name are non sex-linked (NSL) Lutino mutations. As I have discussed elsewhere, no Lutino mutation can survive without at least a trace of melanin and this applies equally to the autosomal recessive forms. Therefore his main reason for denying them status as lutino mutations is flawed. Perhaps Sindel has formed this opinion about NSL Lutino mutations, because in some species the colours being called NSL Lutino are possibly strongly reduced Recessive Lime mutations (eg Princess Parrot). An understanding of the nature of how various genes operate, as well as the genetic interrelationship of certain mutations (eg multiple allelic series), is imperative if we wish to name these mutations correctly.

There are also problems in other areas of his classification system. For instance, for both his 'cinnamon grouping' and his 'dilute grouping' he states that all colours except red show dilution to varying degrees. Neither of these groups alter yellow psittacin pigment quantities under any circumstances. All the colour morphs he discusses in both these groups are melanin altering mutations, without affecting either psittacin pigment or structural colouration.

The other major area of difficulty in the Sindel system involves the use of the names Olive and Greygreen. The Olive (or dark factor) mutation is co-dominant and 'darkens' the plumage in two steps by altering the thickness of the cloudy layer. The Grey mutation (producing Greygreen colour) totally prevents production of a functioning cloudy layer and is inherited as a dominant gene. Homozygous dark factor birds generally have a phenotype very similar to a Greygreen bird. The genetic inheritance is the best way to distinguish them, unless they can be combined with a Blue mutation to visualise the changes to the Blue phenotype, which tends to be more distinct without the yellow psittacin distorting it.

Sindel appears to have encountered difficulties in the application of these names due to the existence of colour morphs in the Scarlet-chested Parrot and the Port Lincoln Parrot that have some features of an Olive mutation, but do not appear to alter blue areas of plumage in the normal way. In both of these so far unique cases, the structural colouration appears lost on areas of the plumage which are normally green, but not apparently in the areas which are normally blue. We currently do not know enough about these mutations to categorise them correctly, but Sindel has decided to use the name 'Olive' for them and has rewritten the definition for this mutation. True Olive mutations (eg Turquoise Parrot) are being called 'Greygreen' by Sindel and are being confused with true Grey mutations (eg Greygreen lorikeets).

The use of the names, Olive and Greygreen, owe their definitions to the Budgerigar and in both cases, all structural colour on the bird is altered by both mutations, albeit in slightly different ways. The Olive mutation produces Cobalt and Mauve colours when combined with Blue mutations. The actual colour in each species depends on more than just these mutations and therefore in some species Olive mutations in double factor blue (Mauve) can appear almost indistinguishable from greygreen blue combinations (Grey). I reiterate that an understanding of the genetic behaviour and the gene action of each mutation is essential to identify different mutations correctly.

Sindel has also introduced another erroneous concept with his Olive classification system. He believes that these mutations can have three genes for this trait. As chromosomes occur in pairs, a mutation with three genes would have to be controlled by duplicate genes, in which case a bird would be able to have as many as four genes for the mutation. Because Sindel relies solely on phenotypes to investigate the nature of mutations, I believe he is mistakenly assigning too many different phenotypes for these colours. The variation that he, and the breeders of the birds, believe they are seeing is likely to be within that expected for any mutation, or else other

P ODEKERKEN

*'Cinnamon' Ruppell's Parrot (background) – another new colour morph that has yet to be studied.*

factors are coming into play. Budgerigar breeders will be horrified to know that he claims that the Olive mutation in this species can also have three factors in the one bird!

### Addendum

*During publication, another new title dealing with colour morphs and genetics in parrots has come to my attention. It is called 'Colour Breeding of Parrots Made Easy' by John Warne and distributed in association with the Parrot Society of New Zealand. The book attempts to explain some of the basics behind colour mutations, lists a large number of colour mutations for various species of parrots and has extensive tables of mating results for combining two different mutations. Unfortunately, whilst the genetic tables are on the whole accurate, much of the other information in the book is either inaccurate or outdated.*

*The issue of correct naming is not dealt with, which is a reasonable decision considering the scope of the book. However, the author has chosen to perpetuate a large number of inaccurate name choices, thereby adding to the ongoing problems we have with the use of incorrect names. In particular he lists a large number of colour morphs under the names assigned by Stan Sindel, whose troubled system I have already discussed. There is also duplication of some mutations in the list under the differing names used in different countries. Overall, the 'known colour mutation' list requires much more research and refining to make it a useful part of the book.*

*If that were the limit of the problems, the book might still be useful, however there are a large number of serious errors in the other main sections of the book. The first section dealing with 'colour production in feathers' is based on very old work and a number of ideas have since been proven to be incorrect. When dealing with feather structure, the author incorrectly views melanin as being restricted to the medulla. There is no mention of the presence of melanin in the cortex of the feather barb to create black areas of the plumage and this missing knowledge then affects the understanding of the action of a number of different colour mutations including melanistic mutations. The author also believes the old theory of melanin types whereby feathers contain both grey and brown melanin and Cinnamon is a schizochroic mutation eliminating grey melanin. As discussed previously, we now* know that brown melanin is merely a precursor stage of black eumelanin, rather than a distinct melanin type of its own and that Cinnamon is an albinistic rather than a schizochroic type mutation.

Another old belief that has crept into this book is the fallacy that 'red pigment' is involved in the production of the Violet colour morph. In certain non-Psittacine species, violet colouration can be produced by constructive interference overlying a 'red pigment'. The best example is the purple of the Gouldian Finch's chest area. However, the red pigment is in fact the chestnut red of phaeomelanin, not red carotenoid pigment that is never present in the medulla of feathers. Psittacine species are unable to produce phaeomelanin and therefore cannot produce violet or purple colours in this manner. Instead Violet colour morphs in Psittacine species are produced by altering the shape of the feather barb cross-section, thereby altering the light frequency produced via constructive interference. There are no pigment changes in a Violet colour morph, only structural changes. The light distortion effect is also recorded incorrectly as Tyndall effect, but this is forgivable, as the true nature of the physical effect involved has had little publicity in avicultural circles.

Other areas of contention include a classification system for Pied colour morphs that is not a standard recognised system, use of the term 'Pastel' incorrectly (we can now say that the misuse of the name 'Pastel' is an ANZAC tradition, not just an Australian one), failure to recognise Pearl as a form of opaline and instead grouping both Pearl and Clearhead incorrectly as forms of Pied.

The author's understanding of basic genetics seems sound and he clearly understands the concept of multiple alleles and also gene linkage. However, consideration of crossover rates is not mentioned and this is particularly relevant for cinnamon and ino crossover. The author does not seem aware that Lacewing is a combination colour involving cinnamon and ino. No attempt has been made to distinguish the two different types of linkage in 'double splits'. No mention is made of the gene linkage between dark factor and blue loci and the author incorrectly states that Paleface and Whiteface in Cockatiels are not allelic. There are also other instances where unrelated alleles are listed incorrectly as allelic.

Overall there are so many inaccuracies, that they outweigh any benefit a reader may obtain from the book. I therefore cannot recommend any breeder reading the book due to the confusion and misconceptions it will cause.

# Building Blocks of Colour

The methods by which colours are produced in parrots are well documented scientifically. Good descriptions can be found at either Clive Hesford's web site or the Mutavi web site. It has also been described by Jim Hayward in his book *Colour Mutations in Parrots* and in the Budgerigar bible *Genetics for Budgerigar Breeders* by Taylor and Warner, which is essential reading for everyone interested in mutations of colour in parrots. The following is a brief outline of colour production in parrots.

Melanin pigments in different forms help form body colour (blue in combination with structural aspects, greys and browns when these are absent) and foreground colour (blacks and dark browns), depending on whether they are present in the cortex or the medulla of feather barbs. Black is the normal melanin produced in most species. Other colours of melanin are generally abnormal, and some shades such as grey are produced only by the depth and concentration of the black melanin pigment. Some species do naturally have a proportion of brown melanin within their wildtype phenotype.

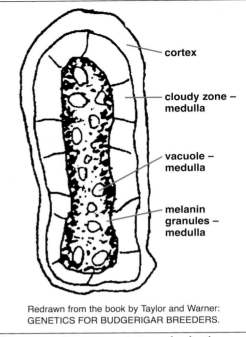

Redrawn from the book by Taylor and Warner:
GENETICS FOR BUDGERIGAR BREEDERS.

*Diagrammatic representation of a feather barb cross-section.*

Psittacin pigments form the ground colour (yellow, red, pink and orange). I consider yellow to be the base psittacin, with the other shades (advanced psittacins) modified from it. Ground colour can be seen in its natural state in some species, but often is simply one part of the body colour. Yellow psittacin, when combined with the blue colouration produced by feather structure and melanin, creates bright shades of green or, when structural colour is not present, duller grey-green shades.

## Addendum

*Psittacin pigment has finally been isolated and identified by scientists, confirming that it is different from carotenoid pigments found in the feathers of other avian species. The pigments producing red in the feathers of the Scarlet Macaw Ara macao have been identified as **linear polyenals** (Stradi et al, 2001). The biochemical pathway is yet to be determined, but will be unique amongst animal species. Dietary carotenoids are not involved in the production of these pigments. The researchers also believe that the polyenal molecules interact significantly with the feather keratin to create a particular colour. Their research is continuing.*

Structural colour is probably the most important aspect. As mentioned in Part One of this book, this phenomenon has always been known as the Tyndall effect. However, recent research by Dr R. Prum (Prum *et al*, 1999) has shown the true nature of the light distortion to be *constructive interference*. With its effect produced by the cloudy layer of the medullary cells, structural colouration allows the vast range of shades of green (in combination with psittacin and melanin) and blue (when psittacin is absent, but melanin is still present). The production of colour can and should be studied much further than this brief outline, and therefore I refer the reader to the book and web sites mentioned in the introduction to this section and noted in the bibliography.

*The following diagrams represent the arrangement of pigments and the structure of feather barbs of differently coloured feathers.*

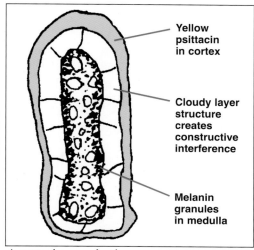

Yellow psittacin in cortex

Cloudy layer structure creates constructive interference

Melanin granules in medulla

*A typical green feather.*

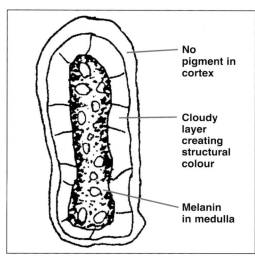

No pigment in cortex

Cloudy layer creating structural colour

Melanin in medulla

*A typical blue feather.*

Psittacin in cortex

Structure normal

However, no structural colour due to the . . .

. . . absence of melanin

*A typical yellow feather.*

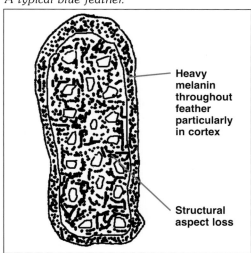

Heavy melanin throughout feather particularly in cortex

Structural aspect loss

*A typical black feather.*

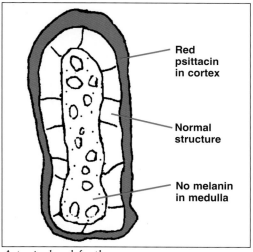

Red psittacin in cortex

Normal structure

No melanin in medulla

*A typical red feather.*

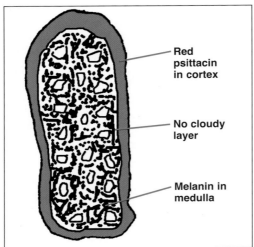

Red
psittacin
in cortex

No cloudy
layer

Melanin in
medulla

*A typical maroon feather.*

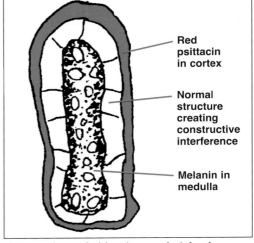

Red
psittacin
in cortex

Normal
structure
creating
constructive
interference

Melanin in
medulla

*A typical purple-blue (not violet) feather.*

# Classification of Melanin

Two different systems are used by scientists to classify the various melanin types. Each system uses different terminology. The first system, described by Paul Buckley (1982) classifies three types of melanin as follows:

**Eumelanin**: dark grey melanin.

**Phaeomelanin**: brown melanin.

**Erythromelanin**: red-brown melanin.

In this system, parrots are believed to carry both grey and brown melanins (with some species also possibly having erythromelanin). The combination of the two types of melanin in high concentrations creates visible black colour. According to Buckley, schizochroism (separation of the colours) will remove the grey melanin to produce a *fawn variant (non-eumelanin schizochroic)* that we know as the Cinnamon phenotype. Conversely, brown melanin can be removed by *non-phaeomelanin schizochroism* to create a *grey variant*. This sounds simple and logical at first, except that no known Grey phenotype (that I am aware of) in parrots or other species is a schizochroic. Many colour morphs produce a Grey phenotype (once the structural colour and psittacin are removed by other alleles), yet in every case they can be freely combined with the cinnamon allele to produce a 'Cream' (lighter brown) phenotype. Under the schizochroism theory, combining a fawn variant and a grey variant would produce a bird without either grey or fawn melanin – the Ino phenotype in other words. This is clearly not the way things work in parrots, or other birds for that matter.

The alternative classification system has general acceptance in Europe, but this is far from universal. In this system there are only two types of melanin:

**Eumelanin**: black melanin, but can come in shades of brown.

**Phaeomelanin**: red-brown melanin.

The potential for confusion between the two systems amongst breeders is obvious. What is erythromelanin in one system is phaeomelanin in the other, whilst phaeomelanin in the first system is simply a form of eumelanin in the second. In Zebra Finches there is a colour morph known as 'Phaeo' that originally created problems for me because I was only aware of the first system. This mutation has all grey and brown melanin removed, but retains red-brown melanin. Using the first system, the bird has no phaeomelanin left, so how did the name come about? Then I was introduced to the second system, which explained the choice of names. (Actually, Phaeo is a combination of the true non-eumelanin schizochroic mutant allele called isabel and a pigment redistribution allele known as black-breasted.) This particular mutation (the true Isabel) also illustrates that both grey and brown melanins share a common metabolic pathway, separate from the pathway for red-brown melanin.

In the second system, brown melanin is created by various failures of melanin to be metabolised correctly. The Cinnamon and Brown phenotypes are produced by dysfunction of the last steps in eumelanin production, Fallow phenotypes being created by dysfunction of earlier steps in the process. Phaeomelanin (red-brown in this case) is produced via a second pathway diverging from the eumelanin pathway at an early stage. The ino locus acts near the start and therefore removes both eumelanin and phaeomelanin. But the cinnamon locus has no effect on phaeomelanin production because it acts at the end of eumelanin production. This fits perfectly with the nature of the cinnamon allele in Zebra Finches (known in aviculture as Fawn), where the red-brown (phaeomelanin) is not altered, but the plumage is changed from grey to brown. This discussion illustrates perfectly my point that studying the action of various mutant alleles and the phenotypes they produce will shed light on the mysteries of how the body functions. By considering the appearance of various colour morphs across species, as well as how they interact with one another, we are able to decide logically which theories are valid, thereby increasing our knowledge and refining our theories to a more precise form.

The following diagram helps illustrate the differing pathways taken in production of eumelanin (black and brown melanin) and phaeomelanin (red-brown melanin) as well as identifying various enzymes that are inactivated by mutations of various loci. Tyrosinase is the enzyme known to be controlled by the non-sex-linked (NSL) ino locus. It is also believed to be the point of action for some fallow alleles. Dopachrome Tautomerase is the enzyme controlled by the cinnamon locus and Tyrosinase related Protein-1 is the point where the brown locus acts.

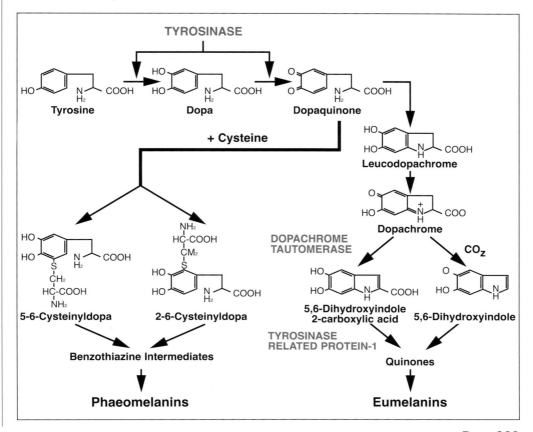

# The Process of Pigmentation, Genetic Control and Colour Mutations

Colour morphs occur through genetic mutation which happens purely by chance. How these mutations act, though, is not random. Their effects are very specific and produced by altering the genetic control of pigmentation. Although the plumage colouration of the wildtype bird is under complex genetic control, study of colour mutations allows the identification of different steps in this process. Careful observation of the changes caused by mutant genes can allow much to be determined about this genetic control. Slowly, with the appearance of each new colour morph, we are able to piece together information about how pigmentation is produced and controlled. The full picture may never be complete, but already we are able to determine much about these processes.

Psittacin is believed to be modified from naturally occurring carotenoids in the diet. We can deduce that this process has only a few basic steps under simple genetic control, as few loci have been found that control psittacin production. The main one is the blue locus, with the slight possibility of a second blue locus in one species. With the exception of the orange locus (which controls only a small area of pigment on the Cockatiel and may be simply a distribution gene) and the tangerine locus (which controls face colour in the Peachfaced Lovebird) no other gene loci alter the outcome of psittacin production. It seems impossible to turn off yellow psittacin without stopping all other forms, therefore yellow must be the base colour. Other advanced psittacin pigments have been removed by some alleles (eg the Cockatiel and Peachfaced Lovebird forms mentioned above).

It is not known which cells control advanced psittacin (red, pink and orange) production, but it appears that melanocytes may have an involvement of some kind. It is known that when melanocytes are removed by certain Pied mutations, feather areas normally devoid of yellow psittacin will start producing yellow pigment. There is also circumstantial evidence that the loss of melanocytes, particularly in the Black-eyed Clear phenotypes, is associated with reduction or loss of red psittacin production. This could suggest that melanocytes are responsible for conversion of yellow psittacin into red psittacin. However, typical pied markings are not found in red areas of Pied mutations, suggesting that only small numbers of melanocytes are needed to convert yellow into red and that the pigment is then transported over large distances to where it is needed. This is in contrast to melanin, which is produced and deposited by melanocytes only in their immediate vicinity. Another explanation is that many pied loci have pleiotrophic behaviour, meaning the genes are master genes controlling multiple functions. The loss of red psittacin could be attributable to another unidentified function of these loci.

In contrast, melanin production is a complex process. A number of steps are necessary for the raw product to be processed to the final stage of black melanin granules for deposition. Mistakes may happen at any number of these steps. The ino locus may fail to initialise melanin production or may do so poorly. The cinnamon locus may stop melanin conversion from brown to black. The fallow loci may stop melanin development even earlier, creating weak pale browns and no pigment in the eyes. Even after all these steps are negotiated, the melanin still has to be successfully deposited under the control of the dilute loci. And before any of these steps can begin, we need correctly functioning melanocytes. Leucistic loci (pied, black-eyed clear, spangle) play a role in controlling some of these functions. Many phenotypes can therefore occur, but often combinations of mutant alleles may produce effects similar to those of another melanin locus earlier in the process.

Structure of the feather barb is also subject to change under genetic control. There are at least three structural loci that must carry two alleles that are both 100% functional to create normal feather barb medullary cell structure. One locus controls the very presence of a cloudy layer (the grey locus), without which the medullary cells are not organised in a functional way for constructive interference. The second locus controls the depth of the cloudy layer (the dark factor locus), so that light of the correct wavelength is reflected. Finally the third locus (the violet locus) finetunes the shape of the cloudy layer and the feather barb. A fourth locus (the slate locus) determines the size and distribution of vacuoles within the medullary cells. These are necessary for the reflective properties of the cloudy layer and must be small enough to match the short wavelengths of blue and violet light. When the slate locus is non-functional these vacuoles can be enormous. There also appear to be a number of recessive loci in at least some species, which alter structural colour in ways that have yet to be studied.

Once all these components of colour are correctly produced, it still remains to be determined where, within the plumage of the bird, they should be placed. This is where we can assume that numerous species-specific control genes determine the distribution pattern. However, one locus that is common to at least a number of Australian species, if not all, has been identified. Its presence illustrates the close genetic relationship of these species and is particularly interesting to note in the case of the Cockatiel, thus demonstrating its familial links to other parakeets rather than the traditional cockatoo family. This is the action of the opaline locus. Recently a colour morph has appeared in other groups of parrots that could also belong to this locus.

There are also two specialised distribution genes, the melanistic locus that alters melanin restrictions and the red/orange suffusion locus that controls distribution of psittacin pigments. Neither of these loci actually creates new pigment. They simply alter and remove previous boundaries for their respective pigments (ie a loss of a boundary).

All these colour mutations result from damage or inactivation of an existing gene normally involved in colour production. To create from scratch a new gene which alters the appearance of the bird, is almost impossible. Therefore the number of possible loci responsible for colour mutants is set and finite. Some of these loci may have large numbers of possible multiple alleles, but the number of distinct phenotypes for each species is not that large. In a fully domesticated species like the Budgerigar, nearly all possible colour mutations will have shown themselves already. This is not to say that new ones are not possible, but the belief of many *that anything is possible* is just not so. The fact that the same mutations are appearing repeatedly in so many different species highlights this aspect: **that colour mutants occur from damage to genes inherited from common ancestors**.

Only those building blocks which are already present in the wildtype genotype can be altered and, although phenotypes may sometimes suggest otherwise, a new colour mutant can only be created by taking away or damaging one of those original building blocks.

## Assigning a Mutation to the Correct Locus

Allocating a new colour morph to the correct locus presents the breeder with a number of difficulties. Rarely is it possible to simply look at a colour morph and determine without doubt what it is. It is quite simply a case of too many layers to a bird's colour, making visualisation of the actual changes caused by the new mutant impractical. To see the true changes, the aspects to colour that are not involved must be removed so that a clear view of the changes can be seen.

For a melanin altering mutant phenotype it is especially difficult. The psittacin pigment needs to be removed using blue alleles and the structural colour changes need to be stopped using grey alleles. If this could be done for every new mutant, answers would come quickly. However at this time, not many species of parrots have mutant alleles of both these two loci.

For this reason we must study closely the appearance of the colour morph, paying particular attention to any feathers that lack structural colour and psittacin pigments naturally. It is impossible to make any judgement on what effects are happening if all that we can observe are green or blue feathers.

For a psittacin altering mutant phenotype, determination is generally easier from the start. However combination with the ino locus or, if unavailable, the most reduced melanin altering locus, will allow full visualisation of the pigment changes involved. Structural colour interacts only vaguely with psittacin pigments and therefore does not need to be deleted.

To explore structural colour changes, removal of psittacin pigments using blue alleles and combinations with any other structural colours available, will help place the mutant into the correct locus.

Despite these facts, most new mutants are immediately given an attractive name to enhance their appeal and financial worth. Unfortunately most of these names are incorrect. It then takes years to correct the damage and teach aviculturists the true name. In addition we have names that mean different things in different countries. There are efforts among most knowledgeable international authors on the topic of avian colour mutations to be consistent.

The symbols used in writing this book are mostly those used by Budgerigar geneticists. They have precedence and therefore should be more readily accepted; however in some instances their choices have been influenced by the limitation of studying only one species. In some cases I have chosen differing symbols which I feel are more appropriate for the whole range of parrot species. Budgerigar geneticists also use the same symbol for both recessive and sex-linked inos. I have avoided this by using a slightly different symbol for each of the sex-linked loci.

Authors are also confronted with the two different systems of symbolisation in use. Australian, UK and USA authors use the method I have employed. Continental European authors use the method employed by microbiologists (ie using $^+$ to indicate the wildtype allele and writing all alleles as uppercase if the mutants are dominant and lowercase if the mutants are recessive. They also use a vertical line to separate gene pairs from other non-linked gene pairs when writing genetic formulae). This method has some advantages but it is not standard in Australia for either mammalian or avian geneticists, and therefore can be confusing for anyone not familiar with the system. The confusion caused by the use of two systems has resulted in some authors inadvertently using a blend of both. As you can see, there is still a long way to go!

# LOCI FOR COLOUR IN PARROTS

## Common Loci

### Sex-linked ino locus – $X^{ino}$

The sex-linked ino locus would have to be the most recognisable gene locus associated with pigment production in parrots and other bird species. The mutant allele is sex-linked recessive and when homozygous, prevents production of melanin pigments. In yellow ground birds, such as most parrots, the colour produced by the mutant allele is Lutino. In a white ground bird, the ino allele produces Albino. Albino is the only result in mammals, as they do not produce the psittacin pigments necessary for yellow production. It is important to understand that the ino allele only affects melanin production. No single gene locus controls both melanin and psittacin production, therefore in parrots, the Albino phenotype will never appear from a single acting gene. The wildtype allele ($X^{INO}$) codes for an early stage in the production of melanin. Therefore when it is totally replaced with the defective allele ($X^{ino}$), the resultant outcome is the inability to produce any melanin at all. Common features of these individuals include red eyes and pink legs. No trace of any

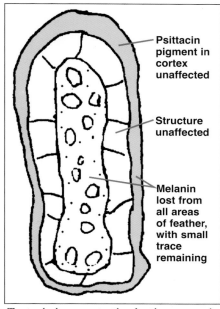

*Typical changes to the feather caused by the ino allele.*

melanin should be visible in the plumage or body. However, it is probable that no Ino phenotype can be totally devoid of melanin and still produce a functional organism because melanin is required for important body functions as well as pigmentation. That means that no colour morph is ever likely to fit this very strict definition.

Another feature of this locus is its ability to produce multiple alleles. In these cases, partially effective alleles occupy the locus and a subnormal amount of melanin is produced. Theoretically, any degree of melanin production (from none to full) would be possible from different alleles in the series. It is possible that some alleles in some parrot species that are currently seen as the full Lutino may in fact be short of a totally non-functional gene. This would help explain the existence of the Cinnamon Ino phenotype. (Refer also to page 271.)

The intermediate alleles have been given various names in different species and are in desperate need of clarification. They have been called Lacewing (Indian Ringnecked Parrots), Isabel (Scarlet-chested and Red-rumped Parrots), Clearbody (Budgerigar), Yellow (Red-rumped

*Sex-linked Lutino Plum-headed Parrot – the non sex-linked (NSL) Lutino was the first to appear, but is much more difficult to breed than the sex-linked form.*

Image labels:
- Psittacin pigment in cortex unaffected
- Structure unaffected
- Melanin lost from all areas of feather, with small trace remaining

Parrot), Cinnamon (Peachfaced Lovebird) and Platinum (Cockatiel and Red-rumped Parrot). Lacewing is totally inappropriate as this name signifies the Cinnamon Ino combination. Isabel is a contentious name, which has never been defined in English and is used for multiple unrelated mutations. It should in fact refer to a mutation that is a 'non-eumelanin schizochroic', retaining only phaeomelanin, which is not present in parrots. The name Isabel should therefore be restricted for use in finch species carrying both eumelanin and phaeomelanin. Platinum is more original, but has been used for the dominant dilute blue combination (Whiteface Dominant Silver) in Cockatiels in some countries. Clearbody is a very species-specific name and would not be easily applied to other parrots. Yellow is clearly wrong because it refers to autosomal loci with different actions and Cinnamon refers to a different sex-linked locus.

Later I will discuss the non sex-linked (NSL) ino (a) locus, which has also produced an intermediate allele. This phenotype has been called Lime in Australia.

I am therefore of the opinion that lime should be adopted for partially functional alleles in parrots with structural green and platinum in parrots or combinations without structural green. In Red-rumped Parrots I believe that there are two alleles that fall in this range, so for now I will continue to call the Australian version by its current name of Platinum.

The list of alleles in various species would be as follows:

| SYMBOL | ALLELE | SPECIES |
|---|---|---|
| $X^{INO}$ | wildtype | All species |
| $X^{inol}$ | lime | Indian Ringnecked Parrot, Scarlet-chested Parrot, Red-rumped Parrot and Peachfaced Lovebird |
| $X^{inopl}$ | platinum | Cockatiel and Red-rumped Parrot |
| $X^{inocb}$ | clearbody | Budgerigar (but perhaps should also be lime) |
| $X^{ino}$ | lutino or ino | All species |

All the intermediate alleles exhibit co-dominant inheritance when heterozygous with the ino gene, except the clearbody allele. The resultant phenotype for the heterozygous outcome is midway between the two homozygous phenotypes. This will cause much confusion if multiple intermediate alleles are eventually recognised in many species. All mutant alleles are recessive to the wildtype allele. The ino allele when homozygous, masks the expression of other melanin altering loci because it stops melanin production at such an early stage.

There are also a number of alleles in other species that are most likely lime alleles, but are still in need of confirmation (sometimes because no sex-linked ino exists to test mate with). These species include the Quaker and Swift Parrots.

## Non Sex-linked (NSL) ino locus – a

There exist in a number of species, mutants which show a typical Ino phenotype but which have autosomal recessive inheritance. Many of these do not fit the true ino definition as they show traces of residual melanin (eg Princess Parrot). There is evidence that some are multiple alleles with a recessive dilute in their species (eg lime and ino in the White Eye-ring Lovebird group). Inte Onsman (Mutavi) has theorised that the NSL ino in the Budgerigar is multiple allelic with one of the fallow alleles in that species. Breeders commonly refer to these birds as Recessive Lutino.

George Smith (AVES 1995) has reported the occurrence of an NSL ino in the Indian Ringnecked Parrot, which he believes is multiple allelic with the 'Buttercup' gene. Recent study suggests that the Buttercup is a fallow allele. From these examples it is obvious that there is still much to be studied. However, it may eventually prove that many recessive Dilute and Fallow phenotypes are allocated to this locus as we discover

*The NSL Ino mutation of the Blue and Gold Macaw is also known as 'Golden'. The name 'Golden' is also used for a distinct mutation in Asia that is similar in appearance to the 'Golden' Eastern Rosella. (See page 38.)*

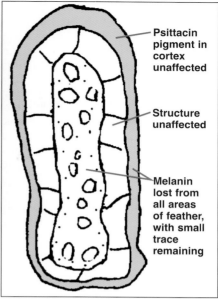

Psittacin pigment in cortex unaffected

Structure unaffected

Melanin lost from all areas of feather, with small trace remaining

*Typical changes to the feather caused by the NSL ino allele are indistinguishable from the sex-linked ino.*

new alleles and learn about their interaction with one another.

In the *Agapornis* White Eye-ring group (Masked, Nyasa, Fischer's and Black-cheeked Lovebirds) it has been shown that the NSL ino locus has a second allele, which in Australia has been known as lime. I have therefore adopted the name lime for all partial ino alleles, both sex-linked and autosomal. Like the sex-linked lime alleles, the autosomal form produces a midway bird when heterozygous with the ino allele. In other words, they exhibit a co-dominant effect with one another, although all alleles are recessive to the wildtype allele.

Many Australian breeders have recently spoken against naming the ino allele in the Princess Parrot a Lutino because of significant apparent green suffusion. It is possible that this bird is in fact a recessive lime allele and that one day the true recessive ino allele will appear. It is also possible that more than one allele of this locus already exists in the Princess Parrot population. It is unacceptable to call this colour morph 'Yellow', because both the Dilute and the Black-eyed Yellow have black eyes and are not albinistic mutations, which this one clearly is.

Below is a list of alleles and their symbols:

| SYMBOL | ALLELE | SPECIES |
|---|---|---|
| A | wildtype | |
| a$^l$ | NSL lime | *Agapornis* White Eye-ring group, Princess Parrot? |
| a | NSL ino | *Agapornis* White Eye-ring group, Elegant Parrot, Pacific Parrotlet |

## Cinnamon locus – X$^{cin}$

The cinnamon locus is perhaps the most common site for mutation of colour across all species of birds. The mutant allele is sex-linked recessive and when homozygous interferes with a step in melanin synthesis, preventing brown melanin from being converted into black melanin. In yellow ground birds, such as most parrots, the mutant allele creates a phenotype known as Cinnamon. When present in a white ground species or combination, the phenotype is known as Fawn or Ivory. Unfortunately a number of white ground combinations in various species have been inappropriately called 'Silvers'. Translation problems from Dutch publications can be blamed for this misnaming, although the Dutch themselves would not use the term. The use of the name 'Silver' for cinnamon blue combinations should cease. Silver is an important term referring to a different combination of mutations. (See page 268.)

It is also important to realise that the Cinnamon phenotype cannot produce black melanin or shades of grey. A number of autosomal recessive dilute or albinistic mutations have been occasionally called 'Recessive Cinnamon'. **These loci are NOT cinnamon** as grey colours are produced. A strict definition must be maintained to avoid confusion. Another area of confusion occurs because prominent Australian breeder and author, Stan Sindel, refers to any mutation that produces a 'yellowing effect' as 'Cinnamon'. It is also popular among some breeders in the USA to refer to mutations in this way. This implies that all these diverse loci operate in the same way. This is not the case and Cinnamon is definitely not a synonym for either the term Yellow or the term Dilute.

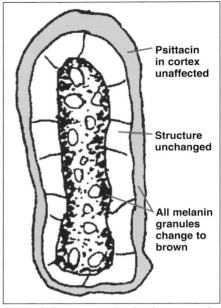

*Typical changes to the feather caused by the cinnamon allele.*

As yet, no multiple alleles have occurred for this locus. Whether this will always be the case is uncertain. The nature of the gene probably gives a clue. If the pigment conversion process is only one step, then brown is either converted or not converted, with no partial steps. Therefore it is unlikely that other alleles of this locus will ever occur. In some species, different strains of Cinnamon seem to vary in intensity and depth of colour. Whether this represents differing alleles or merely variant strains caused by other factors, is (and probably always will be) unclear.

The cinnamon locus does not prevent the expression of any other known locus and, in fact, produces an unexpected combined phenotype with the sex-linked ino allele in some species. (See page 271.) Common features include the conversion of wildtype grey down to brown and ruby-coloured eyes on hatching that darken as the chick ages.

*Cinnamon Plum-headed Parrots – this colour is also known incorrectly as 'Isabel' (cock right, hen above).*

# Dilute (yellow) loci – dil

Dilute loci are widespread in parrot species. When the wildtype gene is replaced with the least functional allele, a mostly yellow bird with a slight green suffusion and a dark eye results. This phenotype is still able to produce melanin but has trouble depositing it in sufficient quantities into feathers. It is the transfer of melanin between the melanocytes in the follicles and the melanosomes in the feathers that is inhibited (quite distinct to the changes caused by various albinistic alleles). Where melanin is present, it is in low concentration, but other-

*Suffused Indian Ringnecked Parrot – this is a typical Dilute colour morph.*

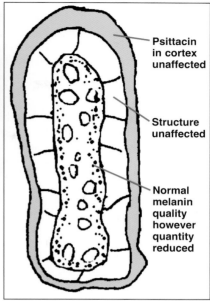

Psittacin in cortex unaffected

Structure unaffected

Normal melanin quality however quantity reduced

*Typical changes to the feather caused by a dilute allele.*

wise unchanged. This is referred to as a quantitative change. Therefore, yellow ground birds generally retain faint traces of green through their plumage and white ground birds retain faint traces of blue. The Dutch and Belgians prefer the name suffused for these lighter alleles and pastel for darker alleles. When the darker dilute alleles are in combination with the grey allele and/or the blue allele (preferably both), the result could be called a Silver.

Multiple alleles for one locus are known in some species (such as the Budgerigar) and will no doubt show up in other species as well. In the English language, the locus for the Budgerigar has been traditionally labelled 'c' for Clearwing. However, if we are to apply symbols across all parrot species, it is more logical to use the 'dil' symbol that has been adopted in Europe. All mutant alleles are autosomal recessive in inheritance. Alleles are listed in descending order of greater recessiveness.

The list of alleles in different species is as follows:

| SYMBOL | ALLELE | SPECIES |
| --- | --- | --- |
| DIL | wildtype | All species |
| $dil^g$ | greywing | Budgerigar (co-dominant with $dil^w$). |
| | pastel or dilute | Other species |
| $dil^w$ | clearwing | Budgerigar (co-dominant with $dil^g$) |
| dil | dilute | Budgerigar |
| | suffused (yellow) | Other species |

In species where more than one dilute locus exists, new symbols need to be given to those that are not alleles of the original form. The difficulty is in knowing which allele belongs to the equivalent of the dilute locus in Budgerigars. Studies of feather structure would probably help resolve this issue, as different Dilute phenotypes are without doubt produced by different gene action if they are not alleles of the one locus. In Budgerigars where three alleles exist for one locus – all are merely partial expressions of one

S HOUSE

another. The greywing allele produces a 50% melanin reduction (equivalent to the pastel definition) and the dilute allele produces an 80–90% reduction in melanin (equivalent to the European suffused definition). The clearwing allele is interesting because it shows differential deposition for different regions of the feather structure, with full deposition being retained in medullary areas, but virtually none in cortical areas. It shows that the gene product has different portions controlling melanin deposition into different regions of the feather.

## Faded (isabel) locus – fd

There also exists a group of colour morphs that are dark 'dilutes' or more precisely dark albinistics. These colours have often been called 'Recessive Cinnamon'. They do not appear to be alleles of the dilute (dil) locus. In phenotype they are slight reductions of the wildtype and I have no doubt that they represent the expression of another locus. They do however need a name and I have previously adopted the name Isabel, which is commonly used in Australia for them. The name Isabel has been widely misused worldwide and in this book I decided to 'bite the bullet' and try to 'kill off' the name Isabel in parrots. However, it should only be replaced by a more suitable name. Breeders should not return to the practice of using other poorly chosen names.

The Dutch originally used the name Isabel during the 1960s as their word (in their language) for Cinnamon or Fawn mutations in species such as the canary and the Zebra Finch. Since then, in the English language, it has fallen into common usage for any bird that looks Cinnamon but is not. It has also been used for the lime allele as well as the faded locus and is currently used in other species for totally unrelated loci. The current Dutch and Belgian system for mutational names classifies Isabel as a partial phaeomelanin schizochroic; in other words, a mutation that retains phaeomelanin but removes all or most eumelanin. If we accept this definition, and we should as they created the name, the name Isabel should only be used in species with phaeomelanin (chestnut-red melanin) in the wildtype plumage. This rules out all parrots.

To avoid the confusion created by the name Isabel, I will assign the Budgerigar name of 'Faded' to this locus and define it as being an albinistic gene with only slight reduction of melanin, retaining black melanin production but often with brownish tones to its melanin. The mutant allele is inherited as an autosomal recessive. *It should be noted also that this colour morph is an albinistic mutation. That means that it affects melanin pigment in all areas of the bird (eyes, feet, skin and feathers) in a qualitative manner. This correlates to the locus being responsible for a facet of melanin production, rather than deposition like dilution mutations or melanoblast migration like leucistic mutations. The faded locus produces the 'darkest' known albinistic colour morphs and they can sometimes almost be mistaken for normals.*

When combined with white ground it produces dark Silver. In Australia, this mutation in Cockatiels is known as the 'West Coast' or 'Western Australia Silver'. The Faded in the Red-rumped Parrot has been called 'Recessive Cinnamon'. In Turquoise Parrots it is known in Europe as Isabel.

In the Budgerigar it is already known as Faded. Perhaps 'Faded' provides a better name for the locus, however only time will tell whether breeders are willing to accept a new name.

## Dominant dilute locus – DD

There are currently two dominant type colour morphs that alter melanin deposition, the Dominant Silver Cockatiel and the misnamed 'Fallow' or 'Isabel' Indian Ringnecked Parrot. Both mutations cause variable decrease in melanin deposition particularly on the wings. In the Cockatiel the colour morph is autosomal co-dominant, with the homozygous mutant phenotype being significantly lighter than the heterozygous phenotype. In the Indian Ringnecked Parrot the colour morph is autosomal dominant. Therefore, grouping the two colour morphs together is more for convenience than signifying a real genetic relationship. I have read reports of a 'Dominant Dilute' mutation in Eastern Rosellas which were similar to the description for the Indian Ringnecked Parrot colour morph, however I am unable to verify the authenticity or existence of this colour morph. The dominant dilute allele in the Indian Ringnecked Parrot has been also called a 'Dominant Cinnamon' in the USA. This is clearly wrong, as the action involved is distinctly different to that of the true cinnamon locus. Unfortunately it has become popular in some sections of aviculture to label every new mutation as a 'Cinnamon'. This only demonstrates a lack of understanding of the true nature of mutations and how different loci act and behave.

How this Dominant Dilute colour morph relates to the recessive dilute locus (such as the 'Pastel Silver', as it is known in Australia) in Cockatiels is totally unknown. The 'Pastel Silver' is the typical true Silver created by the recessive dilute locus well known in other parrot species. It seems unlikely to be allelic for the dominant dilute locus. A study of the feather structure of the colour morph would be extremely interesting for comparison with other known dilute alleles.

The dominant dilute allele in Indian Ringnecked Parrots is producing strange results when combined with other colour morphs. One unusual interaction occurs in combination with the Cinnamon colour morph, where chicks carrying mutant alleles for both loci lack the typical 'ruby'-coloured eye of the Cinnamon colour morph. Differences in expected colouration are less noticeable in fledglings or adult birds, but this does raise a question about gene interaction between these two loci. It also suggests that the Dominant Dilute colour morph may not be a true dilution type mutation, but may be an albinistic type mutation. It is clear that much further research is needed before we can determine the true nature of these colour morphs. And a few more examples in other species would help significantly with collecting the needed information.

Another aspect to consider is whether the Dominant Dilute mutation in Indian Ringnecked Parrots can exist as a homozygous genotype and whether it has a varying phenotype from the heterozygous genotype. The best known form of Dominant Dilute in aviculture occurs in the Zebra Finch, where I (Martin, 1995) have proved beyond doubt that it is homozygous lethal. This form of inheritance is known also as **semi-dominant lethal** and only time will tell if this form of inheritance exists in parrots.

## Fallow loci – f

The fallow loci can be defined by the following phenotype description. Adult birds have red eyes and melanin production is altered so that only faded brown melanin is produced. This results in a yellow-green bird with brown in areas of visible melanin. The mutant alleles are all autosomal recessive. It is important to realise that eye colour alone does not constitute a fallow allele. It must have the melanin change as well. Many other mutations of quite different loci also produce red eyes, but these should never be called Fallow mutations.

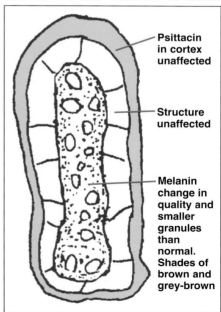

Psittacin in cortex unaffected

Structure unaffected

Melanin change in quality and smaller granules than normal. Shades of brown and grey-brown

*Typical changes to the feather caused by a fallow allele.*

Pale Fallow Moustache Parrot.

Bronze Fallow Turquoise Indian
Ringnecked Parrot.

Bronze Fallow Indian
Ringnecked Parrot.

Bronze Fallow Blue Indian
Ringnecked Parrot.

## Addendum

Once again, increased knowledge must change our understanding. My definition for fallow comes from observation of the Fallow Budgerigar in Australia, as well as definitions used by authors such as Taylor and Warner. But I have now been made aware that the 'English' Fallow Budgerigar, as well as the Fallow mutations in Peachfaced Lovebirds and some other species reduce black melanin to grey-brown, not brown like the common forms I previously knew. I must therefore relent and allow certain flexibility in the classification of Fallow mutations. However, there is a distinct difference between Fallow mutations that change melanin to brown and those changing it into grey or grey-brown. In fact, there could be as many as four or even more distinct loci producing different fallow-like phenotypes (Martin, 2001a).

An international discussion group based on the internet has proposed the following names for different fallow types to attempt to separate the differences into groups. **Ashen** or **Smokey** for 'grey' fallow, **Dun** for 'grey-brown' fallow, **Bronze** for 'brown' fallow and **Pale** (or perhaps **Beige**) for 'pale brown' fallow.

To qualify as a fallow type colour morph, the mutation must be autosomal recessive and be albinistic which implies that the affected loci plays a role in melanin metabolism. As a result melanin granules undergo qualitative changes (altered in colour, size or shape) throughout the body as well as the plumage. The final colour of this melanin may vary, with different loci (altering different spots in the metabolic process) producing different phenotypes ranging from light grey *through grey-brown and brown to pale brown. Melanin in the eyes is particularly affected with adult birds retaining a 'red' eye colour into adult plumage. There are other autosomal recessive albinistic colour morphs that have dark eyes in adults, which are best classified as belonging to the faded locus.*

*One other feature of some Fallow colour morphs is the absence or retention of the 'white iris ring' found in some species. This feature is best known in Budgerigars, where dun fallow (English fallow) loses the white iris ring, but the bronze fallow (German fallow) retains the white iris ring. Most species of parrots with Fallow colour morphs do not have white iris rings in the wildtype phenotype, therefore no observation of this change is possible, however in the Indian Ringnecked Parrot we have two Fallow colour morphs that differ in their iris rings. The 'Recessive Cinnamon' colour morph retains the white iris ring, which correlates perfectly with the bronze fallow category, whilst the 'Buttercup' or 'Yellowhead' colour morph loses the iris ring, which places it in the dun fallow classification, or possibly the ashen fallow group.*

In Budgerigars, more than one loci can produce this or a similar phenotype, therefore it is impossible to determine the correct designation for fallow in other species. Inte Onsman (Mutavi) has suggested that one of the fallow alleles is an allele of the recessive ino locus. If this is the case, then other fallow alleles in different species may also follow this pattern. Only genetic investigation of the nature of the interaction between mutations can determine this. The only species in which this has been tested is the Pacific Parrotlet where the fallow has proven not to be allelic for the NSL ino locus. Only time and opportunity will allow the theory to be tested in other species.

### Addendum
*Recent test matings in Cockatiels between the NSL ino and the bronze fallow have indicated that these two mutant genes are alleles of a single locus, thereby adding support to Inte Onsman's theory.*

Due to poor definitions for fallow in aviculture there are a number of colour morphs in different species that have been given the name incorrectly. The variety commonly called 'Fallow' in Indian Ringnecked Parrots is clearly not a fallow. It probably fits the description for the dominant dilute locus. But the Yellowhead phenotype known as 'Buttercup' is a fallow mutation! The so-called 'Cream' or 'Yellow' Bourke's Parrot is also a fallow colour morph. In Green-cheeked Conures the 'Fallow' colour morph is sex-linked and therefore not a true fallow allele. It is most likely an allele of the sex-linked ino locus, a lime allele.

## Blue locus – b
Mutant alleles of this locus produce some of the most attractive colour morphs in parrots. It is also one of the most frequent loci to be mutated. The blue locus is autosomal and all mutant alleles follow recessive inheritance. The locus represents the main control for production of psittacin pigment. When homozygous for the blue allele, the genetic pathway is non-functional and the bird cannot produce any psittacin pigment at all. As a result, all areas of green become blue in colour and the ground colour changes from yellow to white. It is one of the most important mutations for combination with other colour mutants. All psittacin production stops, so reds, oranges and pinks are also eliminated by the homozygous blue allele. The locus could be viewed as the companion of the ino locus and when combined together the Albino phenotype is produced.

As with the ino locus, multiple alleles are common. In some species more than two alleles have been identified. In the Budgerigar at least four occur (including two b alleles). In the Peachfaced Lovebird two mutant alleles exist (but neither is the b allele) and in the Scarlet-chested Parrot there are possibly three mutant alleles (although evidence in

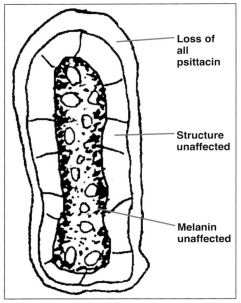

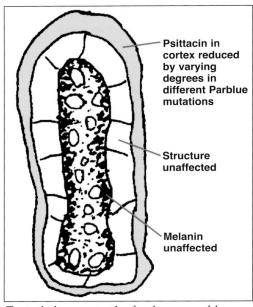

*Typical changes to the feather caused by a blue allele.*

*Typical changes to the feather caused by a parblue allele.*

Australia suggests that we may have a gene occupying another unrelated locus).

Because of the large number of alleles in different species, much confusion has occurred about the inheritance systems for them. Budgerigars in particular have presented much confusion and the best explanation (developed by Peter Bergman, 1998) is that there are two different b alleles that combine in a surprising way to create a Parblue phenotype. The most widely recognised form of the blue allele is possibly the abnormal one when taken in context with other species. The other blue allele is generally incorrectly called the Yellowface mutant 1 (b$^{yf}$ m1) allele. In fact this second blue allele could be the direct analogue of the blue allele present in the Indian Ringnecked Parrot, the Scarlet-chested Parrot, the Cockatiel and probably other species.

For a full explanation of the function of the various alleles in the Budgerigar, I refer the reader to the excellent article on the internet by Peter Bergman (Bergman, 1998), found at Clive Hesford's web site.

Peter Bergman's explanation involves a discussion of

*The 'Creamface Blue' Budgerigar, also known as 'Yellowface mutant 1' is the heterozygous pairing of two different blue alleles. When either allele is homozygous, they are indistinguishable from one another.*

**heteroalleles** and how they interact to produce their gene product. The concept involves alleles of the blue locus that are damaged in different sections of their DNA sequence. Each produces a slightly modified protein structure that when assembled in a heterozygous fashion results in an increase in protein function that neither allele had on its own. The increased activity of the heterozygous gene product is known as **complementation**. The two partial blue alleles in the Budgerigar (b$^{gf}$ and b$^{yfm2}$) are standard alleles of the second blue allele, but these three are all heteroalleles of the original blue allele. Therefore heterozygous birds which combine two heteroalleles will produce greater amounts of psittacin than either of the individual alleles would under homozygous circumstances. This is in contrast to most alleles with standard co-dominance, that produce an intermediate product when in a heterozygous state.

The Peachfaced Lovebird also has two alleles that interact unexpectedly. In this case both are partial blue alleles and the heterozygous genotype ($b^{pb}$ m1$b^{pb}$ m2) bird produces more psittacin than either allele in homozygous form. Once again this has created significant confusion for breeders. This species shows that the protein produced by the wildtype (B) allele is complex and can be altered in numerous ways. These two partial blue alleles should also be considered heteroalleles.

At least one lovebird author, Dr Alessandro D'Angieri, has suggested that two closely linked loci exist in the Peachfaced Lovebird and that crossover can occur between them. The problem with this theory is explaining why a bird which is double split for the two partial blue alleles is not a normal phenotype. This can only be explained if the two alleles are multiple allelic for the one locus. The crossover that he has observed can theoretically occur in the section between the two heteroalleles, thereby creating a 'new' normal allele and a mutant allele with two damaged sections (one at either end of the chain). This is called an **intragenic crossover** and the chances of this happening are extremely small, but the recombinant frequency quoted by Dr D'Angieri is so low that it fits nicely with the heteroallele theory.

*The Applegreen Peachfaced Lovebird is another example of heteroallelic complementation. This phenotype carries more yellow psittacin pigment than when either allele is found in homozygous genotypes.*

The Scarlet-chested Parrot also presents some difficulty for our understanding. European avian geneticists recognise a total of three alleles, one of which is the blue allele. However, in Australia, whilst we recognise two parblue alleles (Seagreen and Parblue) and a blue allele (White-fronted Blue), it has been suggested that the two parblue genes may not be alleles of each other at all. It is believed by many that when these are combined they form a phenotype almost identical to the true blue allele. To add confusion, I believe that we do have populations of the true blue allele, which would be multiple allelic with one of the partial blues but not the other. If you then consider that all the blue versions have been regularly interbred, you can start to understand the confusion that can occur.

*Turquoise Moustache Parrot – often incorrectly called 'Blue' by breeders.*

We definitely have White-fronted Blue phenotypes that do not breed true and when Seagreens and Parblues are crossed, it is possible to produce wildtype phenotypes, which is impossible with the standard multiple allelic series. Only extensive and deliberate experimentation can shed light on the true situation in Australia.

An alternative theory I have been developing is that the apparent wildtype phenotypes produced by combining the two partial blue alleles, is in fact a heterozygous genotype ($b^{pb}$ m1$b^{pb}$ m2) exhibiting similar gene expression to the same heterozygous genotype in the Peachfaced Lovebird. One of the partial blue alleles in the Scarlet-chested Parrot naturally produces more psittacin than either partial blue in the Peachfaced Lovebird. When combined with a second partial blue allele that is heteroallelic, it could theoretically produce a wildtype phenotype from the hybrid of two defective protein components.

R LOW

P FIELDING

*Turquoise Red-rumped Parrot – this European mutation is a typical Parblue. Note the red psittacin pigment in the rump. Colour combinations with this mutation reveal yellow psittacin retained through most of the plumage.*

Y IMANOTHAI

*Above: Blue Black-cheeked Lovebird.*
*Right: Blue Yellow-naped Amazon.*

The list of alleles for various species is as follows:

| SYMBOL | ALLELE | SPECIES |
|---|---|---|
| B | wildtype | All species |
| b$^{gf}$ | goldenface seagreen | Budgerigar Other species? (a homoallele of b$^{m1}$) |
| b$^{pbm1}$ | turquoise | Most species (Yellowface mutant 2 in the Budgerigar) |
| b$^{pbm2}$ | aqua | Peachfaced Lovebird and some other species |
| b$^{m1}$ | blue | Most species (called Yellowface mutant 1 in the Budgerigar) |
| b$^{m2}$ | alternate blue | Budgerigar (the original Blue) |

**Note**: I have designated the original blue allele in Budgerigars as b$^{m2}$ to bring this species into line with what we see in other parrot species. This is the opposite designation used by most Budgerigar geneticists.

One theory proposes that in the Scarlet-chested Parrot, we have the b$^{m1}$ allele, the b$^{pbm1}$ allele and an ab$^{sg}$ allele (alternate blue locus – seagreen). Therefore a bird with the genotype b$^{pbm1}$ b$^{pbm1}$, ab$^{sg}$ ab$^{sg}$ is phenotypically indistinguishable from a b$^{m1}$ b$^{m1}$ bird (the blue genotype).

My alternative theory involves a b$^{m1}$ allele, a b$^{pbm1}$ allele and a b$^{pbm2}$ allele with the latter being a heteroallele of the first two. These would produce the following phenotypes when combined:

*In Australia some 'White-fronted' Blue Scarlet-chested Parrots carry faint but distinct traces of psittacin pigment. These birds do not appear to be the true Blue colour morph, but may represent the b$^{m1}$ b$^{pbm1}$ genotype. The true Blue colour morph also occurs, but is rarely distinguished by breeders as being different.*

| GENOTYPE | PHENOTYPE |
|---|---|
| $b^{m1} b^{m1}$ | True blue appearance |
| $b^{m1} b^{pbm1}$ | Slight psittacin production, almost true blue |
| $b^{pb\,m1} b^{pbm1}$ | Parblue – typical Partial Blue with 'cream' ground colour |
| $b^{pbm2} b^{pbm2}$ | Seagreen – almost full psittacin production on the back with reduced production on the front of the bird |
| BB, $Bb^{pbm1}$, $Bb^{pbm2}$, $Bb^{m1}$ or $b^{pbm1}b^{pbm2}$ | Normal Green phenotype |
| $b^{m1} b^{pbm2}$ | Unknown/unrecognised phenotype? |

I currently consider that my alternate theory is the more likely of the two. I believe that the first theory is unlikely primarily because no alternate blue loci are known in other species. This is obviously not sufficient and only extensive breeding experiments can determine the true nature of the blue locus in the Scarlet-chested Parrot.

## Dark factor locus – D

A synonym for this locus is the olive locus, but I will use the dark factor nomenclature to remain consistent with the accepted Budgerigar terminology. The mutant dark factor allele is autosomal co-dominant.

The heterozygous phenotype is known as the Dark Green and the homozygous phenotype as the Olive. In some countries the name 'Jade' has been used for the Dark Green and should be considered a synonym, with Dark Green being the correct term. The dark factor locus is the most common site for alteration to the structural colour. The mutant allele alters structural colour through changes in the depth of the cloudy layer in the medulla, immediately under the cortex. As the thickness of this layer changes, different wavelengths of light are scattered and our eyes see different colours. This mutation affects the structure by causing a smaller cloudy layer than exists in the

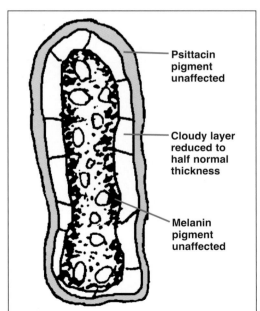

*Typical changes to the feather caused by the heterozygous genotype (Dd) – the phenotype is known as Dark Green.*

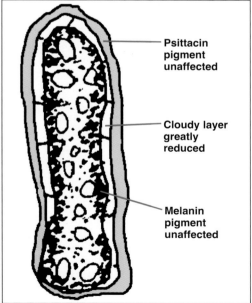

*Typical changes to the feather caused by the homozygous mutant genotype (DD) – the phenotype is known as Olive.*

wildtype bird. The heterozygous (Dd) genotype results in half thickness for the cloudy layer and the homozygous genotype (DD) results in very little cloudy layer production. As a result the phenotypes (in yellow ground birds) change from a brighter (Normal) green, through a darker green and eventually to an olive green. The Olive Green generally varies little from a Greygreen, depending on the species involved. The changes to appearance can be summarised as a loss of brightness and apparent darkening of the shade of colour produced. In a white ground bird, colour changes from light blue, through cobalt blue and eventually to a blue-grey colour, known as Mauve but sometimes incorrectly referred to as 'Slate'.

*Above: Dark Green Fischer's Lovebird.*
*Below: Olive Fischer's Lovebird.*

Correctly identifying dark factor colour morphs has not proven to be as easy as many would have thought. The structural changes are most easily distinguished when psittacin pigment is removed. This can be naturally present in certain plumage regions in some species (eg face and wings of Turquoise Parrots) or can be achieved via combination of the dark factor with a Blue colour morph. Yet even in these circumstances many aviculturists fail to recognise the mauve colour change, instead interpreting this colour as a grey colour change. Their expectations have been for a colour either with more blue in it or perhaps a violet tinge, when in reality the colour created in all species is a blue-grey, even in the Budgerigar where the name Mauve was first coined.

This misconception as to exactly what colour constitutes Mauve has led to a number of Violet colour morphs being incorrectly identified as a product of dark factor alleles. It has even led some authors to suggest that the Olive colour morphs in the Turquoise Parrot and the Peachfaced Lovebird are really Greygreen colour morphs. To distinguish the dark factor locus from the grey locus we have only the inheritance pattern and the appearance of two distinct mutant phenotypes to act as definite

*Cobalt Indian Ringnecked Parrot.*

guides, thereby removing any doubt caused through the interpretation of colours by the human eye. Microscopically the changes that are produced by the two loci are similar, although distinctly different. When this is combined with species-specific changes to phenotype, it is to be expected that the two loci could produce identical phenotypes in some species but slightly differing phenotypes in other species. I would therefore argue that form of inheritance (combined with assessment of gene linkage) is the only reliable method to allocate an allele to the correct locus.

One other aspect of inheritance must also be considered. In Budgerigars there is gene linkage between the dark factor locus and the blue locus. The recombinant frequency is 14%, giving a locus separation of 14 map units. (See page 274.) It would therefore be expected that these two loci would also be linked in other species. This may not always be true, as part of what makes species different can be translocation of genes to new areas of a chromosome. If this occurs over any significant distance, then these two loci could then behave as if they are no longer linked. It is important to realise that chromosomes are hundreds of map units long, but only genes that are relatively close together act as linked genes. A recombinant frequency of 50% follows the Law of Segregation exactly and must be interpreted as unlinked. Recombinant frequency calculations lose accuracy with distance as double crossovers may take place. Therefore tightly linked loci are the most accurate to map.

The grey locus has never shown any linkage to any other locus yet detected. Therefore, if a mutant structural allele shows linkage to the blue locus, we can assume that it lies at the dark factor locus and represents the Dark Green and Olive phenotypes. However the converse is not necessarily true, as I have just discussed.

### Addendum
*Preliminary data collected by myself on recombinant frequencies for the dark factor and the blue loci in Peachfaced Lovebirds indicates a linkage at least as strong as in Budgerigars, confirming that we are dealing with the dark factor locus in this species.*

The function of the dark factor locus is to determine the thickness of the cloudy layer. As the inheritance form is co-dominant, we can assume that two wildtype (dd) alleles are required to produce the full structure of the cloudy layer and one wildtype allele results in incomplete development of the cloudy layer. The dark factor (D) allele can be assumed to be a non-functional allele.

Dr D'Angieri has suggested that the dark factor trait is controlled by three closely linked loci. The purpose of this theory is to explain the variation sometimes seen between different individuals expressing phenotypes of this locus. However, the behaviour of these alleles and their phenotypes is not consistent with either multiple loci or multiple alleles. Therefore, the most plausible explanation is that variations in colour are created by separate 'modifier' genes. Peter Bergman has identified this modifier in the Budgerigar as one which slightly alters the phenotype of both Violet and Dark Factor colour morphs in this species.

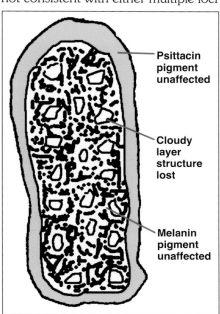

## Grey locus – G
The grey locus is the second most common site for structural colour alteration. It can be considered to control the characteristics of cloudy layer production. The mutant grey (G) allele is autosomal dominant. If the bird is **not** homozygous for the wildtype allele (gg), the cloudy layer does not develop and no structural blue colour is possible. Therefore a yellow ground bird with either one or two grey (G-) alleles is phenotypically a Greygreen and a white ground bird with either one or two grey (G-) alleles is phenotypically a Grey.

Some species, such as the Cockatiel, are natural expressions of the homozygous grey (GG) genotype. Structural colour is therefore

*Typical changes to the feather caused by the grey allele.*

Labels on figure:
Psittacin pigment unaffected
Cloudy layer structure lost
Melanin pigment unaffected

impossible in these species, thereby ruling out any change in appearance (or expression) resulting from alleles at either the dark factor or violet loci. No dark factor form of the Cockatiel can exist unless a reverse mutation allows the grey locus to function again and recreate the structural colours of the bird's ancestors. Similarly, no Blue or Green phenotype is possible. It takes a very fortuitous mutation to reactivate a damaged gene. It is not theoretically impossible, just extremely rare. The hope lies in the locus being present and simply lacking

the start sequence, which could be replaced with a chance translocation of a start sequence from another gene. Significant damage to the DNA sequence in the body of the gene would be almost impossible to reverse without the use of gene splicing technology to introduce a functional wildtype (g) allele from another species. What must be considered (when dreaming of blue and green Cockatiels) is that without selection pressure to maintain functional wildtype (g) alleles, the locus would have deteriorated further once the initial function was lost. Restoration of its function therefore becomes increasingly improbable the longer the time since grey plumage evolved in this species and the ability to produce constructive interference was lost.

*Greygreen Plum-headed Parrot cock and hen (inset).*

It should also be realised, that without selection pressure to maintain green plumage colouration, other loci producing structural features essential for constructive interference to occur (dark factor, violet, slate, etc) could also be damaged. This means that even if the grey locus were repaired in some way, all the other necessary structural loci might then be found to be defective as well. In fact, the likelihood of other loci degenerating would increase in proportion to the length of time since green plumage colouration was lost by the species. If

*Greygreen Alexandrine Parrot (R) produced via hybridisation with the Indian Ringnecked Parrot. It is different from the Recessive Greygreen that is bred in Europe from pure Alexandrine strains.*

a species evolved thousands or even a million years ago, it can be confidently predicted that other structural loci **will** be non-functional. Structural colouration is far too complex a process to ever be reconstructed through random mutation. Therefore the hope of a true Green or Blue phenotype in Cockatiels **is** a forlorn hope!

The classification of a phenotype into either Olive or Greygreen has already been discussed and I refer the reader to the section on the dark factor locus. (See page 245.) Remember also that any new dominant mutation will first appear in the heterozygous form. Therefore, if the first phenotypic change to occur appears to be an Olive – then it is probably actually a Greygreen.

## Violet locus – V

The violet locus is the third locus known to control structural colour and the least common discussed so far. Like the other two loci, it takes two functional wildtype alleles to produce the normal outcome. The mutant violet (V) allele is generally considered as an autosomal dominant gene, however differing phenotypes for heterozygous and homozygous violet genotypes can be visualised. Therefore it should be considered co-dominant.

The action of the gene is to control the shape of the cloudy layer and the shape of the feather barb. The violet allele causes changes that result in altered light scattering from the cloudy layer, changing the light frequencies seen by our eyes. The actual light frequency scattered depends on the exact combination of this allele with alleles of the other structural loci, particularly the dark factor locus. To obtain the classic Visual Violet phenotype in the Budgerigar, the bird requires a genotype of VvDdbb. Other combinations affect the wavelength with each producing slightly different phenotypes.

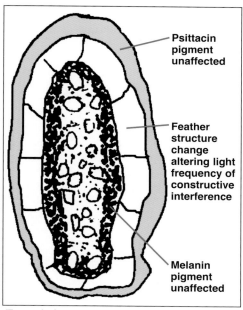

Typical changes to the feather caused by the violet allele.

Recently, Peter Bergman (1999) has been responsible for the 'rediscovery' and further development of earlier work by Taylor and Warner. This demonstrated that the VVbb genotype produces a phenotype very close to the Visual Violet. It has also been suggested that the VVDdbb genotype produces a similar phenotype to the Mauve. The Vvbb genotype produces a phenotype very similar to the Ddbb genotype. Therefore the question must be asked whether the violet locus would have become the dark factor locus by mistake or by default if it had been identified first.

This is the exact situation that appears to have occurred in the Indian Ringnecked Parrot with the so-called Dark Green and Cobalt birds. Further investigation is needed and the Violet theory is far from controversial, but logically it appears to be correct.

Multiple alleles are unknown for any of the structural loci, therefore the suggestion made by some that the European and USA forms differ seems unlikely but cannot be dismissed. In the Indian Ringnecked Parrot it is possible that one is the dark factor locus and the other the violet locus (Smith, D, 1999).

### Addendum

*Recently a USA breeder has produced the Violet phenotype, proving that the USA colour morph is a violet allele. And the latest news is that feather studies of the European colour morph have shown it to be a dark factor allele and breeders have now produced a Mauve phenotype to confirm it. Deon Smith, from South Africa, has been proven correct with his theories.*

P ODEKERKEN

Single Factor Violet Blue Indian Ringnecked Parrot.

## Khaki locus – K

There are now five probable examples of this newly identified colour locus in parrots. The colour morph in Black-cheeked Lovebirds has been called Misty, but in other species the colour is known incorrectly as either Greygreen or Olive. These latter choices are clearly wrong and should be discouraged at all cost, as they are well defined for other established loci. I have chosen to use the name Khaki because it was used by the original breeder of the colour morph in Scarlet-chested Parrots and is reasonably descriptive as well as being distinct. European geneticists have chosen to use the name Misty.

*Khaki Rainbow Lorikeet – this is the 'dark morph' being bred from Khaki lines. The genetic control of this phenotype has yet to be determined.*

*Khaki Rainbow Lorikeet.*

I believe that this locus is a structural locus, like similar appearing dark factor and grey loci. It is also an autosomal dominant (possibly co-dominant) locus. However it has one significant difference in phenotype from these other loci; the effect does not appear to be uniform over the whole plumage.

*Khaki Twenty-eight Parrot.*

In all known examples, the areas of plumage naturally green in the wildtype become a khaki colour (appearing to lose structural colour), whilst areas naturally blue in the wildtype become a lighter blue (appearing to retain some structural colour). In theory, if this allele were combined with a Blue colour morph, we may end up with a 'blue-faced grey' phenotype. And interestingly, a bird fitting this description has appeared in Indian Ringnecked Parrots, which may be a sixth example of this locus.

Unfortunately, respected Australian aviculturist Stan Sindel has attempted to redefine the dark factor locus to fit this colour morph. In his latest book (Sindel, 1999)

*Above: Khaki Scarlet-chested Parrot hen – some individuals are 'dark morphs' which could represent the homozygous genotype.*
*Left: Khaki Scarlet-chested Parrot cock – the more common 'light morph' appears to be the heterozygous genotype.*

1. Seagreen Khaki Scarlet-chested Parrot cock.
2. Misty Grey Indian Ringnecked Parrot cock (right) and hen.
3. A colour morph in the Blue-fronted Amazon known to breeders as 'Olive'. It has features more consistent with the Khaki.
4. Blue Khaki Scarlet-chested Parrot hen.
5. Misty Greygreen Indian Ringnecked Parrot.
6. Misty Indian Ringnecked Parrot.

*Above: Aqua Khaki Scarlet-chested Parrot hen.*
*Left: Aqua Khaki Scarlet-chested Parrot cock.*

he defines Olive mutations as altering only green colours (not blue colours). This is not the case, as anyone who has ever bred Cobalt or Mauve in Budgerigars, Peachfaced Lovebirds, Masked Lovebirds or Lineolated Parrots will testify. But because Sindel has published many books that discuss colour morphs in Australian parrot species, he has added greatly to the level of confusion that exists in aviculture over the true nature of various mutations and how colours should be correctly named.

The species with established colour morphs that appear to fit this locus are the Scarlet-chested Parrot (Olive), Swift Parrot (Greygreen), Black-cheeked Lovebird (Misty), Port Lincoln Parrot (Olive) and the Rainbow Lorikeet (Olive).

The action of this locus is yet to be studied microscopically because there are no examples in Budgerigars, hence I can only theorise at present. But I am confident that in a few years we will be able to talk confidently of a 'new mutation' in parrots that is unknown to Budgerigar breeders.

## Opaline locus – $X^{op}$

Z RANA

The opaline locus is the only known distribution locus that is not species specific. It has only been positively identified in Australian species of parrots to date, although a new mutation in Peachfaced Lovebirds could represent the same locus. There is also a possibility in the Plum-headed Parrot and certain species of conure (Martin, 1999c). The locus controls the distribution of all types of pigment. It has no effect on structural colour, nor does it alter the type of pigments produced. However it does affect distribution of pigment, both overall for each class of pigment (melanin and psittacin) and the relative proportions and spread of different forms of both psittacins and melanins. If 'advanced' psittacins (reds and pinks) are present, along with yellow, their relative distribution is often increased dramatically. Melanins are often reduced in distribution, but may also be spread into previously unoccupied areas of plumage. The exact phenotype is highly variable between species as pigment distribution is also under strict control by the many genes that make a species unique.

*Turquoise Opaline Indian Ringnecked Parrot – a new colour still being studied.*

A number of strong markers which denote the

*Above and right: Opaline Plum-headed Parrot – another new colour still being studied.*

presence of an opaline allele have been identified through research and observation by Clive Hesford (1998) and myself (Martin, 1999b). The first common feature is that all known opaline alleles (in Australian parrots) cause retention of the white underwing stripe (normally present only in hens and immatures) in adult cocks of the mutant phenotype. These stripes are double, one line through the primary and secondary flight feathers, being visible dorsally as well as ventrally, and another through the underwing coverts. The Rose-headed Peachfaced Lovebird does not show this feature which could

indicate that wing stripes are a feature that developed at the time when the Australian species separated from other groups of parrots. More opaline alleles are needed (particularly in Afro-Asiatic and South American species) before this can be fully considered.

The second feature involves changes to the down of chicks. In species where this is normally grey, it becomes snow-white and appears more luxuriant than normal. It is caused by a loss of melanin from the down, but not psittacin. Therefore in species with yellow down, no change will be noted. Interestingly, the Peachfaced Lovebird has both psittacin and melanin in the down and the new mutation in this species called 'Rose-headed' loses the melanin but not the psittacin, creating an altered yellow down in the chicks. In adults with down, it is also lacking in melanin. Opaline chicks are often easier to detect at the down stage, at approximately ten days of age, than after they fully feather.

The third feature is the way melanin is lost from body feathers, generally starting from central areas of the feather and creating either a 'pearl' effect or leaving a faint crescent of melanin on each feather. The expression of this feature is highly variable, with the Opaline being closer to normal phenotype if a larger crescent is retained or is brighter and clearer (showing their ground colour) if the crescent is very thin.

*Above and right:*
*Opaline Indian*
*Ringnecked Parrot –*
*a new colour still*
*being studied.*

The fourth feature is the enhancement of psittacin pigments. As mentioned already, red and pink psittacin pigment is greatly increased in distribution through the plumage. At the same time, yellow psittacin is also increased in distribution if it is not already evenly distributed throughout the plumage of the wildtype. This effect is most noticeable in species such as Red-rumped Parrots and Cockatiels, especially when combined with their Lutino colour morphs.

The fifth feature is the redistribution of melanin pigments, which primarily consists of reduced distribution of foreground melanin in most species and includes reduction of background melanin in some species. Interestingly, a few species have limited areas of increased background melanin. This is seen across the back and wings of the Opaline Budgerigar. In the Bourke's Parrot (Rose) we often see variable areas of blue colouration added through the plumage. This also correlates to the addition of background melanin, as this species' wildtype colouration is predominantly foreground melanin.

The sixth, final and most important feature is its form of genetic inheritance, which is sex-linked recessive. There are only two other common loci (the cinnamon and ino loci) and two rare ones (the slate and orange loci) with this form of inheritance and none can be easily confused with this locus.

The phenotypes produced by the mutant alleles of this locus must be considered some of the most attractive available and they combine readily and distinctively with all other known colour mutations.

## Melanistic locus – m

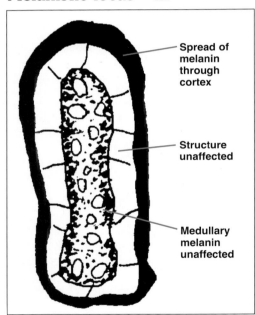

Typical changes to the feather caused by the melanistic allele in the Eastern Rosella.

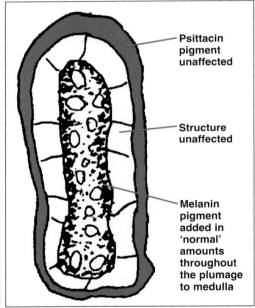

Typical changes to the feather caused by the melanistic allele in lorikeet species.

This appears to be a specialised melanin distribution locus. In its wildtype form it restricts melanin to certain areas of the plumage. When the mutant allele is present, melanin is allowed to cover the entire plumage area. There are currently four examples of this locus, the Black Eastern Rosella, the Blackface Budgerigar, the Melanistic Stella's Lory and the Blue-fronted Rainbow Lorikeet. Whether all these mutations represent alleles of the same locus or different species-specific loci is unknown at present. I suspect that the two lorikeet forms may be analogous, but that the other two forms represent a second and third loci. In species with an even spread of melanin over the whole body, this locus is either not present or is already non-functional. If the locus is non-functional, then possible future reactivation may produce a new pigment pattern, but this seems highly unlikely for most species. Unlike the opaline locus, this locus has no effect on psittacin distribution, although some breeders have hoped that it does remove psittacin pigment (the reason for combining it with the ino allele). Currently there is no evidence to suggest that this will work.

The two lorikeet forms show increased melanin spread through the body colour areas deep within the medulla, but merely filling areas where no melanin previously existed. The Black Eastern Rosella has a spread of melanin through foreground areas, suggesting a loss of control of the foreground markings, but once again there is no increased

D MARSHALL

*Melanistic Eastern Rosellas.*

melanin in pre-existing areas. (It is difficult to tell when the foreground is already black). However the Blackface Budgerigar mutation is possibly the most interesting of all as it exhibits an overall increase of melanin in all areas, resulting in enlargement of facial spots, and also a deepening of body colour caused by increased melanin in areas that already contained melanin. This is distinct from the two lorikeet forms, where areas previously containing melanin are unaltered.

Obviously much is yet to be learnt about these mutations, and with time I suspect that many more Melanistic mutations will occur. It is even possible that more than one type will occur in some species. The Zebra Finch has four genetically and phenotypically distinct melanistic mutations.

## Pied Loci

Pieds comprise a loose grouping of loci that affect pigment deposition. Their effects are not even over the whole body of the bird. Mutant alleles cause random patchy suppression of melanin pigment deposition. This is achieved through defective melanoblast migration in the embryo. Areas of the body lacking melanocytes cannot deposit melanin pigments. Patterns vary between species and even between individual birds of a single species.

The term pied was defined early on as

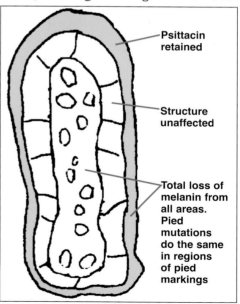

**Psittacin retained**

**Structure unaffected**

**Total loss of melanin from all areas. Pied mutations do the same in regions of pied markings**

*Typical changes to the feather caused by the black-eyed clear allele. Changes caused by pied alleles are similar in the regions of pied markings. Non-pied regions of Pied colours morphs are unaffected.*

representing partial leucism, leucism being the complete loss of melanin pigments from feathers but **not** other body parts. This definition does not strictly apply nowadays, with the appearance of many Pied colour morphs which affect pigments of fleshy body parts such as the feet and the bill. In fact many breeders keen on Pieds look for odd birds with depigmented toes as an indication of a latent pied gene. However, it is important to realise that not all Pied colour morphs show pied toes.

Based upon standard definitions, pied alleles should not alter any psittacin pigments, but as discussed elsewhere, there are some unusual phenotype changes created by certain pied alleles. Apart from the ADM (anti-dimorphism) pied locus, other pieds are recorded as affecting psittacin in some circumstances. Lovebird breeders universally accept that the peach-coloured psittacin in the face is reduced in dispersal. However no typical pied markings are ever seen in the face area, so I am not comfortable labelling these changes as pied effects. At the same time, total (apparent) lack of melanocyte migration in the Black-eyed Clear (Australian Pied) Red-rumped Parrot appears to result in total loss of red psittacin, combined with enhancement of yellow psittacin. The ADM Pieds have shown us that some pied alleles work on loci that have more than one function (ie they are pleiotrophic), therefore some of these other aberrant pied effects may be due to pied loci with as yet unrecognised pleiotrophic effects. Pleiotrophic loci are often control loci, those that turn on or off other loci.

At least four pied loci occur, with possibly more waiting to be recognised. How and whether these pied forms vary in actual molecular action is unknown. However, one pied locus identified and described by myself (Martin, 1999a) is extremely unusual in that it also controls dimorphism in the species in which it occurs.

Some pied forms (called Black-eyed Clear) create a phenotype that is similar to the lightest dilute allele known as suffused (commonly referred to incorrectly as Yellow). The difference is that dilutes are created by evenly reduced numbers of melanin granules in all feathers but these 'Yellow' Pieds have occasional full-coloured feathers but no trace of melanin in other areas.

Another important feature of Pied mutations is whether the melanin is removed fully or partially from 'pied' feathers. The original definition for pied required total removal of melanin or none at all. If feathers showed only a partial loss of melanin (with part of the feather retaining full melanin), then the name Grizzle was given to them. As more pied alleles and loci have become known, it has become apparent that the dividing line between these two names is indistinct. ADM Pied birds show grizzle features and Grizzle birds can have fully pied feathers.

There is also a pied form known as 'Headspot Pied'. As the name suggests, the total pied markings in this mutation comprise a spot on the head. It is believed to be a sex-linked mutation and is known to occur in both the Budgerigar and the Indian Ringnecked Parrot at this time. It has also been theorised in Cockatiels.

H KREMER

*Recessive Pied Crimson Rosella – Dominant Pied Crimson Rosellas have also been established in Europe. The 'pied' pattern in the crimson regions is not typical behaviour for Pied mutations and is not seen in the red plumage of other species such as the Pied Peachfaced Lovebird. The mode of action is yet to be explained, however colour morphs like this one suggest that melanocytes (or the genes that control them) may play a role in the metabolism of red psittacin pigment in at least some species of parrots.*

## Dominant pied locus – P

Dominant pied loci are known in a number of species. In the Budgerigar two separate dominant pied loci are currently known. The phenotypes produced by the two dominant loci can be identified separately with experience, however both are typical pieds in appearance. These loci cause irregular clear areas on the wings, particularly the flight feathers, as well as on restricted areas of the body. One of these dominant loci (known as the Dutch Pied) has a cumulative effect when combined with the recessive pied allele (known as the Danish Pied). This cumulative effect is an unusual form of genetic interaction between unrelated alleles from different loci. It means that the alleles complement each other and, when combined, produce a phenotype beyond what would be expected from combining the two in normal circumstances. Most combinations of mutants from different loci have no direct effect on each other's expression. For example, blue and ino alleles do not interact, both maintain their own function,

*Dominant Pied Fischer's Lovebird. This colour has been called 'Greenwing' in some publications and its inheritance incorrectly recorded as recessive.*

resulting in the straight combination of the two effects. But when Danish and Dutch Pieds are combined, the phenotype produced is a 'Black-eyed Clear'. This is obviously an amplification of the leucistic effect, but neither primary mutation reduces pigment to anywhere near the degree of the combination.

Dominant pied alleles in other species do not necessarily produce phenotypes anything like those in Budgerigars. At this point in time, it is impossible to determine if any of these mutants in differing species are alleles of the one or many different loci. However, in the Red-fronted Kakariki, dominant and recessive cumulative interaction between pied alleles has also been shown, suggesting analogous alleles and loci in this species, to those in Budgerigars.

The Australian Pied is given the genetic symbol (PB) by Budgerigar geneticists.

## Recessive pied locus – r

The recessive pied locus is known in a large number of species, probably more than the dominant loci. No species has been proven to have more than one example of recessive pied loci at present. Therefore it is uncertain whether they all represent one locus or more. I believe that there are probably more, but the problem is finding features unique to a locus so that it can be reliably identified across species.

A common feature of recessive pieds in all species and Families of birds is the phenomenon of reduced penetrance. In a typical recessive mutation, heterozygous individuals should have a normal phenotype. However with most Recessive Pieds we find **some** but not all heterozygous birds showing pied features. Technically, if the proportion of pied heterozygous birds is greater than the proportion of normal heterozygous birds, then it can be said that the pied allele is the one lacking the penetrance and is in fact dominant. It is a fine line where one form of inheritance blends into the other. In practice, to keep things simple and to avoid excessive confusion for the general aviculturist, I believe it is best to call them recessive unless the heterozygous state produces a significant phenotype 100% of the time such as is the case with the co-dominant loci. Some people would like to classify them as co-dominant, but again much confusion occurs for the lay person who asks how a Normal can be split for a dominant. This is the first lesson we all learn!

In most genera of parrots, Recessive Pieds generally show strong pied markings with patchy appearance. I would normally say that no pattern is evident in the markings, but it has been pointed out to me that this is not always so. The patterns are probably under multigenic control and patient breeders have been able to produce symmetrical and beautiful phenotypes through heavy selection pressure.

There is a locus in two *Psephotus* spp. and a few other parrot species, that produces a Black-eyed Clear phenotype when homozygous for the mutant allele. I believe that it should be recognised as a distinctly different locus. However European geneticists generally refer to them as Recessive Pied in a number of lovebird species. They represent full leucism and I therefore view these colour morphs as being related to Pied, but distinct because they lack the randomness of a pied pattern. Another feature that illustrates their relationship is seen through the occasional lack of penetrance that the wildtype allele exhibits over the mutant allele. This results in some birds with heterozygous genotype producing a Pied phenotype and has led to the common misconception that this represents a dominant or co-dominant pied trait. However, this feature is not consistent and is no different from the variable penetrance already discussed for recessive pied alleles. The black-eyed clear locus produces a 'Black-eyed Yellow' phenotype which carries the occasional full coloured feather and heterozygous birds with a Normal phenotype and the occasional clear feather. This is not a dominant trait!

D VAN DEN ABEELE

This Fischer's Lovebird colour morph is classified as a Recessive Pied in Europe and the USA. It appears similar to the 'Australian Yellow' Peachfaced Lovebird. I believe that it is more accurate to call them Black-eyed Clear, which is a subgroup of pied type colour morphs.

## Anti-dimorphism (ADM) pied locus – dm

The anti-dimorphism pied locus is the most recent locus to be identified beyond doubt and forms a new class of mutation because the mutant allele eliminates the plumage dimorphism of the sexes. None of the other pied loci have any effects beyond the altered deposition of melanin. However, the mutant allele of this locus, when homozygous, prevents the occurrence of normal sexual dimorphism. This can result in changes to the distribution of pigments, including psittacins and can even alter structural colour. Whether this locus occurs in non-dimorphic species cannot be determined, but a number of pieds previously called Recessive Pieds have now been reclassified to this locus. Mutant alleles of this pied locus are the only ones, at this time, that can be positively identified across species, with certainty as to where they belong.

Another feature which is becoming apparent for this locus, is that of 'grizzled' feathers. Grizzled feathers are those that are partially leucistic, partially coloured. Other forms of pied do not show this trait, with their feathers being either fully normal-coloured, or fully leucistic.

There are probably many examples of this locus with the best known found in the common Pied colour morphs of both the Red-rumped Parrot and the Cockatiel, two types of Pied notorious for their difficulty in sexing and which exhibit previously unexplained colour changes. At first glance no common link can be seen, until one's point of view is changed and you start to consider dimorphic changes normally present between the two sexes. In both species, the ADM pied allele (designated dm for dimorphism) prevents the appearance of typical cock plumage traits. I wonder if there are any other physiological effects in these colour mutant birds?

In the Red-rumped Parrot, the loss of the red rump and the grey-green appearance of the plumage are both hen features. In the Cockatiel, the hen features include retention of melanin in the face and spread of psittacin yellow through the body area of adult cocks. There are also Pied mutations in the Indian Ringnecked Parrot and the Elegant Parrot that exhibit the ADM pied trait. The Indian Ringnecked Pied mutation lacks the sexually dimorphic neck ring of the cock, whilst the Elegant Parrot cock loses the typical orange vent spot of the Normal cock. No doubt many other Pied mutations also fit this category. Some Recessive Pied Turquoise Parrots lack typical cock markings such as red wing flashes.

### Addendum

*Inte Onsman (Mutavi) believes that the recessive pied allele in Budgerigars may also fit this category. Interestingly, this allele has another pleiotrophic trait in that it alters the structure of the anterior surface of the iris. This results in loss of lipid from this area of the Budgerigar eye, causing recessive pied Budgerigars to have a 'black' eye when the species normally has a 'white' iris. Other pied alleles need to be examined to determine if they also alter the structure of the iris. He has also raised the suggestion that all Recessive Pied colour morphs belong to the one locus, making them all ADM Pieds.*

*There is tremendous opportunity for study of these Pied colour morphs in all species of parrots to aid our understanding. For instance, we need to test the combination of the two Pied colour morphs in Elegant Parrots, the Dominant Pied from Europe and the ADM Pied from Australia. Will they show a cumulative effect when combined? If they do, then that would support the Recessive Pied in Budgerigars and Red-fronted Kakarikis being analogous to the ADM Pied. Changes to the iris structure as noted in Budgerigars also need to be studied in other parrot species.*

For further reading on this locus, please refer to Clive Hesford's web site (Martin, 1999a).

## Uncommon Loci

This group is a haphazard collection of loci that only have single representatives (ie in only one species) at present. With time more examples may occur, or else these loci may represent species-specific loci that play an important part in making a species different.

### Mottle locus – mo

There exists in Budgerigars a mutation known as Mottle. This mutation is a special type of the partial leucistic (Pied) form. As the name suggests, the plumage is mottled in appearance and the degree of pied markings increases with the age of the bird. It has also been called a 'progressive pied'. Inte Onsman (Mutavi) has studied this colour morph and believes that it relates to early cell death of melanocytes, which leads to the increasing leucism of the plumage. It is similar to the greying of human

D VAN DEN ABEELE

D MERVILDE

*Above: Mottle Fischer's Lovebird – an established colour morph in Europe. Left: Mottle Budgerigar. 'Mottling' in this mutation increases with age.*

hair with age. Mottle colour morphs are also recognised in lovebird species.

Another similar appearing colour morph is known as Grizzle. Grizzle alleles are not uncommon in other Families of birds. They occur in poultry, pigeons and finches. How does the Grizzle differ from the standard Pied? In a typical Pied, feathers are either pied or full coloured. However in Grizzles, many feathers are partially clear, partially coloured. They can have coloured bases and clear tips or clear bases and coloured tips. Like other Pieds, Grizzles also vary tremendously in the amount of pied areas carried. Some individuals have only a few marked feathers, others may have an almost full 'clear' appearance. There are some Grizzle colour morphs in certain non-parrot species that have a very fine 'salt and pepper' pattern to their entire plumage colouration, but in other species they retain the irregularity

S NASTASI

*A new Indian Ringnecked Parrot colour morph under development that may be a Mottle.*

K BENTON

*A new Indian Ringnecked Parrot colour morph currently referred to as 'Grizzled'.*

typical of Pieds. Many Grizzle colour morphs are also progressive, like the Mottle colour morph, whilst others are not. All this variation suggests that there is probably more than one type of mutation being called Grizzle in different species of birds. So far there are no examples in parrots, however with time I suspect that we will one day see at least one Grizzle parrot.

## Slate locus – $X^{sl}$

This locus is unique to the Budgerigar so far. It alters the structure of the medulla of feather barbs. The whole medullary cell structure is changed, not just the cloudy layer. The distribution of vacuoles changes and many vacuoles increase tremendously in size. The resultant phenotype has a greatly reduced ability to produce structural colours and, when combined with the blue allele, the bird becomes a shade of bluish grey. The locus is sex-linked, so would provide interesting recombinant frequencies with the other sex-linked loci. It will be very interesting if colour morphs of this locus appear in other species.

D MERVILDE

*Slate Blue Budgerigar.*

## Recessive grey locus – rg

The recessive grey locus is one of the rarest loci identified for structural colour. The recessive grey allele originally occurred in the Budgerigar but was lost due to the greater popularity of the Grey colour morph produced by the dominant grey locus (G). Recently a new Recessive Grey colour morph has appeared and appears to involve a different structural change from the original Recessive Grey, therefore suggesting a second

The 'Dark' Blue Pacific Parrotlet colour morph is the combination of the Blue and the 'USA Dark' mutation which is yet to be classified. It is distinctly different from the Recessive Greygreen and Grey colour morphs bred in Europe.

recessive grey locus. Both recessive colour morphs act differently from the dominant grey gene.

As these mutations are so rare, I will not go into detail, except to point out that they highlight that structural colour can be damaged by mutation at more than one locus. This indicates that the production of functional

'Recessive Greygreen' Alexandrine Parrot (R) – the correct identification of this colour morph is still not certain.

feather structure is a complex process involving multiple loci working in unison to achieve the desired result.

### Addendum

*I have become aware of a number of recessive grey alleles in various species that are known in Europe. The most common is in the Recessive Greygreen in Pacific Parrotlets. There are also reports of a Recessive Grey colour morph in the Turquoise Parrot, however they cannot be confirmed as the primary source of information is in a book filled with numerous inaccuracies. There is a mutation known as 'Olivegreen' from Denmark that could be the colour in question, but the literature reports little except its existence. It could be the same as the dark factor allele (Olive) that appeared in Australia around the same time, or it may be distinctly different. If its inheritance is recessive then it could be a recessive grey. I encourage readers to contact me with any available information on this colour morph.*

## Slaty locus – SLT

There are new colour mutant genes appearing in quite a few species, which produce a blue-grey phenotype when combined with mutant alleles of the blue locus. Some of these do not fit any of the common, recognised loci that produce similar phenotypes (Grey, Slate, Dark Factor, Recessive Grey). Preliminary studies by Inte Onsman (Mutavi) in a few species (ie lovebirds, Indian Ringnecked Parrots) have suggested that there may be two or more new mutations creating these aberrant colour morphs. In different cases, the structure of the feather is being altered in different ways, but the overall result is a partial loss of constructive interference resulting in a change part way between

*A developing colour morph in Indian Ringnecked Parrots that is currently known as 'Slaty'.*

blue and grey. The phenotype change is most noticeable when in combination with Blue, raising the possibility that breeders overlook the mutation when it is present on its own in an otherwise wildtype bird.

The name Slaty has been adopted for these uncertain colour morphs, to distinguish them from other recognised colours and I commend the breeders who have resisted the temptation to use an established name for a colour we know little about. Many of these mutations appear to be dominant in inheritance, like the majority of other structural altering mutations.

## Spangle locus – S

Another locus that is also unique to the Budgerigar at the present time is the spangle locus. The mutant allele is co-dominant and controls pigment deposition within feathers. The heterozygous genotype (Ss) creates a phenotype whereby only part of each feather forming the markings has normal melanin deposition. Melanin loss is primarily from foreground areas only and in Budgerigars, the remaining pigment forms narrow bands of melanin in foreground areas, giving the appearance of spangles on the wings. Background melanin is changed little in the heterozygous genotype. In the homozygous genotype (SS), almost all melanin deposition is prevented and the resultant phenotype is known in Australia as a 'Black-eyed Clear'. This creates a problem for Budgerigar breeders when faced with a yellow-coloured bird; it can have any one of three completely unrelated genotypes (SS, Pprr or dildil).

I had always viewed the Spangle as a co-dominant total leucistic mutation, with the heterozygous bird producing a 'special pied' form. It may be stretching the definition of Pied too much to call this colour morph a Pied, however it does fit with it being a leucistic mutation. Recent study (Onsman) shows that the homozygous phenotypes (SS) still carry melanin traces in their feathers, found only in grossly deformed melanosomes. It appears that the spangle locus controls an aspect of melanocyte function, possibly early death of melanocytes. This also would be consistent with a leucistic mutation.

One needs to ask what a Spangle would look like in a species with little foreground melanin. Would the heterozygous bird have a distinct phenotype or will only the homozygous spangle be distinctive, and then as a mostly 'clear' bird?

There are colours in the Fischer's Lovebird and the Bourke's Parrot that could be true spangle alleles. In the Fischer's Lovebird the allele is co-dominant and is a strong contender, however European genetisists prefer to call it Dominant Edged and group it with the category I call Dominant Dilute. The Bourke's Parrot colour morph is supposedly recessive, so it seems doubtful. However, considering my previous conjecture, only time will tell the true story.

## Orange locus – X<sup>or</sup>

So far, this sex-linked locus is known only in the Cockatiel where it is responsible for production of the orange cheek spot. The mutant allele can be viewed as non-functional, resulting in the inability to produce the orange cheek patch. This gives the bird a full yellow face, hence its common name of Yellowface. There are two possible explanations for the function of this locus: it is either responsible for conversion of yellow psittacin into orange and possibly other modified psittacins (red and pink) or the locus codes for a 'marking gene', solely to produce a spot on the face and therefore has nothing to do with the metabolic production of orange or other psittacins.

If the latter is correct, then this locus is almost certainly a species-specific gene. However, it may eventuate one day that other species with multiple psittacin pigments will have this locus to control production of their advanced psittacins (those other than yellow). For example, breeders should look for Bourke's Parrots without the pink and Eastern Rosellas without the red. Will these be alleles of this locus? Only time will tell.

# Tangerine locus – T

This is another locus confined to one species, in this case the Peachfaced Lovebird, where it is generally called Orangeface. It prevents conversion of orange psittacin into pink psittacin pigment. In the heterozygous form it is partially effective, therefore the mutation is co-dominant in nature, although the heterozygous form is not the desirable outcome. It is not known to have any relationship to other mutations at present. Overseas it has been combined with most available mutations.

There does exist in Dusky Lories two naturally occurring colours, known as the Red Phase and the Yellow Phase, the Yellow being dominant over the Red. Therefore I am theorising that we might have another example of an allele of this locus. If this is true, then Red (although less common in nature) was the original 'wildtype' form, with the Yellow being a naturally occurring mutant allele.

It is most likely that the tangerine locus codes for an enzyme responsible for the conversion of yellows and oranges into pinks

The Orangeface colour morph combines readily with most other mutations to produce a stunning range of colours such as these Orangeface Olive Lime (Pallid) (above) and Orangeface Olive Pied (below) Peachfaced Lovebirds.

and reds. When inactive, the process is arrested at this step. It suggests that orange psittacin has more in common with yellow psittacin than either red or pink. It may be simply that it is the first step after yellow and before the others, or that it occurs via a different process to the reds and pinks. These are interesting areas of research to consider and I cannot wait until more mutations that alter psittacin production appear.

## Addendum

*There is a new colour morph under development in Red-collared Lorikeets that may also reflect expression of this locus. It still needs to be established and developed but early specimens suggest a change of red psittacin in the normal bird into yellow psittacin in the colour morph. This is not just apparent in areas of red colouration, but also in regions naturally appearing blue that have red psittacin in them. These latter regions become green.*

There is another new colour in the Peachfaced Lovebird known as 'Pale-headed' in Europe. This allele reduces the strength of the pink and red psittacin to lighter pink and red-coloured psittacin. It is a co-dominant allele, with the homozygous being once again the preferred colour. This raises the question as to whether it may be an allele of the tangerine locus. That then raises the difficult question of proving whether dominant alleles belong to the one locus. This is another interesting area for further study.

## Addendum

*Since originally writing this section I have been able to discuss this colour morph with European breeders and examined a number of photographs of the Pale-headed mutation and its combination colours. It is now apparent to me that the pale-headed allele acts in a distinctly different manner from the orangeface allele. Photographs of the combination of the two alleles show a distinct dilution of the orange face colour, without altering psittacin in the body. It is clear that, while the orangeface allele delineates between yellow-orange and pink-red, the pale-headed mutant acts with a psittacin diluting action in the facial area only. The different action of the two alleles would clearly suggest that they belong to different loci.*

*It is interesting that the action of the pale-headed allele is restricted to the head region, not diluting the yellow psittacin of the body. It is almost certainly a locus tied in with production of the distinctive separation of colour in the head/face of the bird. I wonder if similar colour morphs will one day appear in other Afro-Asian species with distinct separation of head/face colour?*

**The following photographs illustrate one of the newest colour morphs in Peachfaced Lovebirds, the Pale-headed mutation. This dominant mutation has unique features not currently seen in mutations in other species of parrots.**

*Pale-headed Lutino Peachfaced Lovebirds – the combination highlights that only head colour is affected by this mutant gene.*

*Pale-headed Cinnamon Dark Green Peachfaced Lovebird.*

*Pale-headed Green Peachfaced Lovebird.*

*Pale-headed Edged Dilute Green Peachfaced Lovebird.*

## Brown locus – br

Currently this locus has only one known example, the Brownwing Budgerigar. It is a recessive equivalent of the cinnamon locus, coding for an enzyme that converts brown melanin into black melanin. When inactive in the mutant form, the bird can only produce brown melanins. It is distinct from the fallow loci that also alter melanin colour to brown.

Whilst parrot breeders have called many mutations 'Recessive Cinnamon', none to date have been the true brown locus. Every so-called 'Recessive Cinnamon' I have seen, still has traces of grey (and therefore black) melanin and cannot be classified as this mutation.

The brown locus is a common mammalian locus and is designated 'b' in mammalian genetics. Inte Onsman (Mutavi), who has studied the Brownwing Budgerigar, assigns it the same 'b' symbol. To do this, we have to assign the blue locus a new symbol. Onsman uses 'bl' as this symbol is used for Blue in other species of birds. However these 'blue' mutations in other species act differently from the blue locus in parrots. They do not control psittacin pigment, which is non-existent in these species. Therefore I am not comfortable using 'bl' for the blue locus.

As the brown locus is still extremely rare in parrots, (and with a small apology to Inte, although I have adopted most of his other symbol suggestions) I will continue to use the English Budgerigar designation of 'b' for the blue locus and 'br' for the brown locus.

## Clearbody locus – CL

There is a locus identified in Budgerigars, producing a colour morph known as Easley Clearbody. The locus controls medullary structure of the feather, with the mutant allele causing loss of normal medulla structure including both cloudy layer and background melanin pigment. This results in a total loss of all body colour elements; hence the name Clearbody is very appropriate. There are other colour morphs in Budgerigars also known by names including the term Clearbody (Texas Clearbody, Australian Clearbody). In these cases the colour morphs involved do not obliterate body colour like the Easley Clearbody, but merely reduce it strongly through either the process of albinism and/or dilution. Logically the name Clearbody should be reserved for this dominant structural locus.

I quote Inte Onsman (Mutavi) on this colour morph: 'I did investigate the

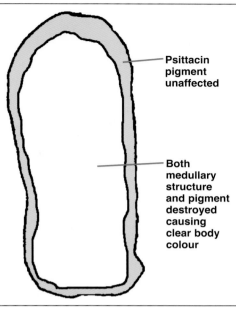

*Typical changes to the feather caused by the clearbody allele.*

mutation several years ago and made cross-sections from SF dominant Clearbodies (AKA Easley Clearbodies). The result was that all cross-sections showed complete absence of the medulla. In some cross-sections small traces of spongy zone and/or medullary cavities were seen but the overall impression is that the medulla including the spongy zone are (almost) completely suppressed by the action of this mutation, that is for SF birds. I presume that this suppression is complete in DF birds. Feather barbs in these birds are like icicles, foreground pigmentation is unaffected, background pigmentation is very much suppressed especially in DF birds'.

Overall, it is a very interesting locus and I cannot wait until we discover mutant alleles of this locus in other parrot species.

*(Easley) Clearbody Budgerigar – a so far unique mutation for which the Clearbody name should be reserved, to use when it appears in other species.*

# Special Case Loci

## Red-Orange suffusion locus/loci – RO

I have left these birds until last as there has been much debate about their nature. They have been labelled as 'merely a selective trait' by some, recessive by others. I have experience with breeding two forms: the Full Red-fronted Scarlet-chested Parrot and the Full Red-fronted Turquoise Parrot. Even just calling them red or orange causes debate. It is true that the Turquoise Parrot does not have the same red colour as the Scarlet-chested Parrot, but the colour is

*Red Suffused Red-rumped Parrot.*

far redder than what I personally view as orange. It is all in the eye of the beholder and I think it should be settled as red-orange!

Without doubt, this trait is under multigenic control in these two species. This is not to deny gene control. I believe that a locus exists that either allows or does not allow red production. It is then increased under selection pressure on numerous modifier genes. This control gene for red-orange is dominant in nature. In my experience you cannot breed red-orange from two 'Yellow-bellied' Turquoise or Scarlet-chested Parrots. But you can breed 'Yellow-bellied' birds from two Red-fronted birds.

This mutation could be viewed as the psittacin equivalent of the melanistic mutations. Could we call it *psittacistic?*

Red-orange suffusion also occurs in the Princess Parrot, the Peachfaced Lovebird and the African Grey Parrot. In these species and others, it is not believed to be inherited, but merely a function of the general health of the bird. There is no reason however, to prevent someone from one day establishing a mutation that mimics this effect.

*Red Suffused Cinnamon Red-rumped Parrot.*

### Addendum

*There are strains of Princess Parrots that may have a genetically controlled form of Red Suffused. There is also a Red-fronted colour morph established in Swift Parrots. Breeders are also working on Red Suffused in the Red-rumped Parrot.*

## Modifier Loci

Modifiers are genes which have only slight effects on wildtype phenotype, or in some cases, act only when in combination with mutant alleles of another locus. These genes are many and are responsible for all the slight variations we see in a normal phenotype. In some instances however, the effect of a modifier may be enhanced when combined with alleles of a colour loci, (eg a modifier unnoticed in a Normal phenotype being transferred to a mutant phenotype when outcrossing, suddenly producing a 'new' colour.)

What must be considered in these cases is whether the modifier produces a significant phenotype, or whether it might amount simply to a 'fault' in colour. I am often asked to comment on 'new' colours that are simply the result of modifiers and obviously their worth (aesthetic, not simply monetary) will be related to their visual appeal. This can be difficult for the breeder to accept, when all their hopes are placed on the success of *their new mutation.*

Some modifiers are used to 'improve' an existing colour variety. These are the ones that enhance or strengthen a colour. For instance, some modifiers enhance the colour of the pink on an Opaline (Rose) Bourke's Parrot. They will be relatively invisible when carried by birds of Normal phenotype, but can then be transferred onto offspring of the Opaline phenotype to produce 'more attractive' youngsters.

The converse also exists with modifiers that produce undesirable changes to phenotype. There is a modifier that has been identified and called a Body Colour Intensity Reducing Factor (BCIRF) (Bergman, 1999). This reduces the intensity of colour in Dark Factor and Violet phenotypes in Budgerigars. It is also apparent in lovebirds and is responsible for birds which carry dark factor and/or violet alleles being wrongly identified. Then when the modifier is dropped out during breeding, strange results appear because a dark factor allele or a violet allele may mysteriously show itself. Peter Bergman considers this modifier to have a dominant inheritance pattern.

## Darkwing locus

The mutant allele of this locus is one of the most distinct modifiers known and one of the few that can be documented in its mode of action. The darkwing allele is expressed only in combination with mutant alleles of the dilute locus in Budgerigars. Its effect is to produce an enhancement of the foreground melanin markings, thereby partially countering some of the effect of respective alleles of the dilute locus. The effect is not evident when combined with wildtype alleles of this locus (because you cannot get blacker than black), but is apparent in conjunction with the greywing, the clearwing and the dilute alleles.

In each case it results in darker grey foreground markings than is normal for the variety. However, the most recognised combination of the darkwing allele, is with the dilute allele and the cinnamon allele to produce a 'Cinnamonwing Yellow', a once popular Australian bird. Ken Yorke is the breeder responsible for elucidating the true nature of this colour combination, by showing that the darkwing modifier has action in combination with all mutant alleles of the dilute locus and that it is the presence of the cinnamon allele that changes the foreground melanin into a brown shade. The darkwing allele follows a dominant inheritance pattern.

Cinnamon Darkwing Dilute Budgerigar – exhibited as the 'Cinnamonwing Yellow'. The result of this three-way combination is to reduce body colour as much as possible whilst retaining some foreground colour.

Darkwing Dilute Budgerigar – the Darkwing modifier enhances deposition of foreground melanin, partially reversing the action of mutant alleles of the dilute locus.

Cinnamon Darkwing Dilute Blue Budgerigar – exhibited as the 'Cinnamonwing White'.

# COMBINATION COLOURS

This topic has been discussed in Part Two of this book. There are only a few points that require technical discussion.

The correct name for a combination of mutations is becoming an increasingly annoying problem. Many people, particularly in Europe, are reverting to using a simple combination name of the colours involved. This is without doubt the safest thing to do. However, there are instances where a simple name for a combination is clear and easily understood. Albino is the perfect example. This is a blue ino combination. Unfortunately a number of names have been misused. I suspect that translation is to blame as a number have originated from Europe where the breeders are generally very conscientious, but language barriers with English speakers have led to mistakes.

Isabel, whilst not used for combinations, is a perfect example. In the 1960s European authors often swapped the terms Cinnamon or Fawn for Isabel. The name sounded catchy in English and has been adopted but not for what it originally meant.

Silver is also a commonly misused term. European literature translated into English has primarily been to blame. It is now common in Australia and other countries to use the name Silver for cinnamon blue combinations. However, Silver is a totally inappropriate name for a light brown and blue bird. Silver is a shade of diluted grey and that is exactly what it should be used for – Dilute Grey. A Grey 'Lacewing' Indian Ringnecked Parrot (apart from the misuse of the name 'Lacewing') is closer to the silver colour, although technically, it still would not be the true Silver combination, which involves the Dilute (suffused) mutation (which does not exist in Australia) combined with Grey. A Cinnamon Grey Indian Ringnecked Parrot is a Fawn (white ground version of the Cinnamon).

Budgerigar breeders have, overall, avoided the use of special names for combinations and therefore have avoided much confusion. In Australia, lovebird breeders have used them to some degree and have managed to use most of them correctly. However, in the USA there is a strong move to remove special names for combinations. If only the rest of the parrot fraternity could follow suit either by using names correctly or abandoning combination names.

Lists of names that apply to combinations and that have set definitions are as follows:

| | |
|---|---|
| **Albino** | – blue ino |
| **Ivory** | – cinnamon blue |
| **Fawn** | – white ground cinnamon (ie cinnamon grey blue) |
| **Silver** | – dilute grey blue or dilute blue |
| **Cream** | – dilute fawn |
| **Creamino** | – parblue ino |
| **Mustard** | – olive cinnamon, also used for cinnamon greygreen |
| **Lacewing** | – cinnamon ino |
| **Grey** | – grey blue |
| **Cobalt** | – dark factor blue |
| **Mauve** | – double dark factor blue |
| **Visual Violet** | – violet cobalt |

---

*The diagrams on the following three pages represent typical changes seen in different combination colours.*

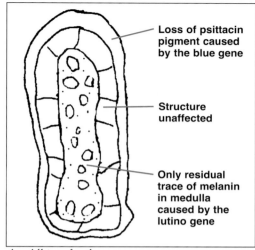

Loss of psittacin pigment caused by the blue gene

Structure unaffected

Only residual trace of melanin in medulla caused by the lutino gene

*An Albino feather.*

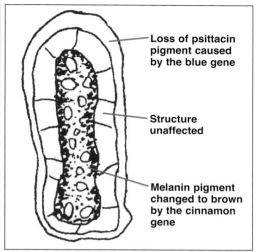

Loss of psittacin pigment caused by the blue gene

Structure unaffected

Melanin pigment changed to brown by the cinnamon gene

*A Cinnamon Blue (Ivory) feather.*

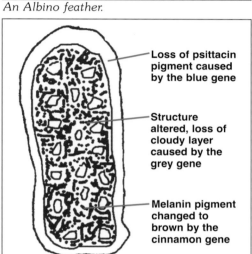

Loss of psittacin pigment caused by the blue gene

Structure altered, loss of cloudy layer caused by the grey gene

Melanin pigment changed to brown by the cinnamon gene

*A Fawn feather.*

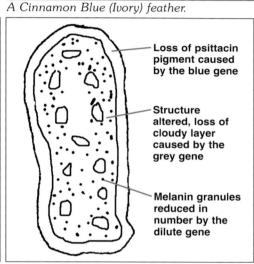

Loss of psittacin pigment caused by the blue gene

Structure altered, loss of cloudy layer caused by the grey gene

Melanin granules reduced in number by the dilute gene

*A Silver (Dilute Grey) feather.*

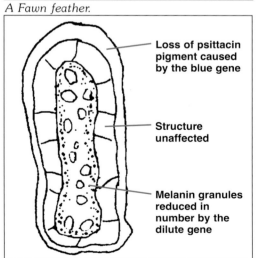

Loss of psittacin pigment caused by the blue gene

Structure unaffected

Melanin granules reduced in number by the dilute gene

*A Dilute Blue feather.*

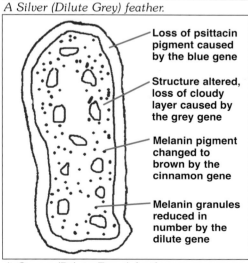

Loss of psittacin pigment caused by the blue gene

Structure altered, loss of cloudy layer caused by the grey gene

Melanin pigment changed to brown by the cinnamon gene

Melanin granules reduced in number by the dilute gene

*A Cream (Dilute Fawn) feather.*

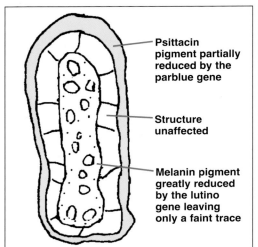

Psittacin pigment partially reduced by the parblue gene

Structure unaffected

Melanin pigment greatly reduced by the lutino gene leaving only a faint trace

*A Creamino feather.*

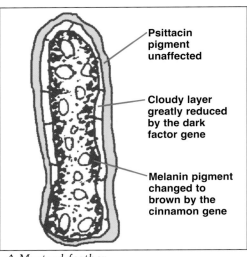

Psittacin pigment unaffected

Cloudy layer greatly reduced by the dark factor gene

Melanin pigment changed to brown by the cinnamon gene

*A Mustard feather.*

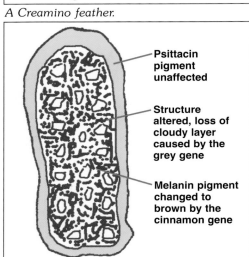

Psittacin pigment unaffected

Structure altered, loss of cloudy layer caused by the grey gene

Melanin pigment changed to brown by the cinnamon gene

*A Mustard (Greygreen) feather.*

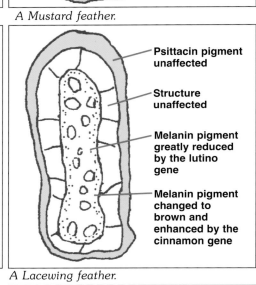

Psittacin pigment unaffected

Structure unaffected

Melanin pigment greatly reduced by the lutino gene

Melanin pigment changed to brown and enhanced by the cinnamon gene

*A Lacewing feather.*

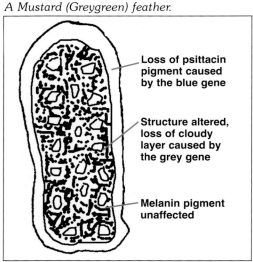

Loss of psittacin pigment caused by the blue gene

Structure altered, loss of cloudy layer caused by the grey gene

Melanin pigment unaffected

*A Grey feather.*

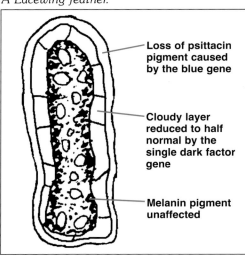

Loss of psittacin pigment caused by the blue gene

Cloudy layer reduced to half normal by the single dark factor gene

Melanin pigment unaffected

*A Cobalt feather.*

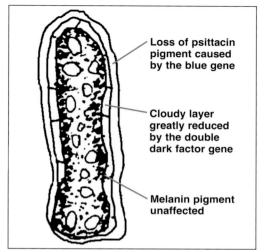

Loss of psittacin pigment caused by the blue gene

Cloudy layer greatly reduced by the double dark factor gene

Melanin pigment unaffected

*A Mauve feather.*

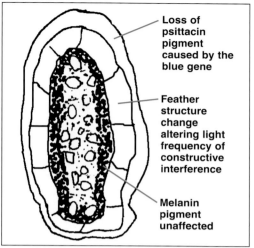

Loss of psittacin pigment caused by the blue gene

Feather structure change altering light frequency of constructive interference

Melanin pigment unaffected

*A Violet feather.*

Cinnamon ino combinations deserve a special mention. Theoretically they should not produce a distinctive phenotype as the ino allele prevents all melanin production. In reality they do create a distinct phenotype as has been proven in the Budgerigar with the Lacewing colour morph. This is partly through the inability of the ino alleles to turn off all melanin production. If they did, life possibly could not function. As a result, the race has been on to recognise similar combinations in other species. In Cockatiels there are ino birds with a faint cinnamon suffusion that could fit the description. However I have mated a cock of this phenotype back to a Cinnamon hen and produced Normal chicks – impossible if the theory were correct. Similar results have been obtained by other breeders. I am yet to determine exactly what causes this phenotype.

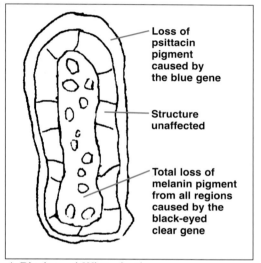

Loss of psittacin pigment caused by the blue gene

Structure unaffected

Total loss of melanin pigment from all regions caused by the black-eyed clear gene

*A Black-eyed White feather.*

In the Indian Ringnecked Parrot there is a phenotype known by the misnomer 'Yellowhead Cinnamon'. Without doubt, there are at least two genotypes that create phenotypes that fit this description. One has white flight feathers and has the genotype ($X^{ino^l} X^{ino}$), a heterozygous limeino (Lime is incorrectly called 'Lacewing' in this species). Obviously only cocks of this genotype and phenotype can exist.

The second genotype has a very similar phenotype but with faint beige flight feathers. Hens of this phenotype do exist. This bird is either a third allele of the ino locus or more likely the true Lacewing (cinnamon ino) combination. If the second possibility is the correct one, then we have the crazy situation where the name 'Lacewing' has already been used but for the wrong bird. The breeder who prematurely gave the name 'Lacewing' to the lime allele should not be forgiven too quickly! The confusion that will develop around this group of phenotypes will haunt us all for a long time to come.

### Addendum

*There is now solid evidence that the second genotype is the true cinnamon ino combination.*

P ODEKERKEN

*This Indian Ringnecked Parrot may be the first recorded example of crossover combining the Lime (Pallid) and Cinnamon colour morphs in Indian Ringnecked Parrots. The full description for this bird is believed to be Cinnamon Lime TurquoiseBlue.*

Deon Smith has been investigating the nature of birds with this phenotype and found evidence for a possible third genotype. In this case, a dominant modifier acts on alleles of the sex-linked ino locus in a variable fashion. It is possibly a 'post-transcription modifier' of the ino locus gene product. Its presence makes ino alleles more effective and lime alleles less effective, in each case producing birds fitting the 'in-between' category.

A situation similar to the Cockatiel exists in the Peachfaced Lovebird where birds known as 'Lacewing' exist, but which do not produce results consistent with a cinnamon ino genotype. In this species we also have a Lime mutation that is generally incorrectly named 'Australian Cinnamon'. Overseas, some breeders have started calling it 'Australian Ino', but this is also inaccurate as it is a partial ino allele, not a full ino allele. However, its existence as well as its interaction with the true cinnamon allele and the ino allele is probably responsible for most of the confusion in this species. A heterozygous bird ($X^{ino^l}$ $X^{ino}$) split for Cinnamon can have either type 1 or type 2 linkage between the ino and cinnamon alleles and as a result look like a Lacewing (as do all LutinoLime colour morphs) but produce a multitude of genetic outcomes. Consider the following matings:

**$X^{ino^l,cin}$ $X^{ino,CIN}$ (LutinoLime/Cinnamon Type 2) mated to $X^{ino,cin}$ Y (Lacewing)**
= 48.5% $X^{ino^l,cin}$ $X^{ino,cin}$ (Cinnamon LutinoLime cocks)
        and $X^{ino,CIN}$ $X^{ino,cin}$ (Lutino/Cinnamon cocks)
+ 1.5%  $X^{ino^l,CIN}$ $X^{ino,cin}$ (LutinoLime/Cinnamon Type 1 cocks)
        and $X^{ino,cin}$ $X^{ino,cin}$ (Lacewing cocks)
+ 48.5% $X^{ino^l,cin}$ Y (Cinnamon Lime hens) and $X^{ino,CIN}$ Y (Lutino hens)
+ 1.5%  $X^{ino^l,CIN}$ Y (Lime hens) and $X^{ino,cin}$ Y (Lacewing hens)

**$X^{ino^l,CIN}$ $X^{ino,cin}$ (LutinoLime/Cinnamon Type1) mated to $X^{ino,cin}$ Y (Lacewing)**
= 48.5% $X^{ino^l,CIN}$ $X^{ino,cin}$ (LutinoLime/Cinnamon Type 1 cocks)
        and $X^{ino,cin}$ $X^{ino,cin}$ (Lacewing cocks)
+ 1.5%  $X^{ino^l,cin}$ $X^{ino,cin}$ (Cinnamon LutinoLime cocks)
        and $X^{ino,CIN}$ $X^{ino,cin}$ (Lutino/Cinnamon cocks)
+ 48.5% $X^{ino^l,CIN}$ Y (Lime hens) and $X^{ino,cin}$ Y (Lacewing hens)
+ 1.5%  $X^{ino^l,cin}$ Y (Cinnamon Lime hens) and $X^{ino,CIN}$ Y (Lutino hens)

When you consider that the Lacewing, LutinoLime and probably the Cinnamon Lime all have very similar phenotypes, it is no wonder that breeders are confused.

Returning to the problem of these unexplained 'Lacewing' phenotypes, one relatively simple theory would be that this colour is produced by a second allele of the ino locus, without any involvement of the cinnamon locus. However, it appears that all examples of these birds carry at least a single cinnamon allele. Under ordinary circumstances, a cock carrying a single cinnamon allele shows no evidence of the allele's presence because it is a recessive trait. However, we already know that the cinnamon locus interacts in some way with the sex-linked ino locus, to partially 'by-pass' the blockade on melanin production normally created by the sex-linked ino allele and hence create the Lacewing phenotype. We could therefore explain the situation in Cockatiels (and probably other species as well) if the 'suppressed' heterozygous cinnamon allele, whose function is hidden by its wildtype allele counterpart, was actually still functioning, thereby continuing to interact in some way with the ino alleles and creating the by-pass which leads to the beige suffusion in these birds. This would mean that the cinnamon allele is not a non-functional allele as I normally view most mutant alleles of colour loci, but that whilst losing function to convert eumelanin from brown into black, gains the ability to increase function of the sex-linked ino locus. Possibly the cinnamon locus has more than one function that includes a 'supporting role' in conjunction with the sex-linked ino locus? Another consideration that should be kept in mind is the possibility that the bird homozygous for ino and heterozygous for cinnamon may have a slightly different phenotype from the true Lacewing (cinnamon ino). This would result in the following table of genotypes and corresponding phenotypes.

| GENOTYPE | PHENOTYPE |
|---|---|
| $X^{cin}\, X^{cin}$ | Cinnamon cock |
| $X^{ino,cin}\, X^{ino,cin}$ | Lacewing (cinnamon ino) cock |
| $X^{ino,cin}\, X^{ino,CIN}$ | 'Lighter' Lacewing (ino/cinnamon) cock |
| $X^{ino}\, X^{ino}$ | Ino cock |
| $X^{cin}\, Y$ | Cinnamon hen |
| $X^{ino,cin}\, Y$ | Lacewing (cinnamon ino) hen |
| $X^{ino}\, Y$ | Ino hen |

If this theorised genetic interaction does occur, then it would result in significant confusion for breeders trying to make sense of breeding results, particularly if the situation is made more complicated by the existence and intermingling of lime alleles as well. This is exactly the situation we have in Indian Ringnecked Parrots and Peachfaced Lovebirds.

# CROSSOVERS AND RECOMBINANT FREQUENCIES

When two genes reside at loci found on the same chromosome and within close proximity, they remain bound together during meiosis, unless a crossover event occurs between them. Crossovers occur frequently whenever meiosis occurs and may occur in many places along homologous chromosomes. Because of this high frequency, unless the two loci are close together in position, they will be separated virtually every time that gametes (reproductive cells) are produced. With this in mind and considering that chromosomes are hundreds of map units long, it is theoretically possible that nearly all colour loci are on the one chromosome but separated by great distance. Alternatively, as birds have large numbers of microsomes (small chromosomes believed to carry few genes), it is possible that colour loci are all on different chromosomes. The truth is probably somewhere in between.

The rate at which crossovers occur is known as the *recombinant frequency (RF)*. It is calculated as the percentage of young that show crossover between linked genes. If the RF is low it will be a true indication of the distance between the two loci. The distance is measured in *map units* (MU), an arbitrary distance that relates to an RF of 1%. Therefore an RF of 7% indicates that the two loci are seven map units apart. An RF value of 50% indicates no functional linkage. If we had three linked loci, two 60 map units apart and one in between, the outer two would behave as if not linked with one another, but both would behave as if linked to the third, creating an apparent paradox.

A grasp of algebra is certainly needed to fully comprehend some aspects of this inheritance.

RF values have been roughly determined for the four sex-linked recessive traits of Budgerigars. They are as follows:

$X^{cin}$ and $X^{ino}$ – 3%
$X^{cin}$ and $X^{op}$ – 33%
$X^{ino}$ and $X^{op}$ – 30%
$X^{cin}$ and $X^{sl}$ – 7%
$X^{op}$ and $X^{sl}$ – 40%
$X^{sl}$ and $X^{ino}$ – 10%

If we drew a linear map of the X chromosome it would look like this. ▶

In Budgerigars, the blue locus and the dark factor locus are linked:

D and b – 14%

These crossover rates are important when trying to produce combinations of colours. Depending on the RF value, type 1 and type 2 double splits have different breeding (and perhaps commercial) values. If the RF is low, then a type 1 double split (for two recessive traits) is many times more valuable than a type 2. If the RF is high, then it is not as important. What do *type 1* and *type 2* mean? They refer to the linkage present in the bird's genotype. Type 2 genotype has the two dominant (or

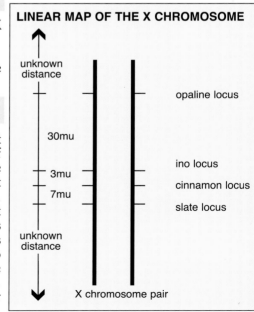

LINEAR MAP OF THE X CHROMOSOME

unknown distance

opaline locus

30mu

ino locus

3mu

cinnamon locus

7mu

slate locus

unknown distance

X chromosome pair

recessive) alleles (for two different loci) on separate chromosomes of the pair, which are effectively separate with only one being inherited by a youngster unless a crossover takes place. Birds with the type 1 genotype have the two dominant (or recessive) alleles (for two different loci) already linked together on one chromosome of the pair and the alleles will be inherited together unless another crossover takes place.

If the aim is to produce a combination of recessive colours, then using type 1 birds is very important. If the dark factor allele is being combined with the blue allele, then type 2 birds are required as one allele is dominant and the other is recessive. Remember that crossover only takes place during meiosis, so is only relevant in double split birds and works both ways, to combine and to separate. It is a common mistake to think that once it happens it is permanent.

I am currently trying to collect data for RF values in as many other species as possible. Personally I am working on RF values for the Red-rumped Parrot.

With time, studying the recombinant frequencies for the various linked loci in different species may give further clues as to the genetic relationship of those species. These studies would give a small insight into the true genotypes for these birds, before the era when gene mapping becomes readily available to study these things further.

# BIBLIOGRAPHY

## Recommended Reading
## for Colour Mutation and Genetic Information

Andersen, D., Cross, P., *A Guide to Cockatiels and their Mutations*,
    ABK Publications, 1994.

Buckley, P.A., *Diseases of Cage and Aviary Birds* in Avian Genetics Ch. 4, Petrak,
    M. (ed), 2nd edn., Lea and Febiger, 1982.

Hayward, J., *The Manual of Colour Breeding*, The Aviculturist Publications, 1992.

Hunt, C., *A Guide to Australian White Cockatoos*, ABK Publications, 1999.

Kremer, H., *Australian Parakeets and their Mutations*, Uitgeverij 'Ornis', 1992.

Martin, T., *A Guide to Neophema and Psephotus Grass Parrots*, rev. edn.,
    ABK Publications, 1997.

Martin, T., *Semi-lethal Dominant Dilutes*, Zebra Times, SEQZFS, 1995.

Odekerken, P., *A Guide to Lories and Lorikeets*, rev. edn.,
    ABK Publications, 2002.

Smith, D., *Indian Ringneck – Genetics made Easy*, Sunbird Press, 1999.

Smith, S. & J., *A Guide to Asiatic Parrots*, rev. edn., ABK Publications, 1997.

Taylor, T.G., Warner, C., *Genetics for Budgerigar Breeders*, 2nd edn.,
    The Budgerigar Society (UK), 1986.

The African Lovebird Society of Australia, *Lovebird Genetics*, 1986.

## Web Sites with Valuable Information
## on Parrot Mutations and Genetics

Belgian Lovebird Society Homepage – www.agapornidenclub.be/
    Up-to-date information on genetics and mutations of lovebird species.

Mutavi – www.euronet.nl/users/hnl
    Onsman, I., various articles on the correct naming and the scientific investigation
    of colour mutations, covering Budgerigars, lovebirds, Indian Ringnecked Parrots
    and Cockatiels, 2001.

Psittacula World – www.psittaculaworld.com
    Rana, Z., discusses mutations in all Psittacula (Asiatic) species.

The Genetics of Colour in Budgerigars and Related Parrots –
    http://www.parrotgenetics.info
    Hesford, C., covers the latest theories on parrot colour morphs and genetics in an
    approachable format for the average breeder.

Bergman, P., *Gene Function in Yellowface Budgerigars Pts 1 and 2*, 1998.

Bergman, P., *The Facts about Violet Budgerigars*, 1999.

Hesford, C., *The Opaline Factor in Australian Parakeets*, 1998.

Martin, T., *An Update on the Opaline Locus*, 1999c.

Martin, T., *Classifying and Defining Fallow Colour Morphs in Parrots*, 2001a.

Martin, T., *Nature of the Opaline Locus*, 1999b.

Martin, T., *The Pied Red-rumped Parrot – a Mysterious Combination*, 1999a.

Martin, T., *Unexpected Behaviour of the Cinnamon Allele*, 2001b.

## Other Books Covering Parrot Mutations

*A Guide to Rosellas and their Mutations*, ABK Publications, 1990.

Alderton, D., *A Birdkeeper's Guide to Cockatiels*, Tetra Press, 1989.

Alderton, D., *A Birdkeeper's Guide to Long-tailed Parrots*, Tetra Press, 1989.

Alderton, D., *Lovebirds – Their Care and Breeding*, K and R Books, 1979.

Bastiaan, T. & G.J.J., *Ringnecked Parakeets and their Mutations*, 1995.

Cooke, F., Buckley, P.A., *Avian Genetics: A Population and Ecological Approach*, Academic Press, 1987.

D'Angieri, Dr A., *The Colored Atlas of Lovebirds*, TFH Publications.

Laubscher, C., *The Swift Parrakeet*, The Parrot Society UK, 1999.

Sindel, S., *Australian Lorikeets*, Singil Press, 1986.

Sindel, S., Gill, J., *Australian Broad-tailed Parrots, the Platycercus and Barnardius Genera*, Singil Press, 1999.

Sindel, S., Gill, J., *Australian Grass Parrakeets*, Singil Press, 1992.

Sindel, S., Gill, J., *Australian Grass Parrakeets, the Psephotus and Northiella Genera*, Singil Press, 1996.

Sindel, S., Lynn, R., *Australian Cockatoos*, 2nd edn., Singil Press, 1996.

Smith, G.A., *Lovebirds and Related Parrots*, Inkata Press, 1979.

Wilson, K., *A Guide to Australian Long and Broad-tailed Parrots and New Zealand Kakarikis*, ABK Publication, 1990.

Zomer, H.P.M., *Grass Parakeets and their Colour Mutations*, Gwendo – Arnhem Publications, 1989.

## Papers

Pearson K., Nettleship E., Usher C.H., *A Monography on Albinism in Man*, Draper's Company Research Memoires Biometric Series 6 8 9: Parts 1 2 4, London Dulau, 1911–1913.

Prum, R.O., Torres, R., Williamson, S., Dyck J., in the *Proceedings of the Royal Society Biological Sciences Series – 266* (1414) Jan 7 1999, pp. 13–22.

Smith, G., AVES Convention held by the Northern Rivers Avicultural Society, Grafton, New South Wales, Australia, 1995.

Stradi, R., Pini, E., Celentano, G., *The Chemical Structure of the Pigments in Ara Macao Plumage*, Elsevier Science Inc., Comparative Biochemistry and Physiology Part B 130 (2001), pp. 57–63.

# INDEX OF PRIMARY MUTATIONS BY SPECIES

This index lists all the primary mutations known for all species of parrots. It does not list any colour combinations as the number of possible combinations is enormous and probably beyond tabulation. Every new primary mutation established in a species effectively doubles the possible colour combinations, with over 100 combinations possible from merely seven different primary mutations (Note: not all combinations are worth producing).

| Mutation | Common Names<br>'names in inverted commas<br>are incorrect usage' | Distribution | Availability<br>under dev. =<br>under development | Page<br>Text, **Photographs**,<br>Technical Reference |
|---|---|---|---|---|
| **Budgerigar** *Melopsittacus undulatus* | | | | |
| Blue mutant 1 | Blue | worldwide | common | 41, **41**, 241 |
| Blue mutant 2 | 'Yellowface mutant 1' | worldwide | common | 41, **41**, 241 |
| Parblue mutant 1 | 'Yellowface mutant 2' | worldwide | common | 46, 241 |
| Parblue mutant 2 | 'Goldenface' | worldwide | common | 46, **46**, 241 |
| Sex-linked Lutino | Lutino | worldwide | common | 51, **51**, 233 |
| Sex-linked Par-ino | 'Texas Clearbody' | worldwide | established | 56, **57**, 233 |
| NSL Lutino | 'Recessive Lutino' | Europe | extinct | 58, 234 |
| Cinnamon | 'Cinnamonwing' | worldwide | common | 61, **63**, 235 |
| Dilute mutant 1 | Greywing | worldwide | common | 67, **67**, 237 |
| Dilute mutant 2 | Clearwing | worldwide | common | 67, **67**, 237 |
| Dilute mutant 3 | Dilute | worldwide | common | 67, **67**, 237 |
| Faded | Faded | Australia | under dev. | 72, **74**, 238 |
| Bronze Fallow | 'German Fallow' | worldwide | common | 76, **77**, 239 |
| Dun Fallow | 'English Fallow' | Europe | common | 76, **139**, 239 |
| Ashen Fallow? | 'Scottish Fallow' | Europe | extinct | 76, 239 |
| Dark Factor | Dark Green and Olive | worldwide | common | 81, **81**, 245 |
| Grey | Greygreen | worldwide | common | 85, **86**, 247 |
| Recessive Grey | Recessive Greygreen | Australia | under dev. | 87, 260 |
| Violet | Violet Green | worldwide | common | 88, **89**, 249 |
| Slate | Slate | Europe | established | 108, **108**, 260 |
| Opaline | Opaline | worldwide | common | 89, **90**, 252 |
| Dominant Pied | 'Australian Pied' | worldwide | common | 93, **93**, 257 |
| Dominant Pied | 'Dutch Pied' | worldwide | established | 93, **93**, 257 |
| Recessive Pied | 'Danish Pied' | worldwide | common | 96, **96**, 257 |
| Mottle | Mottle | worldwide | established | **259**, 259 |
| Spangle | Spangle | worldwide | common | 101, **101**, 262 |
| Melanistic | 'Blackface' | Europe | established | 103, **104**, 254 |
| Clearbody | 'Easley Clearbody' | Europe, USA | established | **265**, 265 |
| Darkwing modifier | Darkwing,<br>'Cinnamonwing Yellow' | Australia | established | **267**, 267 |

| Mutation | Common Names<br>*'names in inverted commas<br>are incorrect usage'* | Distribution | Availability<br>*under dev. =<br>under development* | Page<br>Text, **Photographs**,<br>Technical Reference |
|---|---|---|---|---|
| **Bourke's Parrot** *Neopsephotus bourkii* | | | | |
| Sex-linked Lutino | Lutino | Europe | established | 51, **51**, 233 |
| Cinnamon | Cinnamon | Europe | established | 61, **64**, 235 |
| Dilute | 'Yellow Pastel' | Europe | uncertain | 67 |
| Faded | 'Dilute' | Australia | under dev. | 72, **73**, 238 |
| Bronze Fallow | 'Cream' or 'Yellow' | worldwide | common | 76, **77**, 239 |
| Dun Fallow? | Fallow | Europe | established | 76, 239 |
| Opaline | 'Rose' | worldwide | common | 89, **90**, 252 |
| Recessive Pied | Pied | Australia | under dev. | 96, **99**, 257 |
| Uncertain designation | 'Spangle' | Europe | established | 101, **102**, 262 |
| **Turquoise Parrot** *Neophema pulchella* | | | | |
| Seagreen (Parblue) | Parblue | Europe | uncertain | 46, 241 |
| Cinnamon | Cinnamon | Europe | established | **31**, 61, **63**, 235 |
| Dilute | 'Yellow' | worldwide | common | 67, **69**, 237 |
| Faded | 'Isabel' | Europe | established | 72, **73**, 238 |
| Dun Fallow | 'Isabel' type 1 | Australia | established | 76, **78**, 239 |
| ? Fallow | 'Isabel' type 2 | Australia | established | 76, **78**, 239 |
| Dark Factor | 'Jade' and Olive | Australia | common | 81, **83**, 245 |
| Uncertain designation | 'Olivegreen' | Europe<br>(Denmark) | uncertain | 88 |
| Grey | Greygreen | Europe | established | 85, **86**, 247 |
| Opaline | Opaline | worldwide | established | 89, **91**, 252 |
| Recessive Pied | Pied | worldwide | under dev. | 96, **99**, 257 |
| Red Suffusion | Red-bellied, Red-fronted | worldwide | common | 105, **105**, 265 |
| Uncertain designation | 'Fallow' | Europe | established | 80, **80** |
| **Scarlet-chested Parrot** *Neophema splendida* | | | | |
| Blue | 'White-fronted Blue' | worldwide | common | 41, **41**, 241 |
| Turquoise (Parblue) | 'Parblue' | worldwide | common | 46, **47**, 241 |
| Seagreen (Parblue) | Seagreen | worldwide | common | 46, **47**, 241 |
| Sex-linked Lutino | Lutino | Europe | established | 51, **51**, 233 |
| Sex-linked Lime | 'Isabel' | Europe | common | 56, **56**, 233 |
| Cinnamon | Cinnamon | Europe | common | 61, **61**, 235 |
| Ashen Fallow | 'Isabel' | Australia | established | 76, **79**, 239 |
| Dun Fallow? | Fallow | Europe | established | 76, 239 |
| Grey | Greygreen | Europe | established | 85, **88**, 247 |
| Khaki | 'Olive' | Australia | established | 84, **84**, **250**, 250 |
| Dominant Pied | Pied | worldwide | under dev. | 93, 257 |

| Mutation | Common Names<br>*'names in inverted commas<br>are incorrect usage'* | Distribution | Availability<br>*under dev. =<br>under development* | Page<br>Text, **Photographs**,<br>Technical Reference |
|---|---|---|---|---|
| **Scarlet-chested Parrot – continued** | | | | |
| Recessive Pied | Pied | worldwide | under dev. | 96, **99**, 257 |
| Red Suffusion | Red-fronted | worldwide | common | 105, **105**, 265 |
| Uncertain designation | 'Fallow' | Australia | under dev. | 80, **80** |
| **Elegant Parrot** *Neophema elegans* | | | | |
| NSL Lutino | 'Recessive Lutino' | worldwide | common | 58, **59**, 234 |
| Cinnamon | Cinnamon | worldwide | common | 61, **61**, 235 |
| Sex-linked Lime | 'Cinnamon Yellow' | Australia | extinct | 56, 233 |
| Dun Fallow | Fallow | Europe | common | 76, **79**, 239 |
| Dominant Pied | Pied | Europe | common | 93, **94**, 257 |
| ADM Pied | 'Recessive Pied' | Australia | common | 100, **100**, 258 |
| Uncertain designation | 'Lacewing', 'Greywing' | Europe | common | **142** |
| **Rock Parrot** *Neophema petrophila* | | | | |
| Cinnamon? | 'Cinnamon Yellow' | Australia | wild | 61 |
| Fallow | 'Cinnamon' | Australia | under dev. | **66**, 76 |
| **Blue-winged Parrot** *Neophema chrysostoma* | | | | |
| Blue | Blue | Australia | common | **23**, 41, **41**, 241 |
| Uncertain designation | 'Cinnamon' | Australia | under dev. | 72, **74** |
| **Red-rumped Parrot** *Psephotus haematonotus* | | | | |
| Blue | Blue | Australia | common | 41, **42**, 241 |
| Turquoise (Parblue) | 'European Blue' | Europe, USA | established | 46, 241, **244** |
| Sex-linked Lutino | Lutino | worldwide | common | 51, **52**, 233 |
| Sex-linked Lime | 'Yellow', 'Isabel',<br>'UK Cinnamon' | worldwide | common | 56, **56**, 233 |
| Sex-linked Platinum | Platinum | Australia | established | 56, **56**, 233 |
| Cinnamon | Cinnamon | Australia | common | 61, **61**, 235 |
| Faded | 'Recessive Cinnamon' | Australia | extinct? | 72, **73**, 238 |
| Dun Fallow? | Fallow | Australia | under dev. | 76, **78**, 239 |
| Bronze Fallow? | 'Golden Fallow' | Australia | under dev. | 76, **78**, 239 |
| Grey | Greygreen | Australia | under dev. | 85, **87**, 247 |
| Opaline | Opaline | Australia | common | 89, **91**, 252 |
| ADM Pied | 'UK Pied' | worldwide | common | 100, **101**, 258 |
| Black-eyed Clear | 'Aust Pied'<br>'Dominant Pied' | Australia | established | 94, **95**, 258 |
| Red Suffusion | Red Suffusion | Australia | under dev. | 105, **265**, 265 |

| Mutation | Common Names<br>'names in inverted commas<br>are incorrect usage' | Distribution | Availability<br>under dev. =<br>under development | Page<br>Text, **Photographs**,<br>Technical Reference |
|---|---|---|---|---|
| **Hooded Parrot** *Psephotus dissimilis* | | | | |
| Seagreen (Parblue)? | 'Blue' | Australia | under dev. | 46, 241 |
| Bronze Fallow | 'Cinnamon' | Australia | established | 76, **77**, 239 |
| Black-eyed Clear | 'Dominant Pied' | Australia | common | 94, **95**, 258 |
| Recessive Pied | Pied | Australia | under dev. | 96, 257 |
| Uncertain designation | 'Olive' | Europe | uncertain | **36** |
| **Mulga Parrot** *Psephotus varius* | | | | |
| Dilute mutant 1 | Dilute type 1 | Australia | under dev. | 67, **68**, 237 |
| Dilute mutant 2 | Dilute type 2 | Australia | under dev. | 67, **68**, 237 |
| Pied | Pied | Australia | uncertain | 96, **99**, 257 |
| **Blue-bonnet Parrot** *Northiella haematogaster* | | | | |
| Sex-linked Lutino | Lutino | Australia | extinct | 51 |
| Cinnamon | Cinnamon | Australia | under dev. | 61, **66**, 235 |
| Dilute | Dilute | Australia | under dev. | 67, 237 |
| **Mallee Ringnecked Parrot** *Barnidius barnardi* | | | | |
| Blue | Blue | worldwide | common | 41, **42**, 241 |
| Dark Factor | Dark Green and Olive | Europe | under dev. | 81, **83**, 245 |
| Dominant Pied | Pied | Australia | under dev. | 93, **94**, 257 |
| **Port Lincoln Parrot** *Barnidius zonarius*<br>including the subspecies known as the **Twenty-eight Parrot** *B.z. semitorquatus* | | | | |
| Blue | Blue | worldwide | common | 41, **42**, 241 |
| NSL Lutino | Lutino | Australia | under dev. | **55**,58, 234 |
| Cinnamon | Cinnamon | Australia | established | 61, **66**, 235 |
| Khaki | 'Olive' | Australia | under dev. | 84, **250**, 250 |
| Pied | Pied | Australia | under dev. | 96, 257 |
| Uncertain designation | 'Cinnamon' | Australia | under dev. | 61 |
| Uncertain designation | 'Dilute' | Australia | under dev. | 67 |
| **Cloncurry Parrot** *Barnidius macgillivrayi* | | | | |
| Uncertain (albinistic) | unnamed | Europe | uncertain | **37** |
| Uncertain designation | 'Melanistic' | Australia | under dev. | 104 |
| **Eastern Rosella** *Platycercus eximius* | | | | |
| Blue | Blue | Australia, Europe | under dev. | 41, **44**, 241 |
| Parblue | Parblue | Europe | under dev. | 46, **181**, 241 |
| Sex-linked lutino | Lutino | worldwide | common | 51, **52**, 233 |

| Mutation | Common Names *'names in inverted commas are incorrect usage'* | Distribution | Availability *under dev. = under development* | Page Text, **Photographs**, Technical Reference |
|---|---|---|---|---|
| **Eastern Rosella – continued** | | | | |
| NSL lutino | 'Recessive Lutino' | Australia | extinct | 58 |
| Cinnamon | Cinnamon | worldwide | common | 61, **62**, 235 |
| Dilute mutant 1 | Pastel | Europe | common | 67, **68**, 237 |
| Dilute mutant 2? | Dilute | Australia | under dev. | 67, **68**, 237 |
| Dominant Dilute | | Europe | uncertain | 75 |
| Faded | unnamed | USA | under dev. | 72, 238 |
| Opaline | 'Red' | worldwide | common | 89, **90**, 252 |
| Dominant Pied | 'White-winged' | Europe | established | 93, 257 |
| Melanistic | 'Black' | Australia | established | 103, **104**, 254, **255** |
| Uncertain designation | 'Golden' | Europe | under dev. | **38** |
| Uncertain designation | 'Black-eyed Yellow' | UK | under dev. | **25**, 94, 258 |
| Uncertain designation | 'Yellow-headed' | worldwide | established | **28** |
| **Pale-headed Rosella** *Platycercus adscitus* | | | | |
| Blue | Blue | Australia | under dev. | 41, **43**, 241 |
| Uncertain | 'Dilute' | Australia | uncertain | 67 |
| Pied | Pied | Australia | under dev. | 96, **99**, 257 |
| **Crimson Rosella** *Platycercus elegans* | | | | |
| Blue | Blue | worldwide | common | 41, **43**, 241 |
| Turquoise (Parblue) | Parblue | Australia | under dev. | 46, **49**, 241 |
| Aqua (Parblue) | 'Orange' | Europe | established | 46, **49**, 241 |
| Sex-linked Lutino | Lutino | Europe | established | 51, 233 |
| NSL Lutino | 'Recessive Lutino' | Australia | extinct | 58 |
| Cinnamon | Cinnamon | Europe | established | 61, **62**, 235 |
| Dilute | Dilute | Australia | uncertain | 67, **72**, 237 |
| Pied | Pied | Europe | established | 96, **99**, 255, **256** |
| Black-eyed Clear? | 'Yellow' | Europe | established | **26**, 94, 258 |
| **Adelaide Rosella** *Platycercus adelaidae* | | | | |
| Sex-linked Lutino | Lutino | Australia | under dev. | 51, **52**, 233 |
| NSL Lutino | Lutino | Australia | under dev. | 58, **59**, 234 |
| Cinnamon | Cinnamon | Australia | established | 61, **62**, 235 |
| **Yellow Rosella** *Platycercus flaveolus* | | | | |
| Dilute | 'Yellow' | Australia | uncertain | 67, **72**, 237 |
| Lutino | Lutino | Australia | extinct | 51 |

| Mutation | Common Names _'names in inverted commas are incorrect usage'_ | Distribution | Availability _under dev. = under development_ | Page Text, **Photographs**, Technical Reference |
|---|---|---|---|---|
| Cinnamon | Cinnamon | Australia | extinct | 61, 235 |
| Dominant Pied | Pied | Australia | under dev. | 93, **94**, 257 |

### Western Rosella _Platycercus icterotis_

| Mutation | Common Names | Distribution | Availability | Page |
|---|---|---|---|---|
| Blue | Blue | Europe | established | 41, **43**, 241 |
| Turquoise (Parblue) | 'Blue' | Australia | under dev. | 46, **48**, 241 |
| Sex-linked Lutino | Lutino | Europe | under dev. | 51, **55**, 233 |
| Cinnamon | Cinnamon | Europe | established | 61, **64**, 235 |
| ? | Cinnamon | Sth Africa | under dev. | 61 |
| Faded? | 'Isabel' | Europe | under dev. | 72, 238 |
| Dun Fallow | Fallow | USA | under dev. | 76, 239 |
| Bronze Fallow | 'Cinnamon' | Australia | under dev. | 76, **80**, 239 |
| Dark Factor | Dark Green and Olive | Europe | under dev. | 81, **81**, 245 |
| Opaline | Opaline | Europe | under dev. | 89, **173**, 252 |

### Princess Parrot _Polytelis alexandrae_

| Mutation | Common Names | Distribution | Availability | Page |
|---|---|---|---|---|
| Blue | Blue | worldwide | common | 41, **42**, 241 |
| Parblue | Parblue | Australia | under dev. | 46, 241 |
| NSL Lutino | Lutino, 'Yellow' | worldwide | common | 58, **60**, 234 |
| NSL Lime | 'Yellow' | worldwide | common | 60, **60**, 234 |
| Faded | 'Cinnamon' | Australia | established | 72, **74**, 238 |
| Pied | Pied | | uncertain | 96 |
| Red Suffusion | Red Suffusion | worldwide | under dev. | 105, **106**, 265 |

### Superb Parrot _Polytelis swainsonii_

| Mutation | Common Names | Distribution | Availability | Page |
|---|---|---|---|---|
| NSL Lutino | Lutino | Australia | under dev. | 51, **55**, 58, 234 |
| Cinnamon or Lime? | 'Isabel' | Europe | established | 61, **66**, 235 |
| Uncertain designation | 'Greygreen' | Australia | under dev. | 85, **87**, 247 |
| Uncertain designation | 'Yellow' | Australia | uncertain | 67, **71** |

### Regent Parrot _Polytelis anthopeplus_

| Mutation | Common Names | Distribution | Availability | Page |
|---|---|---|---|---|
| Dilute | 'Yellow' | Australia, Europe | uncertain | **36**, 67, 237 |

### Crimson-winged Parrot _Aprosmictus erythropterus_

| Mutation | Common Names | Distribution | Availability | Page |
|---|---|---|---|---|
| Cinnamon | Cinnamon | Australia | established | 61, **61**, 235 |
| Uncertain designation | 'Greygreen' | Australia | under dev. | 85, **88**, 247 |

| Mutation | Common Names<br>'names in inverted commas<br>are incorrect usage' | Distribution | Availability<br>under dev. =<br>under development | Page<br>Text, **Photographs**,<br>Technical Reference |
|---|---|---|---|---|
| **King Parrot** *Alisterus scapularis* | | | | |
| Blue or Turquoise? | Blue | Australia | under dev. | **19**, 41, **45**, 241 |
| Cinnamon | Cinnamon | Australia | under dev. | 61, **61**, 235 |
| Dilute | Pastel, Dilute | Europe | established | 67, **68**, 237 |
| Black-eyed Clear | 'Yellow' | Australia | under dev. | 67, **68**, 237, 258 |
| **Eclectus Parrot** *Eclectus roratus* | | | | |
| Blue | Blue | Europe, USA | under dev. | 41, **43**, 241 |
| Uncertain designation | 'Cinnamon' | Europe | under dev. | 61 |
| Lutino | Lutino | Asia | uncertain | 51 |
| **Cockatiel** *Nymphicus hollandicus* | | | | |
| Blue | 'Whiteface' | worldwide | common | 41, **43**, 241 |
| Parblue | 'Pastelface' | worldwide | established | 46, **50**, 241 |
| Sex-linked Lutino | Lutino | worldwide | common | 51, **52**, 233 |
| Sex-linked Platinum | Platinum | Australia | common | 56, **57**, 233 |
| NSL Lutino | NSL Lutino | Europe | established | 58, 234 |
| Cinnamon | Cinnamon | worldwide | common | 61, **63**, 235 |
| Dilute mutant 1 | 'Pastel Silver' | Australia | common | 67, **70**, 237 |
| Dilute mutant 2? | 'Spangle Silver' | Australia | established | 67, **70**, 237 |
| Dominant Dilute | Dominant Silver | Europe, USA | common | 75, **75**, 238 |
| Faded | 'West Coast Silver' | Australia | established | 72, **74**, 238 |
| Ashen Fallow | 'Recessive Silver' | Europe, USA | common | 76, **79**, 239 |
| Bronze Fallow | Fallow | Europe, USA | established | 76, **79**, 239 |
| Opaline | 'Pearl' | worldwide | common | 89, **91**, 252 |
| ADM Pied | Recessive Pied | worldwide | common | 100, **100**, 258 |
| Yellowface | Yellowface | Europe, USA | established | 108, **108**, 262 |
| Uncertain designation | 'Olive' | USA | under dev. | **26** |
| **Galah** *Elophus roseicapillus* | | | | |
| Blue | 'White-fronted' | Australia | established | 41, **43**, 241 |
| Sex-linked Lutino | 'Rubino' | Australia, Europe | common | 51, **52**, 233 |
| Cinnamon | Cinnamon | Australia, Europe | established | 61, **63**, 235 |
| Dilute | Silver | Australia | under dev. | 67, 237 |
| Faded | 'Isabel' | Australia | under dev. | 72, **74**, 238 |
| Fallow | Fallow | Australia | under dev. | 76, 239 |
| Black-eyed Clear | 'Black-eyed White' | Australia | under dev. | 67, **72**, 237, 258 |
| Pied | Pied | Australia | under dev. | 96, **98**, 257 |

| Mutation | Common Names<br>'names in inverted commas are incorrect usage' | Distribution | Availability<br>under dev. = under development | Page<br>Text, **Photographs**, Technical Reference |
|---|---|---|---|---|
| **Red-tailed Black Cockatoo** *Calyptorhynchus magnificus* | | | | |
| Pied | Pied | Australia | wild | **98** |
| Uncertain designation | 'Par-ino' | Australia | wild | **37** |
| **Yellow-tailed Black Cockatoo** *Calyptorhynchus funereus* | | | | |
| Lutino? | Lutino | Australia | wild | |
| Pied | Pied | Australia | under dev. | 96 |
| Pied | Pied | Australia | wild | |
| **Yellow-fronted Kakariki** *Cyanoramphus auriceps* | | | | |
| Sex-linked Lutino | Lutino | | uncertain | 51 |
| **Red-fronted Kakariki** *Cyanoramphus novaezelandiae* | | | | |
| Sex-linked Lutino | Lutino | worldwide | under dev. | 51, **54**, 233 |
| Cinnamon | Cinnamon | Australia, Europe | common | 61, **63**, 235 |
| Dominant Pied | Dominant Pied | Europe | common | 93, 257 |
| Recessive Pied | Recessive Pied | Europe, Australia | established | 96, **98**, 257 |
| **Swift Parrot** *Lathamus discolor* | | | | |
| Faded | 'Pastel' | Europe | established | 72, 238 |
| Sex-linked Lime | 'Yellow' | Europe | uncertain | 56 |
| Khaki | (Misty) 'Greygreen' | Europe | established | 84, 250 |
| Red Suffusion | 'Red-fronted' | Europe | established | 105, **106**, 265 |
| **Rainbow Lorikeet** *Trichoglossus haematodus* | | | | |
| Blue | Blue | Australia | extinct | 41, **44**, 241 |
| Sex-linked Lutino | Lutino (hybrid) | Australia | established | 51, **52**, 233 |
| Cinnamon | Cinnamon | Europe | uncertain | 61, **65**, 235 |
| Dilute | 'Cinnamon' | Australia | common | 67, **71**, 237 |
| Bronze Fallow | 'Pink' Fallow | Australia | under dev. | 76, **78**, 239 |
| Dun? Fallow | 'Purple' Fallow | Australia | under dev. | 76, **78**, 239 |
| Grey | Greygreen (hybrid), 'Olive' | Australia | common | 85, **85**, 247 |
| Khaki | 'Jade', 'Olive' | Australia | under dev. | 84, **84**, **250**, 250 |
| Dark Factor? | 'Jade' | Australia | under dev. | 81, **85**, 245 |
| Recessive Pied | Recessive Pied | Australia | established | 96, **98**, 257 |
| Black-eyed Clear | Yellow | Australia | under dev. | 94, **95**, 258 |
| Melanistic | 'Blue-fronted' | Australia | common | 103, **103**, 254 |
| Uncertain designation | 'Aqua' | Australia | under dev. | **25** |

| Mutation | Common Names<br>*'names in inverted commas<br>are incorrect usage'* | Distribution | Availability<br>*under dev. =<br>under development* | Page<br>Text, **Photographs**,<br>Technical Reference |
|---|---|---|---|---|

**Red-collared Lorikeet** *Trichoglossus haematodus rubritorquis*

| Mutation | Common Names | Distribution | Availability | Page |
|---|---|---|---|---|
| Sex-linked Lutino | Lutino (hybrid) | Australia | established | 51, **53**, 233 |
| Dilute | 'Cinnamon' | Australia | established | 67, 237 |
| Grey | Greygreen (hybrid), 'Olive' | Australia | established | 85, **85**, 247 |
| Pied | Pied | Australia | under dev. | 96 |

**Scaly-breasted Lorikeet** *Trichoglossus chlorolepidotus*

| Blue | Blue | Europe | under dev. | 41, **44**, 241 |
|---|---|---|---|---|
| Sex-linked Lutino | Lutino | Australia | established | 51, **54**, 233 |
| Dilute | 'Cinnamon' | Australia | established | 67, **71**, 237 |
| Grey | Greygreen, 'Olive' | Australia | established | 85, **85**, 247 |

**Musk Lorikeet** *Glossopsitta concinna*

| Grey | Greygreen (hybrid), 'Olive' | Australia | common | 85, **85**, 247 |
|---|---|---|---|---|

**Purple-crowned Lorikeet** *Glossopsitta porphyrocephala*

| Dilute | 'Cinnamon' | Australia | established | 67, **71**, 237 |
|---|---|---|---|---|

**Varied Lorikeet** *Psitteuteles versicolor*

| Uncertain designation | 'Pied' | Australia | extinct? | |
|---|---|---|---|---|

**Stella's Lory** *Charmonsyna papou*

| Melanistic | Melanistic phase | worldwide | established | 103, **103**, 254 |
|---|---|---|---|---|

**Red-flanked Lorikeet** *Charmonsyna placentis*

| Uncertain designation | 'Cinnamon' | Europe | uncertain | **220** |
|---|---|---|---|---|

**Dusky Lory** *Pseudeos fuscata*

| Uncertain designation | 'Yellow phase' | worldwide | common | 107, **107**, 263 |
|---|---|---|---|---|

**Chattering Lorikeet** *Lorius garrulus*

| Black-eyed Clear? | unnamed | Asia | extinct | **96** |
|---|---|---|---|---|

**Masked, Nyasa, Fischer's and Black-cheeked Lovebirds** *Agapornis personatus ssp*

Note: Debate still exists over the taxonomy of the White Eye-ring group. Added to this, all members have been frequently hybridised to transfer mutant colour genes. I have therefore grouped all four together.

| Blue | Blue | worldwide | common | 41, **44**, **45**, 241, **244** |
|---|---|---|---|---|
| NSL Lutino | Lutino | worldwide | common | 58, **59**, **60**, 234 |
| NSL Lime | Lime, 'Pastel', 'Dilute' | worldwide | common | 60, **61**, 234 |
| Fallow | Fallow | Europe | established | 76, 239 |

| Mutation | Common Names<br>*'names in inverted commas*<br>*are incorrect usage'* | Distribution | Availability<br>*under dev. =*<br>*under development* | Page<br>Text, **Photographs**,<br>Technical Reference |
|---|---|---|---|---|
| Dark Factor | Dark Green and Olive | Europe | established | 81, **82**, 245, **246** |
| Violet | Violet<br>'Dark Green' 'Cobalt' | Europe, USA<br>Australia | common<br>established | 88, **88**, 249 |
| Khaki (Misty) | Misty | Europe | established | 84, 250 |
| Uncertain designation | Dominant Edged,<br>'Spangle' | Europe, USA | established | 101, **102**, 238, 262 |
| Dominant Pied | Dominant Pied,<br>'Greenwing' | Europe | established | 93, **257**, 257 |
| Recessive Pied | Pied | Europe, USA | established | 96, **98**, 257, **258** |
| Mottle | Mottle | Europe | established | **259**, 259 |
| Slaty | Slaty | Europe | under dev. | 261 |
| Uncertain designation | 'Avocado' | Australia | under dev. | **25** |

**Peachfaced Lovebird** *Agapornis roseicollis*

| Mutation | Common Names | Distribution | Availability | Page |
|---|---|---|---|---|
| Turquoise (Parblue) | 'Whiteface Blue',<br>'Creamface' | worldwide | common | 46, **47**, 241 |
| Aqua (Parblue) | Seagreen, 'Dutch Blue' | worldwide | common | 46, **47**, 241 |
| Sex-linked Lutino | Lutino | worldwide | common | 51, **53**, 233 |
| Sex-linked Lime | 'Australian Cinnamon' | worldwide | common | 56, **57**, 233 |
| Cinnamon | 'American Cinnamon' | worldwide | common | 61, **63**, 235 |
| Dilute mutant 1 | Edged Dilute,<br>'American Yellow' | worldwide | common | 67, **71**, 237 |
| Dilute mutant 2 | Japanese Yellow | USA, Japan | rare | 67, **71**, 237 |
| Bronze Fallow | 'West German Fallow' | Europe | established | 76, **78**, 239 |
| Pale Fallow | 'East German Fallow' | Europe | established | 76, **78**, 239 |
| Dark Factor | Dark Green and Olive | worldwide | common | 81, **82**, 245 |
| Violet | Violet | Europe, USA | established | 88, **166**, 249 |
| Opaline | 'Rose-headed' | USA | established | 89, **90**, 252 |
| Dominant Pied | Pied | worldwide | common | 93, **94**, 257 |
| Black-eyed Clear | 'Australian Yellow' | Australia | established | 94, **95**, 258 |
| Orangeface | Orangeface | Europe, USA | established | 107, **107**, 263 |
| Pale-headed | Pale-headed | Europe | established | 263, **264** |

**Abysinnian Lovebird** *Agapornis taranta*

| Mutation | Common Names | Distribution | Availability | Page |
|---|---|---|---|---|
| Fallow | Fallow | Europe | under dev. | 76, 239 |
| Dark Factor | Dark Green and Olive | Europe | established | 81, **82**, 245 |
| Khaki (Misty) | Misty | Europe | under dev. | 250 |

**Red-faced Lovebird** *Agapornis pullarius*

| Mutation | Common Names | Distribution | Availability | Page |
|---|---|---|---|---|
| Lutino | Lutino | Europe | extinct? | |

| Mutation | Common Names<br>'names in inverted commas<br>are incorrect usage' | Distribution | Availability<br>under dev. =<br>under development | Page<br>Text, **Photographs**,<br>Technical Reference |
|---|---|---|---|---|
| **Madagascan Lovebird** *Agapornis canus* | | | | |
| Dilute? | Yellow | USA | extinct | 67, **71**, 237 |
| **Indian Ringnecked Parrot** *Psittacula krameri* | | | | |
| Blue | Blue | worldwide | common | 41, **20**, **44**, 241 |
| Turquoise (Parblue) | Turquoise, 'Pastel' | worldwide | established | 46, **47**, 241 |
| Sex-linked Lutino | Lutino | worldwide | common | 51, **54**, 233 |
| Sex-linked Lime | Pallid, 'Lacewing' | worldwide | established | 56, **58**, 233 |
| Cinnamon | Cinnamon | worldwide | established | 61, **63**, 235 |
| Dilute | Suffused, 'Citron' | Europe, USA | established | 67, **72**, **237**, 237 |
| Dominant Dilute | 'Fallow', 'Isabel' | worldwide | established | 75, **76**, 238 |
| Dun Fallow | 'Buttercup' | Europe, USA | established | 76, **80**, 239 |
| Bronze Fallow | 'Recessive Cinnamon' | Europe, USA | established | 76, 239, **240** |
| Dark Factor | Dark Green and Olive | Europe, Sth Africa | established | 81, **83**, 245 |
| Grey | Greygreen | worldwide | common | 85, **87**, 247 |
| Violet | 'Dark Green', 'Cobalt' | USA | established | 88, **89**, 249 |
| Khaki (Misty) | Misty | Europe | under dev. | 250, **251** |
| ADM Pied | 'USA Pied' | USA | established | 100, **100**, 258 |
| Other Pieds | various | worldwide | under dev. | 96, **97**, 257 |
| Uncertain designation | 'Clearhead-Cleartail' | Europe | established | **27**, **113**, **221**, **223** |
| Opaline? | Opaline | Europe | under dev. | 89, 252, **253** |
| Slaty | Slaty | worldwide | under dev. | **261**, 261 |
| **Alexandrine Parrot** *Psittacula eupatoria* | | | | |
| Blue | Blue | Europe | established | 41, **44**, 241 |
| Turquoise (Parblue) | Parblue | Australia | under dev. | 46, **47**, 241 |
| Sex-linked Lutino | Lutino | worldwide | established | 51, **54**, 233 |
| Recessive Grey | Greygreen | Europe | under dev. | 260, **261** |
| Dark Factor or Violet | Dark Green | Europe | under dev. | 81, 88, 245 |
| Dun Fallow? | Fallow, 'Yellowhead' | Europe | under dev. | **38**, 76, 239 |
| Cinnamon? | Cinnamon, 'Isabel' | Europe | uncertain | 61, 235 |

The mutations listed above have occurred as primary mutations of the Alexandrine Parrot, however a number of mutations have also been introduced into this species via hybridisation with the Indian Ringnecked Parrot. They include specimens of Blue, Lutino, Dominant Grey, Cinnamon and Pallid. Unfortunately these hybrid Alexandrines are gradually mixed through the general population. **248**

| Mutation | Common Names<br>*'names in inverted commas<br>are incorrect usage'* | Distribution | Availability<br>*under dev. =*<br>*under development* | Page<br>Text, **Photographs**,<br>Technical Reference |
|---|---|---|---|---|
| **Plum-headed Parrot** *Psittacula cyanocephala* | | | | |
| Blue | Blue | Europe | uncertain | 41, 241 |
| Turquoise (Parblue) | Turquoise | Europe | under dev. | 46, 241 |
| Sex-linked Lutino | Lutino | USA | under dev. | 51, **233**, 233 |
| NSL Lutino | Lutino | Europe | established | 58, 234 |
| Cinnamon | Cinnamon, 'Isabel' | Europe | under dev. | 61, 235, **236** |
| Fallow | Fallow | Europe | established | 76, 239 |
| Grey | Greygreen | Europe | established | 85, 247, **248** |
| Opaline? | Opaline | Europe | under dev. | 89, 252, **253** |
| Pied | Pied | worldwide | under dev. | 96, 257 |
| Dilute | Suffused, 'Yellow' | Europe | under dev. | 67, 237 |
| **Moustache Parrot** *Psittacula alexandri* | | | | |
| Blue | Blue | Europe | under dev. | 41, **45**, 241 |
| Turquoise (Parblue) | Turquoise, 'Blue' | Europe | established | 46, 241, **243** |
| NSL Lutino | Lutino | Europe | extinct? | 58 |
| Cinnamon? | Cinnamon, 'Isabel' | Europe | under dev. | 61, 235 |
| Dun Fallow | Fallow | Sth Africa | under dev. | 76, 239 |
| Pale Fallow | Fallow | Europe? | under dev. | 76, 239, **240** |
| Grey | Greygreen | Europe | established | 85, 247 |
| Pied | Pied | Europe | uncertain | 96, 257 |
| **Slaty-headed Parrot** *Psittacula himalayana* | | | | |
| NSL Lutino | Lutino | Europe | established | 58, **60**, 234 |
| **African Grey Parrot** *Psittacus erithacus* | | | | |
| Blue | Blue | Europe | uncertain | 41, 241 |
| Sex-linked Lutino | 'Albino' | Japan | uncertain | 51, 233 |
| Cinnamon | Cinnamon | USA, Europe | under dev. | 61, 235 |
| Uncertain designation | 'Red Pied' | Sth Africa | under dev. | **37** |
| **Senegal Parrot** *Poicephalus senegalus* | | | | |
| Dominant Pied | Pied | Europe, USA | established | 93, **94**, 257 |
| Uncertain designation | 'Cinnamon' | Sth Africa | under dev. | 61 |
| Uncertain designation | 'Yellow' | Sth Africa | under dev. | 67 |
| **Red-bellied Parrot** *Poicephalus rufiventris* | | | | |
| Pied | Pied | Europe | under dev. | 96, **97**, 257 |

| Mutation | Common Names<br>*'names in inverted commas*<br>*are incorrect usage'* | Distribution | Availability<br>under dev. =<br>under development | Page<br>Text, **Photographs**,<br>Technical Reference |
|---|---|---|---|---|
| **Meyer's Parrot** *Poicephalu; meyeri* | | | | |
| Blue | Blue | Europe | extinct? | 41 |
| **Ruppell's Parrot** *Poicephalus ruepellii* | | | | |
| Uncertain designation | 'Cinnamon' | Sth Africa | under dev. | 61, **224** |
| **Pacific Parrotlet** *Forpus coelestis* | | | | |
| Blue | Blue | USA, Europe | common | 41, **44**, 241 |
| NSL Lutino | Lutino | USA, Europe | established | 58, **59**, 234 |
| Dilute mutant 1 | American Yellow | USA, Europe | established | 67, **70**, 237 |
| Dilute mutant 2 | European Yellow | Europe | established | 67, **70**, 237 |
| Dilute mutant 3? | Isabel | Europe | established | 67, **70**, 237 |
| Dun Fallow | Fallow | USA, Europe | established | 76, **79**, 239 |
| Recessive Grey | Recessive Greygreen | Europe | established | 84, 260 |
| Dominant Pied | Pied | Europe | established | 93, 257 |
| Uncertain designation | Recessive American 'dark' | USA | established | 84, **84**, 260, **261** |
| **Blue-winged Parrotlet** *Forpus crassirostris* | | | | |
| Blue | Blue | Sth America | established | 41, 241 |
| Sex-linked Lutino | Lutino | USA | under dev. | 51, **54**, 233 |
| Cinnamon | Cinnamon | Sth America | under dev. | 61, 235 |
| **Green-rumped Parrotlet** *Forpus passerinus* | | | | |
| Dilute | Dilute | USA | under dev. | 67, 237 |
| Dark Factor | Dark Factor | Europe | established | 81, 245 |
| **Spectacled Parrotlet** *Forpus conspicillatus* | | | | |
| Dilute | Pastel | Europe | extinct | 67, 237 |
| Dilute? | Isabel | | uncertain | 67, 237 |
| Pied | Pied | Europe | uncertain | 96, 257 |
| **Lineolated Parrot** *Bolbohynchus lineola* | | | | |
| Turquoise (Parblue) | Blue | Europe, USA | established | 46, **48**, 241 |
| Sex-linked Lutino | Lutino | Europe, USA | established | 51, **54**, 233 |
| Dark Factor | Dark Green, Olive | Europe, USA | established | 81, **83**, 245 |
| Dilute? | Dilute, 'Cinnamon' | Europe, USA | under dev. | **39**, 67, 237 |
| Dominant Dilute<br>(Edged) | 'Cinnamon' | Europe, USA | under dev. | 75, 238 |
| Cinnamon or Lime? | 'Cinnamon' | Europe, USA | under dev. | 61, 235 |

| Mutation | Common Names<br>*'names in inverted commas*<br>*are incorrect usage'* | Distribution | Availability<br>*under dev. =*<br>*under development* | Page<br>Text, **Photographs**,<br>Technical Reference |
|---|---|---|---|---|
| **Plain Parakeet** *Brotogeris tirica* | | | | |
| Blue | Blue | Sth America | uncertain | 41, 241 |
| **Grey-cheeked Parakeet** *Brotogeris pyrrhopterus* | | | | |
| Uncertain designation | 'Mauve' | USA | uncertain | |
| **Scarlet Macaw** *Ara macao* | | | | |
| Blue | Blue | Asia | under dev. | 41, 241 |
| **Blue and Gold Macaw** *Ara ararauna* | | | | |
| Blue | Blue | Sth America | under dev. | 41, 241 |
| NSL Lutino? | Lutino | USA | under dev. | 58, 234, **235** |
| Grey? | 'Black and Gold' | Sth America | under dev. | 85, **87**, 247 |
| Pied | Pied | USA | under dev. | 96, **97**, 257 |
| Uncertain designation | 'Cinnamon' | Europe | under dev. | 61 |
| Uncertain designation | 'Gold' | Asia | under dev. | |
| **Military Macaw** *Ara militaris* | | | | |
| Uncertain designation | 'Cinnamon' | Sth America | under dev. | **36** |
| **Quaker Parrot** *Myopsitta monachus* | | | | |
| Blue | Blue | worldwide | common | 41, **45**, 241 |
| Aqua (Parblue) | 'Aquamarine' | Europe | established | 46, **50**, 241 |
| Turquoise (Parblue) | Turquoise | Australia | under dev. | 46, 241 |
| Sex-linked Lime | Pallid, Lime, 'Cinnamon' | USA | established | 56, **58**, 233 |
| NSL Lutino | Lutino | Europe, USA | established | 58, **60**, 234 |
| Cinnamon | Cinnamon | Europe, USA | established | 61, **63**, 235 |
| Fallow | Fallow | USA | under dev. | 76, **79**, 239 |
| Black-eyed Clear | Yellow | USA | under dev. | 94 |
| **Nanday Conure** *Nandayus nenday* | | | | |
| Lutino | Lutino | Europe | under dev. | 51 |
| Faded | 'Cinnamon' | Australia, Europe | established | 72, **74**, 238 |
| **Sun Conure** *Aratinga solstitialis* | | | | |
| Lutino | Lutino | USA | uncertain | 51 |
| Uncertain designation | 'Pied' | Australia | under dev. | **26** |

| Mutation | Common Names<br>*names in inverted commas<br>are incorrect usage'* | Distribution | Availability<br>*under dev. =*<br>*under development* | Page<br>Text, **Photographs**,<br>Technical Reference |
|---|---|---|---|---|
| **Wagler's Conure** *Aratinga wagleri* | | | | |
| Uncertain designation | 'Cinnamon' | USA | under dev. | 61 |
| **Mitred Conure** *Aratinga mitrata* | | | | |
| Uncertain designation | 'Cinnamon' | USA | under dev. | 61 |
| **Dusky-headed Conure** *Aratinga weddellii* | | | | |
| Blue | Blue | USA | under dev. | 41, 241 |
| Lutino | Lutino | USA | under dev. | 51, **55** |
| **Golden-crowned Conure** *Aratinga aurea* | | | | |
| Blue | Blue | USA | under dev. | 41, **45**, 241 |
| Uncertain designation | 'Cinnamon' | USA | under dev. | 61 |
| **Sharp-tailed Conure** *Aratinga acuticaudata* | | | | |
| Blue | Blue | USA | under dev. | 41, 241 |
| Lutino | Lutino | USA, Sth America | under dev. | 51 |
| **Maroon-bellied Conure** *Pyrrhura frontalis* | | | | |
| Lutino | Lutino | USA | under dev. | 51 |
| Uncertain designation | 'Cinnamon', 'Fallow' | USA | under dev. | **40**, 61 |
| **Green-cheeked Conure** *Pyrrhura molinae* | | | | |
| Blue/Turquoise? | 'Blue' | Europe, USA | established | 46, **46**, 241 |
| Sex-linked Lime? | 'Fallow', 'Cinnamon' | USA | established | 56, **58**, 233 |
| Opaline? | 'Yellowsided' | USA | established | 89, **91**, 252 |
| **Black-capped Conure** *Pyrrhura rupicola* | | | | |
| Opaline | 'Yellowsided' | USA | under dev. | 89, **91**, 252 |
| **Painted Conure** *Pyrrhura picta* | | | | |
| Pied | Pied | USA | under dev. | 96, 257 |
| **Patagonian Conure** *Cyanoliserus patagonus* | | | | |
| Lutino | 'Yellow' | UK | under dev. | 51 |
| **Blue-fronted Amazon** *Amazona aestiva* | | | | |
| Blue | Blue | Europe,<br>Sth America | established | 41, **45**, 241 |
| Sex-linked Lutino | Lutino | Europe,<br>Sth America | under dev. | 51, **55**, 233 |

| Mutation | Common Names *'names in inverted commas are incorrect usage'* | Distribution | Availability *under dev. = under development* | Page Text, **Photographs**, Technical Reference |
|---|---|---|---|---|
| Uncertain designation | 'Cinnamon' type 1 | Europe | under dev. | 61, **65**, 235 |
| Uncertain designation | 'Cinnamon' type 2 | USA | under dev. | 61, **65**, 235 |
| Uncertain designation | 'Cinnamon' type 3 | Sth Africa | under dev. | 61, **65**, 235 |
| Khaki? | 'Olive' | Sth America | under dev. | 250, **251** |

**Yellow-naped Amazon** *Amazona auropalliata*

| | | | | |
|---|---|---|---|---|
| Blue | Blue | USA | under dev. | 41, 241, **244** |
| Uncertain designation | 'Cinnamon' | USA | under dev. | 61 |

**Red-lored Amazon** *Amazona autumnalis*

| | | | | |
|---|---|---|---|---|
| Lutino | Lutino | Europe | under dev. | 51, **55**, 233 |
| Uncertain designation | 'Cinnamon' | USA | under dev. | 61 |

**Double Yellow-headed** *Amazona oratrix*

| | | | | |
|---|---|---|---|---|
| Pied | Pied | USA | under dev. | 96, 257 |

**Mealy Amazon** *Amazona farinosa*

| | | | | |
|---|---|---|---|---|
| Lutino | Lutino | | uncertain | 51 |

**Lilac-crowned Amazon** *Amazona finschi*

| | | | | |
|---|---|---|---|---|
| Pied | Pied | | uncertain | 96, 257 |

**Green-cheeked Amazon** *Amazona viridigenalis*

| | | | | |
|---|---|---|---|---|
| Uncertain designation | 'Cinnamon' | USA | under dev. | 61 |

**Orange-winged Amazon** *Amazona amazonica*

| | | | | |
|---|---|---|---|---|
| Uncertain designation | 'Cinnamon' | USA | under dev. | 61 |
| Uncertain designation | 'Yellow' | USA | under dev. | 61 |
| Pied | Pied | USA | under dev. | 96, 257 |

**Festive Amazon** *Amazona festiva*

| | | | | |
|---|---|---|---|---|
| Lutino | Lutino | USA | under dev. | 51, **55** |

**White-fronted Amazon** *Amazona albifrons*

| | | | | |
|---|---|---|---|---|
| Lutino | Lutino | USA | under dev. | 51 |
| Uncertain designation | 'Cinnamon' | USA | under dev. | 61, **66** |

**White-crowned Pionus** *Pionus senilis*

| | | | | |
|---|---|---|---|---|
| Lutino | Lutino | Europe | under dev. | 51 |

**Scaly-headed Pionus** *Pionus maximiliani*

| | | | | |
|---|---|---|---|---|
| Uncertain designation | 'Cinnamon' | Sth America | under dev. | 61 |

# *The Acclaimed 'A Guide to ...' range*

*Concise, informative and colourful reading for all
bird keepers and aviculturists.*

- **A Guide to Gouldian Finches**
- **A Guide to Australian Long and Broad-tailed Parrots and New Zealand Kakarikis**
- **A Guide to Rosellas and Their Mutations**
- **A Guide to Eclectus Parrots**
- **A Guide to Cockatiels and Their Mutations**
- **A Guide to Pigeons, Doves and Quail**
- **A Guide to Neophema and Psephotus Grass Parrots and Their Mutations (Revised Edition)**
- **A Guide to Asiatic Parrots and Their Mutations (Revised Edition)**
- **A Guide to Zebra Finches**
- **A Guide to Australia Grassfinches**
- **A Guide to Basic Health and Disease in Birds (Revised Edition)**
- **A Guide to Incubation and Handraising Parrots**
- **A Guide to Pheasants and Waterfowl**
- **A Guide to Pet and Companion Birds**
- **A Guide to Australian White Cockatoos**
- **A Guide to Popular Conures**
- **A Guide to Lories and Lorikeets (Revised Edition)**